MW00597534

Station Identification

Station Identification

A CULTURAL HISTORY OF YIDDISH RADIO
IN THE UNITED STATES

Ari Y. Kelman

UNIVERSITY OF CALIFORNIA PRESS
Berkeley   Los Angeles   London

University of California Press, one of the most distinguished
university presses in the United States, enriches lives around
the world by advancing scholarship in the humanities, social
sciences, and natural sciences. Its activities are supported by
the UC Press Foundation and by philanthropic contributions
from individuals and institutions. For more information, visit
www.ucpress.edu.

University of California Press
Berkeley and Los Angeles, California

University of California Press, Ltd.
London, England

Library of Congress Cataloging-in-Publication Data

Kelman, Ari Y., 1971–.
    Station identification : a cultural history of Yiddish radio in the
United States / Ari Y. Kelman.
        p.   cm.
    Includes bibliographical references and index.
    ISBN 978-0-520-25573-9 (cloth : alk. paper)
    1. Radio programs—United States—History and criticism.
2. Jews—United States—Intellectual life.   3. Mass media—United
States.   4. Popular culture—United States.   5. Theater, Yiddish—
United States—History.   I. Title.

PN1991.3.U6K45   2009
791.44'68924—dc22   2008040824

Manufactured in the United States of America

17   16   15   14   13   12   11   10   09
10   9   8   7   6   5   4   3   2   1

The paper used in this publication meets the minimum requirements
of ANSI/NISO Z39.48–1992 (R 1997) (Permanence of Paper).

For A. D.

In bed, early, Miles is jabbering and making jokes about breakfast and porridge in particular. He tells me that for breakfast we have spider porridge, and I ask, "What's that?" and he says *"Spider porridge*—with *spiders* in it . . ." and I say I will feed him helicopter porridge, or something like that, and he threatens me with many other kinds of porridge until at last he gets into this one: radio porridge.

He says we will have radio porridge with voices in it.

All summer we lived in the house with the stars up above it and the earth down below and we ate radio porridge. Immensely filling, the porridge satisfied hunger but left one haunted with voices under the skin.

Tim Etchells

Contents

Illustrations

Acknowledgments

My interest in radio began as I was preparing to teach a course on the history of American popular music. One night, I stumbled across a television documentary about radio disc jockeys during the late 1940s who played a critical role in exposing rural high school students to the urban sounds of rhythm and blues. Although this was not necessarily the intent of the disc jockeys, their broadcasts opened up the airwaves and, in some ways, the lives of their audience. This opened up a whole world of questions for me: How did radio work? Why did the radio dial look the way it did in late-1940s Ohio? Who decided what and who got on the radio? And, perhaps most interesting for me, how did radio broadcasting both transgress and reinforce communal, cultural, and social differences? Amie Dorman, however, can take credit for starting this project by asking a simple question: "Wasn't there Jewish radio?"

And, some ten years on, here we are. Indeed, there was Jewish radio—an acoustic world of broadcast Yiddish that neither looked nor sounded like I had imagined when I decided to write on this topic. I didn't even speak Yiddish at the time. I don't speak Yiddish particularly well now, but I'm a great listener.

I've listened to hundreds of hours of audiotape and become familiar with the voices of a handful of performers whose names we know and a number of actors, singers, and musicians whose names have been lost to us. Nukhem Stutchkoff, Zvee Scooler, Miriam Kressyn, the Barry Sisters, Reyzele and Sheyndele, Ben Fishbein, William Zigenloib, Victor Packer, Mendel Osherovitch, Freydele Oysher, Marc Schwied, Celia Budkin, Rabbi Samuel Rubin, Rabbi Aaron Kronenberg—the list goes on. Howard Dressner opened his home to me one afternoon and talked to me about his experience working on the *American Jewish Hour*. His help, wisdom, and guidance were invaluable. These men and women made Yiddish radio speak from its debut in 1926 through the 1970s, when both performers and audiences succumbed to the inevitable passage of time. To this group of intrepid performers, I owe my deepest debt of gratitude and the most sincere regret that most of them passed on before I had the opportunity to meet them.

I did have the incredible pleasure of getting to know one exceptional member of the Yiddish radio family, Seymour Rechzeit, with whom I spent one afternoon each week talking, listening, trading stories, asking questions, kvetching, and drinking scotch. Cynthia Allen, a mutual friend, introduced us, and Seymour became an important part of this project and an important part of my life. His spark, his honesty, and his love of life remain in my memory, and I owe him a deep debt of thanks. His memory is a blessing.

I am proud to have begun this project as my Ph.D. dissertation in the American Studies Program at New York University, where a remarkable array of scholars, colleagues, and friends taught me how to do scholarly work (although any shortcomings herein are mine alone). I owe them all immense debts of thanks and gratitude, and I'm fortunate to have the opportunity to share some of their teachings with my own students. Hasia Diner is a model scholar and a powerful mentor, and she provided a steady guiding hand and lots of support through the years of this project. I learned some of my best habits and hardest lessons from her. Andrew Ross and George Yudice played critical roles in my intellectual growth and provided important direction as this book took shape. Toby Miller has become a great friend and adviser; his work remains something I aspire to emulate. Jeffrey Shandler is a remarkable colleague and scholar whose assistance on this book (and other projects) has been invaluable. I have had the great pleasure to learn from a number of other outstanding scholars, and I am deeply grateful for their assistance, collective wisdom, and insight: Paul Buhle, Jim Clifford, Steven M. Cohen, Nathaniel Deutsch, Herman Gray, Eric Goldstein, Jenna Joselitt, Barbara Kirsheblatt-Gimblett, Josh Kun, Tony Michels, Derek Valliant, Beth Wenger. And to the colleagues I am also proud to call friends whose impact on this work will be (perhaps) less immediately apparent: Andy Bachman, Alisa Braun, Dan Bronstein, Mia Bruch, Kristen Dombek, Marc Gidal, Rachel Havrelock, Scott Herndon, Stuart Hoke, Tori Langland, Akiba Lerner, Josh Perelman, Eddy Portnoy, Ari Sclar, and Benjamin Stewart.

I am deeply and profoundly indebted to the extraordinary work of a number of archivists and librarians who provided tireless assistance and patient answers to all my questions and requests. And, as importantly, to their institutions, which became my homes during the long hours of often-tedious research: the Robert Wagner Archives, the Tamiment Library, and the Bobst Library at New York University; the Butler Library at Columbia University; and the Dorot Jewish Division and the Performing Arts Division of the New York Public Library. Shane Baker at the Congress for Jewish Culture was a great help early on in the project. Lyn Slome of the American Jewish Historical Society (AJHS) is a great colleague and an incredible resource. Claire Pingel and the staff of the National Museum of American Jewish History made a wonderful home for me and helped to shape this project in many ways. Paul Hamburg at the Bancroft Library of the University of California, Berkeley; Jesse Aaron Cohen at the YIVO Institute; and Jennifer Anna at the AJHS helped with the images for the book. Jeff Place at the Smithsonian Folkways archive of recordings uncovered a treasure trove of material that shaped the later chapters of this book. The YIVO Institute and Loren Sklamberg, sound archivist, in particular, made it possible for this book to be written. Finally, I want to acknowledge Henry Sapoznik's pathbreaking work as a collector, producer, and advocate of Yiddish radio and culture. Henry's stories of rescuing old recordings from dumpsters are the stuff of archival legend, and his Yiddish Radio Project has become both a valuable resource and an invaluable contribution to the long and vibrant life of Yiddish culture in America.

I am incredibly fortunate to have found a home in the American Studies Program at the University of California, Davis, where my colleagues have already taught me so much about teaching, scholarship, and the other work of academic life. I am thankful every day to them for inviting me to join the faculty there and for seeing in me and my scholarship the potential that I sometimes questioned.

My deepest thanks go out to the anonymous readers for the University of California Press, whose tough love and serious critiques of earlier drafts have strengthened and softened the work. Likewise, the attention of Suzanne Knott, project editor, and Sheila Berg, copy editor, significantly improved the work's readability and accuracy. I owe special thanks to Stan Holwitz at the University of California Press, who saw in a chapter of my dissertation a more sophisticated work and had the wisdom and patience to see it through to its current state. Stan's support and honesty through this process have given me more faith in its future than I could muster on my own.

Big, big thanks to my family and friends, whose love, support, and encouragement sustained me often and always. In particular, my parents, proud educators in their own right, taught me the value of learning. I hope I never cease to be a student. Finally, Amie Dorman has been a source of unflagging support, insight, and inspiration. She asked the question that eventually turned into this book, and she came up with the title too. From her I have learned more than I could have imagined, things far more valuable than any number of pages can document.

Note on Romanization

Yiddish terms are generally Romanized according to the YIVO standard, except in citations, which preserve the Romanization of the source. Titles of programs are translated the first time they appear in the text and, following Yiddish, which has neither upper- nor lowercase, are uncapitalized, except for the first words in the titles. To maintain consistency, I have retained nonstandard spellings of names in cases in which those spellings were preferred by the people in question. Programs such as the *Forward Hour* are referred to in the text by their English titles, even when they had Yiddish ones, because I thought this improved the readability of the text. All translations from Yiddish are mine, except where indicated.

Introduction

The wise dialogue and compositions and fine sketches,
and also to hear the always pleasant B. Vladeck it is
doubly enjoyable when one lives in a country between
goyim, where one hears not one Yiddish word. And Sunday
morning one can go and open the radio and hear a good
Yiddish program. . . . I love hearing a Yiddish voice in the
house and it awakens in us a feeling of the olden days.

Letter to the *Jewish Daily Forward*, February 1933

If we ever have pogroms in America, they will be directed
against "The Yiddish Hour" on the radio. Every idiot, every
bonehead that can put two words together is an announcer.
It is a disgrace to the Jewish people, these Yiddish Hours with
which they festoon the airwaves. . . . It's enough to make you
an anti-Semite.

Joseph Rakhlin, in the *Jewish Daily Forward*, August 1932

In November 1936 Mme Bertha Hart wanted to commemorate the eigh-
teenth anniversary of Armistice Day.[1] At the time, Hart hosted a weekly
Yiddish-language amateur program for WCNW, a small Brooklyn-based
radio station, and she thought it appropriate to close that evening's performance by asking the evening's performers and the in-studio audience to

I

join her in singing the "Star-Spangled Banner." She invited her performers to the microphone, and with all the pomp and circumstance befitting
the French-titled hostess of a Yiddish amateur radio program, Mme Hart
introduced the national anthem. Without even a bar of introduction,
her piano player launched into the anthem's opening melodic line as
the performers struggled to catch up. Although the singers found their
collective rhythm, they could never quite get the lyrics to sound right
because, it quickly became apparent, they did not know the words.

With their Yiddish hearts in the right place, Madame Hart's amateurs offered a version of the national anthem more memorable for
the sincerity of its failure than its fidelity to Francis Scott Key's lyrics.
They hummed, vocalized, and even harmonized, and only occasionally
managed to put together a complete line, but the desire, even the need,
to perform America's national anthem and commemorate Armistice
Day echoed louder than their ability to sing the right words. Although
Madame Hart's guests failed to sing the song correctly, they succeeded
in expressing something perhaps more profound and certainly more
illustrative of where they stood within their American and immigrant
communities. They tried to sound American, and they failed. Ironically,
their improvisations and imperfections gave voice instead to the cultural
contradictions of Jewish life in America.

Radio played a critical role in the amplification of this sentiment.
WCNW, like more than fifty other radio stations in the United States
that carried Yiddish programming, entertained millions of Jewish
immigrant listeners who did not necessarily tune in to hear perfect
renditions of popular Yiddish and English tunes but heard, instead,
a more cacophonous chorus, which sounded out the porous limits of
their communities. Madame Hart's orchestration of the "Star-Spangled
Banner" articulated the combined result of mass Jewish immigration
from Eastern Europe, the popularity of the Yiddish theater and the
Yiddish press, the invention of broadcast technology, the growth of the
radio industry, the emergence of popular genres of radio performance,
the influence of vaudeville, the institution of federal radio regulations,
the popularity of radio among immigrants, the interest of sponsors,
the investments of station owners, the demographics of Jews in New
York, the attention of those Jews, and finally the willingness of Jewish

amateurs to stand before the microphone and sing as if WCNW could catapult them to stardom. Out of these various forces emerged Yiddish-language radio programming, which, despite its limited range (in terms of both language and broadcast power), attracted the attention of an ethnic minority. Speaking to the population of Jewish immigrants as part of a mass medium, Yiddish radio became an important cultural venue for the expression and reception of concerns that shaped the ways in which Jewish immigrants imagined themselves.

This book traces those forces throughout the second quarter of the twentieth century in an effort to understand what the radio meant in the lives of Jewish immigrants, their families, and their communities. Radio brought Jewish and non-Jewish cultural content in both English and Yiddish into Jewish homes via the same medium, the same appliance. Unlike theaters and newspapers, which typically featured one language or the other, radio offered both, and the consonance between the two amplified the cultural detail of Jewish immigrant life.

Yiddish radio emerged at the intersection between Jewish immigration and mass media. It drew on the cultures of print and performance, of Jewish religious and secular thought, of entertainment and information, and of community and communal institutions. A complex culture of sound and sensibility developed around radio that resonated with both the experience of Jewish immigrants and broadcast technology. Therefore, this book focuses on Yiddish radio not only as a technological innovation or a commercial enterprise but also as a cultural formation—a site for investment, articulation, and discussion of meaning. More than the sum total of broadcast hours or programmatic offerings, Yiddish radio captured the ways in which Jewish immigrants imagined and constituted themselves, their relationships with one another, and their relationships to their home in the United States.

AUDIENCE, IMMIGRANT, NATION, LANGUAGE

As the first medium to reach a mass audience in what is currently known as "real time," radio held within it the hope that it could unify the American nation by providing high-quality entertainment and edu-

cation to every listener in every community across the country.[2] From
the first recognized broadcast in 1920, the medium promised the perfect combination of technological progress and social uplift, a combination that resonated with the values of the Progressive Era.[3] It could
civilize immigrants, bring rural communities into contact with cities,
and improve the lot of farmers by supplying them with more accurate
weather forecasts. Generally, it could spread the ideals of Progressivism
and "uplift the masses" with lectures, information, education, and
entertainment that were "really worth while."[4] Radio promised never-
before-seen access to the American people and the hope that this would
strengthen the nation by speaking to its citizens en masse. Secretary of
Commerce Herbert Hoover captured the intentions of the industry in
his opening remarks to the third national radio conference, held in 1924.
"For the first time in history," Hoover observed, "we have available to us
the ability to communicate simultaneously with millions of our fellow
men, to furnish entertainment, instruction, widening vision of national
problems and national events. . . . The local station must be able to bring
to its listeners the greatest music and entertainment of the Nation, but
far beyond this it must be able to deliver important pronouncements of
public men; it must bring instantly to our people a hundred and one
matters of national interest."[5]

For some critics, radio did not promise to cure social problems but
rather exacerbate them. They argued that it would add to the fragmen-
tation of American life by bringing entertainment from the public into
the private sphere, by promoting commercialism, and by pandering to
Americans' base interests instead of their aspirations. Hoover again:
"Here is an agency that has reached deep in to the family life. We can
protect the home by preventing the entry of printed matter destruc-
tive to its ideals, but we must double-guard the radio."[6] Hoover's comments reverberated throughout the industry over the next few decades
as attitudes about radio's "audience" often smacked of disdain, tempered by a sense that they needed protection from their own tastes and
preferences.[7]

What is important here, with respect to these competing opinions, is
not whether radio would benefit the United States but that radio repre-

sented an unpredictable and unknown power whose impact could not yet be measured or channeled. It would reach formerly isolated populations with both the best information and the worst entertainment. It would change people's leisure-time habits and expectations, but it would not totally reinvent them. The significant social values attached to the new medium and the hope and fear that it inspired indicated there was far more at stake than merely what was on the air. Ultimately, the question radio's critics sought to address could be reduced to this: What kind of impact would radio have on American listeners, and what power would the medium exert on the nation as a whole? The very prospect of measuring the significance of radio in terms of its impact, however, was rooted in three crucial assumptions about the relationship between radio and its audience in the American context, assumptions that continue to inform contemporary radio criticism.

The first assumption held that radio in the United States would speak English. In order to live up to its social and political potential, radio had to speak the nation's official language. Immigrants, in particular, were expected to become American in English. More revealing and more subtly, almost no governmental, industrial, or regulatory discussion about the growth of radio bothered to mention the possibility that American broadcasters might speak a language other than English on the air or that audiences existed for them.[8] In the mid-1920s, when Secretary Hoover took the first tentative steps toward organizing and regulating radio through a series of national conferences, not a single participant talked about what language radio would speak; it simply went without saying. The second assumption held that the American audience was, in the words of Secretary Hoover, "millions in number, countrywide in distribution."[9] The radio audience was often painted with a broad brush that treated every listener like every other listener and often failed to hear the differences between them. Certainly, as the promise of networks gained traction during the late 1920s, the image of a single audience stretching from coast to coast gained firmer purchase in the minds of programmers, performers, sponsors, and regulators. Third and finally, it was assumed that every American audience would listen to radio in the same way and absorb the same set of meanings from its programs. This belief that the reception of mediated information is generally passive has retained its appeal in conversations about the mass media. Some work on audience and reception studies beginning in the 1990s raised significant challenges to this idea, yet it remains powerful in both scholarly and popular criticism of media in general.[10]

Nevertheless, much scholarship on American radio repeats and reinforces these three assumptions. Critics, from Eric Barnouw, who wrote the classic three-volume study of American broadcasting, to contemporary scholars such as Michelle Hilmes and Jason Loviglio, who edited *The Radio Reader,* have approached American radio as if its history happened almost exclusively on the networks and almost only in English.[11] Even a recent book about representations of Jews on radio likewise focuses almost exclusively on representations in English.[12] Hilmes, Loviglio, and others in radio studies who are highly critical of network radio ultimately reinforce its preeminence by directing their critiques at the networks instead of listening elsewhere for echoes of alternative broadcasting practices. One could argue that voices that did not speak English or that did not broadcast over the major networks did not amount to much in terms of the broader reception or practice of radio.[13] However, attending to these voices forces us to reconsider the scope and sound of radio culture in the United States, which in large measure took shape outside the network system. Moreover, attending to these voices forces scholars and listeners to reconsider the three assumptions that have underpinned so much of radio writing and to find audiences, communities, counterpoint, and culture that do not appear often on the scholarly radio dial.

Tona Hangen's otherwise excellent book is a case in point.[14] Subtitled *Radio, Religion and Popular Culture in America,* it focuses exclusively on Christian evangelical broadcasting, made popular by Aimee Semple McPherson, Charles Fuller, and others, ignoring the presence of Jews and other religious groups on American airwaves. In this way, she inadvertently reproduces the notion that broadcasting in the United States has always only been in English. This omission is indicative of U.S.-based radio scholarship in general, which makes assumptions about radio that do not resonate with the history of the medium. In fact, Hangen's book is an excellent cultural history of the phenomenon and, in many ways, reads well in conversation with this book, as both explore cultures of radio, religion, listening, and community. Hangen writes keenly about the dynamics between a Christian sensibility in tension with modernity and its reliance on modern broadcast technology. She also makes a welcome argument about the importance of listening in the self-conception of listeners as members of a religious community. Our books part ways where the subject of her study ends at the borders of a religious community; mine focuses on the negotiation of precisely those borders for an ethnic community.

Despite the shortcomings of scholarship, radio in the United States has been multilingual practically since the very beginning. Only a few years after the first widely acknowledged radio broadcast in 1920 and before the 1926 debut of NBC's national network, owners of small stations in New York, Philadelphia, Chicago, Los Angeles, and a handful of other cities found audiences in immigrant populations. They began broadcasting programs in Yiddish, Italian, Polish, Russian, German, and a number of other languages spoken by newly settled communities. These stations comprised an alternative radio in the United States by carrying multilingual lineups to immigrant audiences who wanted an aural culture that spoke to them from within their own communities and about the homes they had left behind. Outside the predominantly English-speaking world and partly independent of the networks that crossed the country during the 1930s and 1940s, these stations broadcast in specific neighborhoods and cities, drew largely on local sponsors and talent, and, although bound by the same laws as the larger stations, held an entirely different set of expectations, limitations, and sensibilities with respect to their listeners. Listening for these smaller stations within the broader histories of American broadcasting provides a vital and vibrant counterpoint to accounts of radio's "Golden Age" that begs a reconsideration of the relationship between language, nation, media, popular culture, ethnicity, audience, and community.

I focus on the culture of Yiddish radio in the United States for two reasons. First, unlike Canada or the United Kingdom, the state did not control the radio industry in the United States. Thus the U.S. airwaves proved uniquely open for innovation and entrepreneurs in ways that the radio industries of other countries were not. As a result, there were handfuls of isolated Yiddish programs in countries other than the United States, but they never quite coalesced into an independent cultural formation and always seemed or sounded like appendages of other community structures. There were shortwave Yiddish programs broadcast from the Soviet Union, and Cuba's Jewish community held regular programs for a time in the late 1930s, but no other country could approach the breadth and depth of Yiddish radio as it was heard in the United States.[15] Second, the presence of non-English-language programming on U.S. radio has been almost completely overlooked, and an account of at least one strain of this rich counterpoint in American aural culture is long overdue.

At the heart of much American radio scholarship has been the relationship between radio and the American nation during the twentieth century. For scholars focusing on political economy, American radio has largely been the story of corporate interests using the medium to amass political and cultural power.[16] Critiques of the political economy of radio have, in turn, given birth to alternative accounts of particular heroic presences on radio who disrupted the inertia and influence of capital.[17] Yet both of these versions reduce the development of the medium to a story of insiders and outsiders, of those with power and those fighting it. In this respect, one major contribution of *Station Identification* is its resistance to both of these narratives. Yiddish-speaking radio producers neither had power nor fought against it overtly. Nor did they generally operate according to the logic either of networks such as NBC or of powerful local stations. Though attentive and responsive to developments on mainstream radio, they focused their energies elsewhere and carved out a Yiddish-speaking niche for one particular American community. This is not to suggest that they were above the fray but rather that this alternative aural culture developed around a different set of concerns with respect to the role of radio in the lives of its sponsors, owners, and listeners.

Susan Smulyan's groundbreaking study of the commercialism of radio is a case in point.[18] Smulyan's work is eloquent, insightful, and rigorously argued, yet it, too, pays little attention to the internal variety of radio and the real differences among audiences, especially with regard to language. Accurate with respect to network radio, her argument needs further development when applied to the small radio stations that entertained immigrant audiences; for these stations, the relationships between them, their sponsors, and their listeners articulated communal sensibilities quite different from those on network radio. Most operated on a shoestring budget and struggled to stay out of debt and on the air. To keep themselves afloat, they relied mainly on "time brokers," who worked within the ethnic communities that constituted their audiences to find sponsors in local businesses—Parmet Brothers' Furniture in New York, Harry Kandel's Appliances in Philadelphia, or the oddly named Chicago Pharmacy in Los Angeles. In this context, commercial sponsorship did not line the pockets of large corporations such as Proctor and Gamble, nor did it fill the coffers of increasingly wealthy businessmen who sat atop the radio hierarchy. Instead, in other languages, commercialism became part of a delicate network of local businesses, theaters, performers, and even charities, all of which used radio to speak among and about the communities they served. Moreover, local stations often played an important role in forging and sustaining local relationships between stores and their customers, working, in effect, against the kinds of effects that Smulyan argues characterized commercialism on English-language, network-dominated radio.

Moving from the larger structures of radio to the programs themselves, Fred MacDonald has argued that radio programs during the Golden Age largely functioned as "middle-class morality tales" intended to coach the listening masses about their place in American society.[19] According to MacDonald, popular radio programs subtly, and sometimes not so subtly, taught Americans how to be American and gave regular accounts of what idealized life in America ought to look—and sound—like. This argument ends in radio's complicity with a vaguely defined national identity, as if all of radio sounded the same and ended up meaning the same thing to its listeners, regardless of their particular backgrounds. To Jewish immigrant listeners, programs such as *Clara, Lu and Em* or *The Shadow* may have sounded more foreign than familiar and thus may have reinforced differences instead of interpolating audiences across them. Meanwhile, shows in Yiddish such as *Bay tate mames tish* ('Round the Family Table) and *Der yidisher filosof* (The Jewish Philosopher) presented fictionalized Jewish familial strife for their listeners' enjoyment. By paying attention to other audiences whose experiences of immigration and resettlement informed their reception of mainstream English-language "middle-class morality tales," the stories themselves begin to sound different and nuance understandings of radio more broadly.

Immigrants did not encounter American radio as cultural blank slates but were already familiar with and sometimes fluent in the popular cultures of their home countries or cities. As important, they arrived with the creativity and ingenuity to adapt their cultures to new surroundings. Food, music, literature, dance, poetry, art, social organizations, even economics drew on models they brought with them to the United States.[20] Immigrant groups, in contrast to the hopes of American Progressives, did not leave their tastes for popular culture at the border but instead grafted American media and culture onto immigrant ones, resulting in new combinations, expressions, tastes, styles, institutions, and sounds that both reflected and helped to shape the new communities in which they lived. Those communities did not stop at the border either. Immigrant groups formed strong local associations that fostered powerful ties to their hometowns across the Atlantic, making them both local and global, both transnational and multilingual.[21] These relationships, in turn, drew strength from cultural and economic exchanges that crossed national boundaries with relative ease and fostered further innovations.

Radio provided an ideal medium for these innovations. Already adept at cultural synthesis, immigrants could tune in radio programs in English and in their own languages. Because they could listen to English programming, they were not relegated to radio's margins, but neither were they limited to its mainstream. Instead, they listened to both, and their tastes and preferences took shape around the interactions between the two. The harsh words of Joseph Rakhlin, the critic quoted at the beginning of this introduction, clearly show that Yiddish radio programming did not always fare well compared with mainstream radio, yet audiences continued to tune in. In so doing, they formed an audience distinct from that imagined by Hoover and his radio conferences. Why that audience tuned in is addressed in greater detail below, but what is important to recognize at this point is that the cultural formation of Yiddish radio had material effects that manifested prominently in the ways they made choices about what to listen to, how they related to the medium, and how they related to one another.

THE SOUND OF YIDDISH

Yiddish radio belonged primarily to some 2.5 million Eastern European Jews who immigrated to the United States between 1881 and 1924.[22] Although Hebrew often claimed the status of the Jewish lingua franca, during this time, only a small number of committed Zionists actually spoke Hebrew colloquially as part of a broader nationalist movement. Most European Jews possessed a working knowledge of biblical and liturgical uses of Hebrew but spoke Yiddish in their daily lives. To distinguish between classical and modern Hebrew, Yiddish speakers referred to them differently. Biblical and liturgical Hebrew became known as *Loshn koydesh* (the Holy Tongue), while modern Hebrew was referred to as "Hibreish." In Jewish towns and neighborhoods of Eastern Europe and then again on the streets of America's cities, Jews spoke and heard Yiddish, but nobody ever spoke Yiddish in a vacuum. Itself a mixture of Russian, *Loshn koydesh,* German, and Polish, Yiddish—and Yiddish culture—echoed with influences from other cultures. Klezmer music shared many features with other central European folk musics.[23] Yiddish literature shared aspects of Russian literature, and in the marketplaces and trading routes of Eastern Europe, Yiddish-speaking men and women regularly conducted business with non-Jews, thus requiring the ability to speak, or at least understand, a second and sometimes a third language.[24] Although many Jews spoke Russian or Polish, only Jews spoke Yiddish. In the wake of immigration to the United States, English became another of the languages that coexisted with Yiddish in the minds and mouths of immigrant Jews.

The Yiddish writer Sholom Aleichem captured the resonances of this version of Yiddish bilingualism in his only major work set in America. *Motl, the Cantor's Son*, a Yiddish novella written toward the end of Aleichem's life, follows the mischievous title character as he migrates to America and begins absorbing American culture and the English language into his Yiddish worldview.[25] On his arrival in New York, Motl first registered his new surroundings in sound; New York seemed like Lemberg or Brody, but "everything was just louder and more confusing."[26] As if charting the linguistic trajectory of a new immigrant, Aleichem slowly and steadily introduced English words, transliterated into Yiddish, to Motl's vocabulary, rendering the final third of the novella in a patois of Yiddish and English. While conversations in the street increasingly took place in English, those in his head remained in Yiddish. The effect was one whereby English gained ground in Motl's world even as Yiddish still predominated. Motl and the rest of the novella's characters welcomed the arrival of English even as they joked about the inevitable confusion that arose from words that sounded alike. When Motl's mother tried to cook a "kitshen" in the "tshiken," Motl's only response was to turn to the reader and ask, "You tell me. What language is that?"[27] Sholom Aleichem, who lived his final days in New York, captured the ways in which English penetrated the Yiddish-speaking immigrant world even as that world remained primarily Yiddish.

Motl's generation became Yiddish radio's primary audience. Familiar with English but at home in Yiddish, they tuned in to Yiddish programming not because they had to but because it spoke to them in ways that English programming could not. Yet they engaged in English, spoke it when necessary, often read English newspapers, and understood that their children would likely choose English over Yiddish whenever possible. The historian Deborah Dash Moore explained that "most second generation Jews understood Yiddish, many could read the language, yet few chose to purchase a Yiddish paper. Instead they turned to the English-language press, which gradually expanded its coverage of topics of interest to Jews."[28] Interested in Jewish issues but more comfortable in English, this generation would likely have preferred the sounds of Ozzie Nelson or Rudy Vallee to those of the Yiddish theater composer Alexander Olshanetzky or the great cantor Yossele Rosenblatt. Yet their ability to understand Yiddish and their parents' facility with English captures another key characteristic of the culture of Yiddish radio: It was almost always bilingual.

For radio audiences, language never represented a strict barrier. Both first- and second-generation Jews listened to programming in both languages, even while each preferred one over the other. Thus the culture of radio for immigrants always included at least two languages, which they heard as complementary, not contradictory, sources of entertainment. In fact, the culture of Yiddish radio relied heavily on the direction of English radio. Yiddish-speaking radio audiences began listening to radio even before the first Yiddish broadcast, the Yiddish press reported on and carried listings for English radio programming, and Yiddish-speaking radio performers copied the successful formulas of their English-speaking counterparts. Setting aside, for the moment, the obvious structural situation that Yiddish radio could not have existed without English radio, culturally, too, Yiddish radio owed a significant debt to the conventions of English radio. Yiddish radio relied on English radio for ideas and models of genre, content, and structure. In this way, Yiddish radio provided a venue in which Jewish immigrants could rehearse negotiations between their Jewish communities and their American context.

These negotiations represent one of the major motifs of Jewish life during this period, not only on the radio, but off it as well. Jewish immigrants created a formidable network of cultural institutions, schools, charities, mutual-benefit associations, shops, theaters, synagogues, and landsmanshaftn, all of which served the purpose of helping them make lives in America.[29] For example, landsmanshaftn, or hometown associations that connected Jewish immigrants from the same Eastern European towns to one another while also keeping them in contact with the towns they had left, provided both a material safety net and a venue for practicing all manner of American civil life, from voting to voluntary membership to communal debate. Jewish immigrants also sought ways to balance the power of American public schooling with the importance of maintaining a Jewish education. While public schools became a significant site of socialization and Americanization for immigrants generally and Jews in particular, Jews developed supplemental schools that taught Jewish culture in both religious and secular settings. The first American Yiddish primers were published during the 1910s and 1920s, and by the mid-1930s, Yiddish secular schools accounted for 10 percent of all Jewish supplemental education nationwide and 20 percent of Jewish education in New York City.[30]

These institutions are significant not because they indicate a movement among Jews to stay the prospect of cultural loss in the wake of immigration but because they emerged as part of the process by which Jewish immigrants learned how to be Americans *and* Jews. Moreover, they represent organized responses to the cultural forces of migration and resettlement and offer frames for understanding the processes by which Jewish immigrants constituted themselves and their communities in the United States.

Though not an institution like schools, charities, or *landsmanshaftn*, radio provided another site for Jewish immigrants to rehearse negotiations over culture, language, and community. Radio is no less powerful a site for these rehearsals because it is a mass medium. Rather, the sounds of this community in conversation with itself are a crucial dimension of immigrant Jewish life that has been previously overlooked. The composer and communications scholar Barry Truax is helpful here in his explicit linking of sound and community in his definition of "acoustic community." He writes, "The *acoustic community* may be defined as any soundscape in which acoustic information plays a pervasive role in the lives of the inhabitants. . . . [I]t is any system within which acoustic information is exchanged. . . . [A]coustic cues and signals constantly keep the community in touch with what is going on from day to day within it. . . . The community is linked and defined by its sounds. To an outsider they may appear exotic or go unnoticed, but to the inhabitants they convey useful information about both individual and community life."[31] I want to follow Truax here to argue that the aural dimension of Jewish immigrant culture holds important clues to understanding not only the nature and dimensions of this particular community but also the ways in which the very nature and boundaries of this community were always open for discussion and transgression.

Because Yiddish broadcasting could not have existed without American radio generally, it presents a unique opportunity for exploring the culture of Jewish immigrants in conversation—both literal and metaphoric—with that of their new host nation. Similarly, attending to Yiddish radio broadens the sonic horizons of radio in the United States to account more readily for audiences and performers who engaged radio in their native tongues as well as their adopted ones. As a cultural formation, Yiddish radio amplifies both the distinct sounds of an immigrant acoustic community and its part in a broader conversation about audience, mass culture, and identity.

THE YIDDISH MASS MEDIA

Its relationship to English and operation within a primarily English-speaking medium gave Yiddish radio a unique angle on Jewish life that no other Yiddish mass medium could provide. The nature of radio usage meant that it invited questions about the boundaries between Jewish and non-Jewish culture and communities because it brought the English mass media into Jewish homes and it drew the attention of Yiddish and English speakers alike. Other Yiddish media, like theater, literature, press, and sheet music, circulated primarily among Jewish producers and consumers and did not entertain the same overt relationship to contemporary English-language popular media. Of course, these other Jewish media drew on influences from outside the immediate Jewish context, and thus they, too, gave voice to cultural contradictions of all kinds: stylistic, conventional, formal, and so on. What set Yiddish radio apart, however, was the fact that it could not have existed without its English counterpart; it was structurally dependent on English radio. It would have been possible to attend the Yiddish theater, read the Yiddish press, and sing Yiddish songs exclusively, but radio did not work that way. A radio receiver would pick up whatever signals it could and channel them into homes, regardless of what language people spoke or wanted to hear. Yiddish radio needed English radio, and this intimate relationship gave radio a distinct cultural resonance.

The Yiddish press, for example, engaged American culture from a slightly different angle. Some Yiddish newspapers in the United States, such as the *Jewish Daily Forward,* saw themselves as the first place immigrants could turn for instruction on how to live in America, while more traditional papers such as the *Morgen zhurnal* (Morning Journal) tried to illustrate the compatibility of traditional Judaism and American patriotism. Add to the mix both the Communist *Freiheit* (Freedom) and the more moderate *Der tog* (The Day), and what emerges is a picture of Yiddish journalism in which the paper one read carried a host of political and social attachments and in which the source of news counted in equal measure to the news itself. For all its internal variety and the sometimes significant differences between anarchists, socialists, religious, and secular newspapers, the press as a whole endeavored to explain the wider world to its Jewish readership. The *Jewish Daily Forward* spelled out its mission in its sixty-fifth anniversary edition. "To help the workingman and the Jewish immigrant in this new land were the main reasons for the founding of this paper." The article continued with characteristic hyperbole: "No other paper . . . has been of such help in educating masses of people to a completely new way of life."[32]

Positioning itself at the intersection between Jewish immigrants and American life, the Yiddish press, for all its variety, saw its role as generally educational. Long before it came to own and operate the largest radio outlet for Yiddish programming in America, the *Forward* set the stage for Yiddish radio. Abraham Cahan, longtime editor of the Forward, knew that his audience wanted Yiddish, but he also understood that they did not want to live in a ghetto. By incorporating English words into the *Forward*'s editorial framework, by publishing stories about the seamier side of urban life, and by writing about American politics, Cahan cultivated a newspaper that appealed to an immigrant audience but did not keep them isolated outside the American mainstream. Though his techniques attracted the ire of other journalists, editors, and ideologues who argued that they would weaken the Jewish community, Cahan and his newspaper understood what his audience wanted. In this way, Cahan produced a newspaper that presented a cultural and linguistic sensibility that reached beyond the immigrant community in order to expose it to aspects of American life.

Likewise, the Yiddish theater emerged in the 1880s as another medium for Yiddish culture in the United States. Beginning with the first documented performance in 1881, commercial theaters, amateur theaters, unions, playwrights, actors, and legions of passionately devoted and boisterous fans made up the landscape of Yiddish theater. During its heyday, which lasted from the 1880s until the late 1920s, more than one thousand shows for over two million patrons were staged annually.[33] The theater was a vibrant hub of Jewish cultural and political activity. Located primarily along Second Avenue on Manhattan's Lower East Side, theaters hosted shows on every imaginable subject and in every conceivable style. Producers and performers owned their own theaters; actors and musicians had their own unions, management, and payment structures. They advertised in the Yiddish newspapers (and eventually on radio) and had their own star system as well. And while occasional Yiddish productions found crossover success and a handful of actors managed the same, the world of Yiddish theater belonged almost exclusively to Jewish immigrants.

Although these Yiddish media circulated solely among Jewish communities, they extended to Jewish populations throughout Europe, as well as South Africa and Latin America. The musicologist Mark Slobin and the theater historian Nahma Sandrow have contributed important accounts of the ways in which Jewish diasporic communities shaped and were shaped by Yiddish music and theater, respectively.[34] Sandrow's "world history of Yiddish theater" keenly addresses the ways in which Yiddish theater in the United States not only drew influence and content from Europe and South America but also contributed to them by touring almost continuously. Although her work is less theoretically nuanced than Paul Gilroy's, Sandrow establishes a kind of model for a "Jewish Atlantic" that constituted itself through a Jewish economy of local theaters, company tours, and the publication of scripts and sheet music.[35] Slobin extends Sandrow's observations to the realm of musical culture by examining the ways in which Yiddish music in theaters, in sheet music, and on phonographs participated in a culture that traveled back and forth across the Atlantic. For Slobin, music created a "community of song" that allowed Jewish immigrants to America to express their hopes, dreams, and frustrations as they navigated their way "from Europeans to Americans."[36] For Sandrow and, more subtly, Slobin, Yiddish music and theater were always transnational and always deeply invested in the routes of Jews globally, even as they suited Jewish immigrants in the communities where they lived. From traveling theaters to journalism, Yiddish mass media always articulated a kind of transnational consciousness, even as it existed almost exclusively for Jewish consumption. Thus most Yiddish mass media operated transnationally but along a relatively narrow Jewish wavelength. This tendency would also find expression on Yiddish radio, but in the context of broadcasting, it assumed a different resonance.

In 1920, when the first recognized English-language broadcast aired in Pittsburgh, the Yiddish theater and entertainment world hummed with activity, and Yiddish readers still bought and read their daily papers. But by 1926, when the first Yiddish broadcasts aired, newspaper circulation had declined significantly, and the Yiddish theater world had begun to feel the effects of a bloated and internally divided industry.[37] Radio took advantage of the popularity of both the press and the theater, and it mined both arenas for talent, material, publicity, and financial support. Radio did not so much cause the decline of the theater and the press as it benefited from declines already under way and capitalized on the consumer demand already in place. Shrinking readership and audiences resulted from a number of factors of Jewish life, ranging from the large number of Jews who began moving out of city centers to the growing popularity of English entertainments among the second generation. But radio, which did not need subscribers or an audience to attend its broadcast in person, flourished among urban Jewish communities now divided among a handful of neighborhoods. The support of the newspapers that printed radio listings and advertisements and the availability of writers, singers, musicians, and actors who found fewer and fewer live stages fed the young industry and enabled Yiddish radio to thrive for the next thirty years.

Although radio mined the momentum and power of the press and the theater for material and financial support, it functioned differently than either of its counterparts in five major ways. First, radio receivers provided listeners with both English and Yiddish entertainment just by turning a dial. This fit the emergent tastes of Jewish immigrants, who kept abreast of news from Broadway and Hollywood in regular columns in the *Forward*. Research from the 1920s indicated that more than half of all Jewish immigrants regularly bought and read English-language newspapers in addition to Yiddish ones, suggesting that they turned to English sources for news and entertainment as well.[38] These connections to English-language sources helped to sow the seeds for the success of radio, as they created connections between Jewish immigrant audiences and mainstream American entertainment. Yet radio offered something new and affordable. Unlike movies or plays, for which one had to buy a ticket for each performance, once a family purchased a radio, they could listen to anything and everything that the radio carried. Unlike newspapers, which came largely in either English or Yiddish, the radio spoke both languages (among others) almost interchangeably.

Second, radio was an aural medium. Although people often listened with rapt attention, radio did not demand all of one's facilities. People could listen as they did housework or as they relaxed after work. It presented domesticated sound, tailor-made for listening at home, for a generation struggling to make themselves at home in America. Jewish homes echoed with conversations that frequently slipped back and forth between Yiddish (from parent to child) and English (from child to parent). Each generation understood the other, even as both preferred to speak their own language. For radio, this meant that everyone could listen to and understand all the broadcasts, even as each preferred to listen to the stations that spoke his or her language.

Third, federal regulations influenced the growth of the medium. Unlike a newspaper that anyone could publish, or a play that anyone could produce, radio had rules that were enforced by a federally appointed oversight body. Not only did stations have to earn enough money to remain on the air, but they also had to keep pace with the seemingly endless demands of paperwork, reports, applications, renewals, and laws. Failure to keep up with paperwork could force a station off the air, and federal regulations laid out a standard of broadcast fitness according to the contribution of each station to the "public interest." For stations that broadcast primarily in English, the "public interest" loosely meant following a general code of decency and not permitting their broadcast signals to interfere with the signal of another station. For stations that broadcast in other languages, serving the "public interest" meant providing programming additional intended to "Americanize" their listeners. According to the Federal Communication Commission's (FCC's) usage, "Americanize" meant that programs should actively promote the assimilation of immigrant populations into the American mainstream and advocate the fluency of those populations in American life, custom, and culture.[39] The presence of these regulations meant that stations could not speak however they wanted to whomever they wanted but that they had to operate within fairly specific guidelines with which they did not necessarily agree.

Fourth, Yiddish radio never had its own, dedicated broadcast outlets. There was no such thing as a "Yiddish radio station." Every station that carried Yiddish programming also carried programming in other languages. Even WEVD, the station with the longest and strongest history of Yiddish programming, always carried shows in English and often in other languages, including Italian, German, and Russian. The reason for this was simple: no station could earn enough income from advertising solely to the Jewish community, so they carried whatever programs they could in whatever languages would garner the support of sponsors. Jews often owned stations that carried Yiddish programming, but even then, they carried programs that catered to every immigrant group that wanted to listen. Yiddish radio, as a cultural formation, therefore, existed as part of a loose multilingual alliance within and among the small stations that agreed to carry it.

Fifth, from 1923 to 1953, radio reigned as the single most powerful and popular medium in America. More than film or print media, radio dominated the cultural and political landscape. Radio entertained audiences during the Great Depression, threw itself behind the war effort, and became a key vehicle for President Franklin Delano Roosevelt to rally the support of the American public.[40] Most popular accounts of the medium refer to the 1930s and 1940s as radio's "Golden Age," when performers such as Rudy Vallee, George Burns, Amos 'n' Andy, Fred Allen, Jack Benny, Eddie Cantor, and Gertrude Berg ruled the evening airwaves with their blend of comedy and vaudeville-style skits.[41] Daytime pro-gramming also came into its own behind the creative efforts of people such as Irna Phillips and the husband-and-wife team Anne and Frank Hummert, who created many of the era's most popular soap operas. The NBC, CBS, and Mutual networks rose to prominence and, once joined by ABC, managed to secure the affiliation of 97 percent of all radio stations in America by 1947.[42]

During these twenty years, radio broadcast the sounds of America. Yet radio carried a far more complex and varied sound track than most histories reveal. Part of the same industry but operating on a much smaller scale, non-English-speaking broadcasters represented the voices of some 25 million immigrants during this Golden Age. The roles they played had little impact on the mainstream industry, but their pres-ence on the margin of the radio dial proved crucial to those millions of immigrants who used the most powerful mass medium in America to broadcast and hear voices that sounded like their own. Yet Yiddish radio also emerged out of existing circuits of Jewish mass media. If not for the popular precedents of the publishing, theater, and recording industries, Yiddish radio likely would not have developed at all. Yiddish radio suc-ceeded both because of the structure of English radio and because of the cultural context established by the Yiddish mass media. Thus listeners, when they finally tuned in and began to constitute an audience, already had developed habits within which the radio made cultural sense.[43]

THE CULTURE OF YIDDISH RADIO

"Cultural analysis," warns the anthropologist Clifford Geertz, "is (or should be) guessing at meanings, assessing the guesses, and drawing explanatory conclusions from the better guesses, not discovering the Continent of Meaning and mapping out its bodiless landscape."[44] In other words, cultural analysis is an inexact science because it focuses on the meanings of social life that people ascribe to various symbols and objects, and people are notoriously inconsistent. The meanings people assign to particular symbols change over time, the social circles in which

they travel expand and contract, and how individuals think of themselves in relation to the larger world evolves in significant ways over the
course of a lifetime. By necessity and association, the cultures in which
people participate must also be inconsistent. Yet Geertz did not conclude
that one should not engage in cultural analysis but rather be sensitive
to the "better guesses" and the "explanatory conclusions" that emerge
from patterns of culture. There are internal and sometimes obscured
consistencies that emerge in ways such that seemingly contradictory
behaviors, like a failed rendition of the "Star-Spangled Banner," indicate
a much deeper and more poignant set of concerns and desires. The
goal of cultural analysis is not necessarily to fix culture as a "bodiless
landscape" but to apprehend its ebb and flow.

I recall Geertz's advice because this book is about a particular culture,
and culture, no matter how narrowly defined, cannot be reducible to a
single, static entity. Thus the culture of Yiddish radio is not one particular
thing, but by making informed guesses, we can ascertain what Yiddish
radio meant and how it became a vehicle for creating meaning. Meaning,
like culture, is tricky business, and most of the time it works without
intentional thought. Certain symbols or actions become so familiar that
both they and their meanings are taken for granted. Even when meaning
is contested, as the cultural theorist Dick Hebdidge keenly illustrated
in his account of punk subculture in England during the late 1970s, the
struggle over meaning is rarely rendered wholly logical or rational but
nevertheless succeeds in other ways.[45] Raymond Williams offers one way
of thinking about these other ways by constructing an analysis of culture
that includes the affective alongside the more plainly rational. Williams
refused to consider feelings either wholly "irrational" or "illogical" and
invested instead in an examination of what he called "structures of feeling." Both Geertz and Williams use the term *structure* to explain that
they are looking for the hidden, unspoken, taken-for-granted patterns
that govern the production of meaning. For Geertz, cultural meaning
emerges out of negotiations over symbols; for Williams, affective connections help to constitute meaning according to "specific internal rela-
tions, at once interlocking and in tension."[46] Though they do not always
agree, disagreement, too, produces meaning and often reveals cultural

meaning more readily. In this work, I am invested in a process of uncovering these structures of feeling hidden beneath the sounds of radio. By listening more closely to the structures of radio—as opposed merely to listening to radio itself—the affective investments, communal struggles, and moments of identification become slightly more audible and provide more grounding for better guesses at what it all meant.

The culture of Yiddish radio, as it evolved during the second quarter of the twentieth century, traded in both symbols and feelings. From the overwrought family melodramas of Nukhem Stutchkoff to Madame Hart's amateur performers, Yiddish-speaking broadcasters aired programs that aimed to pull on their audience's heartstrings as much as they hoped to satisfy their sponsors, who pulled on their share of heartstrings as well. At the same time, however, the legal framework of radio kept Yiddish-speaking broadcasters and the stations that hosted them engaged in a kind of meta-performance that assisted in the "Americanization" of the foreign born, when, in fact, foreign-born Jews had already developed strategies for adapting to life in America. Yiddish radio succeeded in attracting listeners despite the presence of English radio because Jews, once comfortable in America, still enjoyed listening to voices that sounded like their own. In this way, Yiddish radio provided a sonic structure of feeling and a cultural formation for ongoing performances of Jewish communal identification by performers and listeners alike. As both vehicle and venue, Yiddish radio captured the sounds of a community in conversation with itself. Drawn affectively to Yiddish programming amid a broader and stronger English-speaking industry, listeners tuned in to hear themselves on the air. When they tuned in, they heard Yiddish-speaking performers faithfully, if hyperbolically, represent versions of Jewish life in America with which they could identify. Supported by symbols and structures of feeling, the audience of Yiddish radio shared in a larger conversation about Yiddish culture and what constituted the outer aural limits of their community of listeners.

Station Identification explores the relationship between membership in an audience and membership in a community. The boundaries that define and determine these two formations are always in flux, always negotiated, and always mediated. Radio, in addition to the press, literature, music, and the theater, became a new venue for the mediation and rehearsal of the interplay between community and audience. Certainly, radio audiences shared some of the characteristics of communities—they engaged a common text with quasi-ritual regularity—and communities shared some of the qualities of audiences—Jewish immigrants made up the majority of Yiddish theater attendance. But the two were hardly congruent. Choosing to listen to Yiddish radio in addition to English radio represented an important act that, in this context, elicited strong communal overtones and reinforced structures of feeling that powerfully underlaid a sense of belonging to a Jewish community. The tension between the mass appeal of the medium and the minority status of Yiddish opens up an analytic space in which to grasp a better understanding of the symbiotic and often-fraught relationship between audience and community.

Benedict Anderson has written eloquently on the relationship between the mass media and the formation of a national consciousness, and he offers a bit of insight into how radio could have fostered a sense of community among Jewish immigrants to the United States. For Anderson, the mass media helped to cultivate a sense of commonality and belonging among populations too dispersed to meet face-to-face.[47] By sharing in the same print culture or by reading the same novels or newspapers, a population developed a common set of references and resources that allowed them to "imagine" themselves into a community. Anderson is helpful here but limited. He offers a way to understand how common bonds are forged across a population regardless of scale, especially with regard to the mass media, as we move here from "print capitalism" to broadcasting. However, his analysis focuses on the moments at which modern nations come into consciousness and their citizens begin thinking of themselves as a unified people. As such, it assumes a kind of conjuring up of nationalist sentiment from a situation in which one did not previously exist. Anderson's ability to trace and explain this phenomenon is one of the strengths of his work, but it reveals its limited if useful application here; Jews arrived in the United States in the years around the turn of the twentieth century with a sense of themselves as

Jews. A sense of commonality, underwritten by a common language, preceded the medium, but the medium allowed for increasingly complex articulations of that sense. The medium did not create the circumstances in which Jewish immigrants began to imagine themselves as a community, ex nihilo. Instead, it emerged within a multilingual medium and alongside a community already in formation, and instead of clarifying the bounds of that community, Yiddish radio complicated them.

The community that formed around Yiddish radio shared cultural traits before radio—or even the press or theater—spoke to them. They shared a common language, a recent history of immigration, a common set of cultural texts and references drawn largely from the Jewish religion. Practically, as well, many lived in the same neighborhoods, sent their children to the same public schools, and socialized, in the main, among other Jews.[48] Most important, however, they shared a common sense of themselves and one another as Jews that translated into certain programmatic conventions on the air. To be sure, the discussion of what does and what does not constitute a community and the power and politics of those distinctions are critically important, but they are not the focus of this book primarily because those people invested in the culture of Yiddish radio did not express this dimension of their communal life in those terms, though they certainly had other outlets for political expression and community mobilization.[49] Specifically with respect to radio, the question of community found its most powerful response through the audience's hopes and intentions for the medium and the culture it fostered. While Yiddish radio provided a venue for imagining—or reimagining—a community, the community that took shape around it did so not as a members of a sovereign, bounded group but as a group aware of its own porous boundaries and in explicit conversation with the broader community that it defined itself, in part, against. Thus this book extends Anderson's argument through an account of a more fluid notion of community, articulated and imagined and broadcast over the radio.

Yiddish radio played a key role in extending the structures of feeling among Jewish immigrants. As a cultural formation, Yiddish radio invited an examination of where the audience ended and where the community began. Not every radio audience constituted a community, and not every community translated into an audience.[50] The audience of Yiddish radio, unlike other American audiences, could be considered a community as they shared a set of concerns greater than those born of listening to the same program at the same time. And their contemporary imaginings of community took root in and translated into additional material effects. More than just an audience and in conversation with communal institutions, economics, and politics, Jewish immigrants heard on radio their community talking to and about itself.

ONE From the Mainstream to the Margin, 1920–1929

Pretty soon Jewish broadcasting stations will be opened and mother will hear all the cantors and rabbis and Jewish actors through the very same radio.

Editorial, *Jewish Daily Forward*, 3 August 1924

One cannot print a magazine for a dozen readers, nor can one broadcast for two hundred listeners, generally speaking. . . . The program will have to appeal to a vast army of listeners, and a proportionately wide range of tastes.

Carl Dreher, radio critic, 1925

By the time the first Yiddish program aired, in 1926, Yiddish-speaking Jewish immigrants had been listening to radio for at least three years; Yiddish newspapers had been publishing daily radio listings, advertisements for radio receivers, and articles about radio; images of radios had been appearing in advertisements for other products; and the radio had become a feature of novelty recordings and other works of art and popular culture. As radio gained in popularity, advertisers, retailers, and manufacturers of receivers began paying special attention to the Jewish immigrant market, targeting them as a discrete audience and consumer base. Owing in part to these efforts, by the end of the decade urban immigrants were among the most likely Americans to own a radio. That there were no Yiddish-language radio programs did not prevent a culture of Yiddish radio from taking root. Instead of an independent industry or a cultural practice born out of linguistic necessity, Yiddish radio grew out of the listening habits of immigrants developed while they tuned in to radio in English. Radio's penetration of Yiddish popular culture indicated that immigrants were involved in mainstream American culture and did not seem to mind that it spoke English exclusively, even while they imagined what Yiddish radio might sound like.

This means that Yiddish radio did not emerge as a thing apart from English-language radio but as an extension of it. Beholden not only to the broader framework of radio as it evolved in the early 1920s but also to the tastes for programming that its intended audience had begun to develop, Yiddish-speaking broadcasters found themselves in a peculiar situation. An audience of Yiddish speakers was in place, but broadcasters still had to develop ways to draw them out of and away from the mainstream audience. In contrast to standard narratives of assimilation that chart the movement of immigrant populations from the margin to the mainstream, the dynamics of Yiddish radio meant a movement from the mainstream to the margin. The development of an audience for Yiddish radio programs meant cultivating a sense of membership in a common audience among listeners who had grown comfortable tuning in to English programs. When they listened, why they listened, what they expected to hear, and what they heard is addressed in detail in the chapters that follow. Here I want to focus on the formation of a culture of Yiddish radio—when Jewish immigrant listeners embraced radio even before radio uttered its first Yiddish word.

LEARNING TO LISTEN TO ENGLISH

Most historians date the beginning of American broadcast radio to November 1920, when Frank Conrad, a radio hobbyist, aired results of that year's presidential election from the roof of a Westinghouse store in Pittsburgh, Pennsylvania.[1] Before Conrad, radio was used mainly by the military or by hobbyists tinkering with kits in their garages and basements. Anyone with a little scientific inclination, some spending money, and some leisure time could assemble a radio set that both broadcast and received signals, like a wireless telephone. Conrad's broadcast has become a fulcrum of sorts in American radio history, signaling a shift from radio as wireless telephony to broadcasting. Whether Conrad or Westinghouse should be properly credited with this shift is a matter of historiographical debate. But what is clear is that in the wake of this broadcast, companies such as Westinghouse and Philco began producing and marketing radio receivers for people wanting to hear what all the fuss was about.[2] In four short years the radio moved from a novelty to a phenomenon and from an esoteric hobby to a national industry. And this despite the fact that there was still very little to hear. In 1920 radio set sales generated $2 million. Four years later they accounted for $350 billion in sales. In 1922 the radio industry reported the sale of some 60,000 receivers. By January 1925 annual sales topped 3.7 million.[3]

Jewish immigrants, for their part, participated in the radio boom as actively as everyone else. Though no specific statistics exist for who bought radio sets, the majority of Jewish immigrants lived in urban areas, where radio signals and sales were strongest. Moreover, Jewish immigrants generally participated in popular culture more broadly, omnivorously consuming news from Broadway, Hollywood, and Tin Pan Alley. Jewish-owned phonograph shops sold recordings of the opera stars Enrico Caruso and Luisa Tetrazzinni, in addition to 78s of Yiddish theater performers and popular cantors. By the 1920s, nickelodeons, which could be found on almost every street on the Lower East Side, had begun to give way to more lavish movie palaces uptown, and younger Jews leaped at the chance to laugh at the antics of Chaplin, Arbuckle, and other stars on screens far larger and more glamorous than they had previously known.[4] Around this same time, Coney Island offered immigrant workers an affordable retreat from city heat, and New York's Hippodrome gave working boys and girls a place to socialize, dance, and spend whatever money their parents surrendered (or they managed to sock away).[5] As the prevalence of newspaper advertisements and listings indicate, Jewish immigrants spent their leisure time and disposable income on the new medium. Stars like Rudy Vallee and Samuel "Roxy" Rothafel became household names both in Yiddish and in English.

By mid-decade, most Jewish immigrants had developed a facility in English that would have allowed them easy access to radio programming. In 1925, the social scientist Mordecai Soltes surveyed readers of the

Yiddish press and found that a significant percentage read and understood English newspapers. Two-thirds of his respondents read English newspapers in addition to Yiddish ones, and another 20 percent could read English but did not read newspapers. Only 13 percent responded that they did not read English at all.[6] If two-thirds of those surveyed could *read* English, then an even greater percentage could *listen* to English-language radio programs, especially since much of radio broadcasting during the mid-1920s featured musical performances.

But Jewish immigrants' acceptance of English as the primary language of radio did not come without some self-consciousness. When the first programs with Jewish content aired in fall 1923, the *Forward* quickly noted that although the programs were Jewish, the medium still was not. These programs, sponsored by United Synagogue, the organizational body of Conservative Judaism in America, commemorated the High Holidays and featured an explanation of "the significance of [the] impending Jewish festivals or holidays, a rendition of the complete musical ritual of the particular service by a leading cantor and choir, and the recital of an appropriate Jewish legend or folk tale from the Talmud."[7] David J. Putterman, "the youngest and only American trained cantor," and his accompanist, Abraham Ellstein, the son of Jewish immigrants and a Juilliard-trained pianist, who were featured on the Yom Kippur program, represented a new generation of American-born Jews who could perform an ideal synthesis of American Judaism.

Despite the programs' significance for Jews, their timing was off. Because Jewish law prohibits the use of electricity on many holidays, neither of United Synagogue's two programs aired on the holidays themselves but a few days before, prompting the *Forward* to comment, "It's a bit too early, but after all, it's a *goyishe* [non-Jewish] station."[8] But would a Jewish station broadcast *on* Yom Kippur in violation of religious law and custom? The newspaper's humorous criticism echoed a sense that even though mainstream, English-language radio could address Jewish subjects, it remained culturally *goyish*. Ironically, the only time the newspaper found radio's *goyishness* important enough to mention was with respect to these two—and at this point, the only two—Jewish broadcasts. Otherwise, radio remained simply radio.

While the *Forward* labeled the medium culturally non-Jewish, at least one other listener recognized something else on the air. Saul Birns, a New York phonograph dealer and Jewish immigrant, heard in the High Holiday programs the possibility for Jewish broadcasting. Already one of the first dealers to advertise radios in the Yiddish press, he ran small bilingual Yiddish-English advertisements that accompanied the *Forward*'s radio listings. They read, "If you took benefit from the aforementioned programs, buy a radio on cash or installments from Saul Birns." The coincidental appearance of Birns's advertisements and the first radio listings suggests that he paid for the listings himself in an attempt to increase interest in the new medium and move more product.

Not content to sell radio receivers, Birns published a full-page advertisement in the *Forward* in October 1923 in which he laid out his vision of a Jewish radio station "through which the millions of Jews who live in New York and in the hundreds of cities and towns around New York City will be able every day to hear on their radio Yiddish music and songs, Yiddish lectures, popular science and all sorts of musical programs" (see figure 1).[9] Thanks to "special permission" from the Department of Commerce in Washington, Birns planned to open "the first and only foreign language broadcasting station," which would carry programs in German, Russian, Polish, and Yiddish. From his yet-to-be-completed studio in the heart of the Jewish East Side at 109 Second Avenue, he predicted that the "Saul Birns radio station [would become] the center of Jewish cultural life in America," adding, "When the Saul Birns radio broadcasting station is finished, it won't only be a mirror for the Jewish East Side, but for the Jews all over the country." As a "center of cultural life," Birns hoped his radio station would be Jewish in both content and context.

Birns's vision for the his Yiddish radio station was not merely one of entertainment or edification; he wanted to facilitate Jewish communal activity nationwide. Birns believed that Jews needed their own radio station that could speak directly to them in their own immigrant tongues. Much like his Progressive counterparts, who believed that radio could unify and uplift the citizens of the United States, Birns believed that his radio station could organize American Jews by providing a singular cultural voice. How much of his message could be attributed to busi-

Figure 1. The "Saul Birns Bulletin" announces, "Saul Birns Will Soon Open the First Yiddish Radio Station." *Jewish Daily Forward,* 6 October 1923, 7. Courtesy of the Forward Association.

ness acumen and how much expressed an honest assessment of the American Jewish population cannot be precisely identified. Nevertheless, his announcement certainly made clear that from the earliest echoes of American radio in Jewish immigrant communities, broadcasters held themselves responsible for providing both content and a community service. Moreover, Birns expressed a sense that English-language radio programs, regardless of content, could not adequately meet the needs and desires of Jewish audiences. For that, Yiddish-speaking audiences would need Yiddish-language programs, even if, for the time being, radio continued to speak English and Jewish audiences continued to listen.

Unfortunately, Birns's dream for radio would have to wait—but not on account of language. A few months later, Birns surrendered his vision, blaming his inability to organize a broadcast station on the "radio trust."[10] Although not, strictly speaking, a "trust," the coordinated interests of General Electric, Westinghouse, RCA, and AT&T effectively directed the growth of the industry and even, eventually, the laws that governed it.[11] Birns returned to his roots as an appliance dealer and wasted no time reminding his customers that "soon, practically no families will be able to get by without a radio, just like no civilized American can understand how one could live without a telephone, electric lights, automobiles, a phonograph, and so on."[12] As a businessman, he reverted to the idea that the real money could be found in selling broadcast hardware, not content, but that in order to sell radios he had to first sell the idea of radio generally and of Yiddish radio specifically. Birns's failure reinforced the fact that if Jewish immigrants were listening to radio, they were listening in English.

Birns, however, was not the only Yiddish speaker to imagine the possibilities of Yiddish radio. A few months before Birns tried to cash in on the radio boom, Baruch Charney Vladeck, managing editor of the *Jewish Daily Forward*, tried to arrange for the construction of a radio station at the Forward Building, the newspaper's Lower East Side home. "My father thought," recalled Vladeck's son, Stephen, "that the circulation then, which must have been about a hundred and fifty thousand, would wane and therefore the *Forward* needed some other way of communication."[13] In August 1923, Vladeck penned a letter to his friend David Sarnoff, chairman of RCA, asking for his assistance in arranging for a broadcast permit: "I am contemplating a broadcasting wireless station for the Forwards [sic] Building. I have been told that some kind of a permit is necessary for the erection of such a station and I wish to ask you to inform me of how to go about it."[14] Vladeck's request went unanswered, but it, along with Birns's advertisements in the Yiddish press, indicated that the culture of Yiddish radio had begun to take root some two and a half years before the first Yiddish-language broadcasts, and it developed in conjunction with a broader acceptance of English as the primary language of radio in America.

While Birns and Vladeck toyed with the idea of a Yiddish-speaking radio station, other writers addressed the medium's emergent popularity and reinforced the primacy of English. In 1924, when the *Forward* published its first full article about radio in the lives of Jewish families, it did so as a column on the newspaper's English-language page, a weekly feature that primarily addressed the English-speaking children of its Yiddish-speaking readers. The article posited the dilemma facing a poor immigrant family: should they buy a radio or a phonograph? "The proper thing," concluded the article, "is to get both a radio and a victrola. The former keeps one in touch with the daily world, the latter affords an opportunity to listen to the world's classics as often as one desires. The older generation could listen to heart's content to Jewish tunes and pieces by Jewish comedians. The younger set could get in touch with any broadcasting station and open floodgates of noise and merriment and fill themselves with dancing to physical exhaustion."[15] The depiction of the conflict between Yiddish-speaking parents and their English-speaking children reaffirmed the primary association between English and radio. Though the author imagined a future for "Jewish broadcasting stations," he never imagined them outside radio's primary function as a source of entertainment for a younger, English-speaking audience.

This attitude found additional support in Yiddish as well. When the New York radio station WHN hired a new announcer who spoke seven languages, including Yiddish, the newspaper treated it as little more than a publicity stunt, commenting, "[He is] the chairman of the air in seven languages—but you still can't understand him."[16] Perhaps most tellingly, when the *Forward* began publishing radio listings in 1923, it tended to give Yiddish transliterations of English program titles. Then, toward the end of 1924, the newspaper started printing its radio listings in English, a practice it continued for a number of months before reverting to transliterations.

Elsewhere, the *Forward*, ever conscious of its mission to help immigrant Jews learn to live in America, promoted the medium through a series of brief articles that explained what a radio set did and how it worked. The articles supplied diagrams of how to build a radio set, explained the difference between a crystal set and a tube set, provided instructions on how to install an antenna, and gave other suggestions about how its readers might enhance their enjoyment of the offerings of the new medium. Like the diagrams of baseball games or voting booths that the *Forward* famously used to teach its readers about life and customs in America, these columns taught readers how to take advantage of new technology so as to keep up with American popular culture.

As radio gained popularity and an audience among Jewish immigrants, it began to appear in other areas of Yiddish culture. In 1924 the B. Manischewitz Company, the matzo baker and producer of kosher food products, used the image of a radio in a series of print advertisements. One advertisement depicted a large globe with the horn of a radio peeking out from the lower right-hand corner (see figure 2). In large lettering, the advertisement boasted, "A name recognized the world over."[17] Despite the fact that few radio stations had the capability to broadcast more than thirty-five miles or so, Manischewitz's vision of itself as a "global brand" matched perfectly the imaginary power of radio that the company hoped to ride into Jewish homes "around the whole world." The combination of radio's wide recognition and its technological promise made it too potent a symbol for advertisers to resist.

Writers and performers began taking advantage of radio's popularity, too. In 1923, Rubin Goldberg, a minor performer in the Yiddish theater and future star of Yiddish radio, recorded a novelty record titled *Shloyme afn radio* (Shloime on the Radio), which likely poked fun at the idea of broadcasting in Yiddish.[18] Three years later, the Yiddish poet and author Avraham Reisen turned to the metaphor of radio as a source of comfort and a cure for isolation:[19]

It will fill your heart with pride
To hear London playing in New York

(London, too, at the same time
will be hearing the jazz that's played here . . .) . . .

Abundance for the rich people,
Only a song for the rest.

Maybe you're lonely like a town
The radio has something joyous for you

Listen to a little speech
And it will bring you a little happiness.

Figure 2. Advertisement for the B. Manischewitz Matzo Company. This is one of the first advertisements to use the image of a radio to promote another product. *Der tog,* 5 March 1924, 10.

By the time radio entered the metaphoric vocabulary of this Yiddish poet, it had spoken its first Yiddish words, yet it had already been speaking powerfully to Jewish immigrants for years, whether it carried messages of music or matzo.

Radio began to make its presence known in the realm of politics as well. A political cartoon from 1924 featured an image of a radio set to comment on a well-publicized speech by Louis Marshall, president of the American Jewish Committee (see figure 3).[20] In a speech carried by one of the New York stations, Marshall spoke in English about the plight of European Jewry in the wake of the Johnson-Reed Immigration Act, which effectively put an end to immigration from Eastern Europe. The following day, *Der tog* responded with a cartoon depicting a man sitting by a radio listening to Marshall's appeal. The man, identified as "American Jew," held a "radio music program" on his lap and listened attentively to the words calling for donations of "$500,000 to save Jewish refugees from disaster" coming from the radio's speaker. The caption read, "The music that must arouse [its listeners]." An editorial accompanying the cartoon linked Marshall's speech to the power of radio to mobilize American Jews in support of their friends and relatives in Europe. The global scale of the issue and the popular fantasies of radio intersected to give this columnist an opportunity to urge his audience to act. The columnist concluded, "The radio brought the moving words of Louis Marshall to the ears of American Jews. And if they cannot again say as they used to—*na'aseh venishma* [lit., "we shall perform and we shall hear"; Exod. 24:7]—so they'll instead say—*nishma vena'aseh*—when they've already heard—now they should do something."[21] By reversing the biblical injunction, he reinforced the ability of radio to speak to Jews and Jewish communal concerns while still primarily speaking English.

The appearance of radio in newspaper articles, advertisements, and entertainment, though they did not add up to a single Yiddish word, cumulatively captured two trends that began to take hold among Yiddish-speaking Americans. First, by the mid-1920s, Yiddish-speaking immigrants embraced radio at a pace similar to their English-speaking counterparts. A set of cultural meanings and habits began to accrue around radio, and the medium began to settle in to the lives of Jewish

Figure 3. Cartoon commenting on a speech by the American Jewish leader Louis Marshall about recent legislation restricting the immigration of Jews from Eastern Europe. The back of the chair reads, "American Jew." And the cartoon is titled "The Music That Must Arouse." *Der tog,* 20 November 1924, 4.

immigrants. Second, the language barrier did not exist. Jewish immigrants embraced radio and participated in it as an English-language medium. Though some writers and businessmen certainly considered the possibilities for radio that spoke specifically to a Jewish immigrant audience, most imagined themselves into the broader emergent American audience, willing to accept English without question, at least for now.

Radio's English roots, in combination with listeners' facility with English, meant that even when Yiddish programs appeared, for most listeners Yiddish remained a choice, an idea captured by a new crop of movies and recordings. *The Lunatic,* a 1927 Yiddish silent film, featured a telling scene in which a couple (played by Ludwig Satz and Paula Klida) argued over what they should listen to.[22] Satz wanted to listen to a Yiddish program; Klida preferred an English one. The dispute concluded in typical vaudeville fashion, as the couple made up in time to perform a musical duet. The following year, Rubin Goldberg adapted *The Lunatic* for a novelty record titled *Moyshe koyft a radio* (Moishe Buys a Radio).[23] Goldberg, who had recorded a similar side in 1923, updated the joke to echo radio's bilingualism. In the recording, Goldberg plays Moyshe, who bought a radio for his wife in honor of her birthday. Turning on the radio to find Caruso, his wife objects, claiming that it sounds too much like the "world to come." He tries a number of other stations before landing on a fictional Yiddish station whose call letters are aleph beis gimel dalet (the first four letters of the Yiddish alphabet), just in time to hear a short speech about why it's better to be a fool than a wise man. This sketch, too, concluded in typical vaudeville style, in a hurry and without much regard for plot development, with Goldberg and his partner performing the popular Yiddish number "Lomir zikh iberbeten" (Let's Make Up).[24]

In theater, radio was the central plot device in Joseph Rumshinsky's 1929 operetta, *Dos radio meydl* (The Radio Girl), which starred Lucy Levin and Molly Picon (see figure 4). The show was a typical Yiddish melodrama about love, confusion, identity, and just deserts. Levin played a popular radio singer whose voice caused a young gentleman to fall in love with her without ever having seen her face. The young man seeks out the object of his affection but mistakes Picon for Levin, and the three spend the remainder of the show straightening things out. The

Figure 4. Newspaper advertisement for Joseph Rumshinsky's musical *Dos radio meydl.* The show featured Lucy Levine as the title character and Molly Picon in a supporting role. *Jewish Daily Forward,* 13 October 1929, II:21. Courtesy of the Forward Association.

show opened at the Second Avenue Theater on Friday, 18 October 1929, and in a stroke of early cross-promotion, Picon and Levin made a guest appearance on WBBC a week before opening night.[25] But even a real radio broadcast could not save the show's unfortunate timing: the stock market began its slide the following Monday, and by Friday, the bottom had fallen out and the Great Depression had begun. To blame the depression for *Dos radio meydl*'s failure would be unfair, however, as it met with lukewarm reviews, although Picon, as usual, stole the show.[26]

This second wave of the use of radio in other media illustrated not only how deeply and how quickly Jewish immigrants accepted radio but also that radio was no easier to decipher once it began speaking Yiddish. If anything, radio became more complicated, as families and audiences now had to choose between English and Yiddish programs. Jewish immigrants were not agitating for Yiddish radio entertainment, but people like Birns and Vladeck saw in them a potential audience and hoped that once radio could speak Yiddish, the audience would materialize.

A *YIDISH KONTSERT*

Audiences, retailers, manufacturers, and Jewish newspapers were so tuned in to English programs that the first Yiddish program passed almost without notice. Buried in the broadcast schedule for Wednesday, 27 January 1926, the *Forward* included a small item about a concert that would air that evening on WHN.[27] This "Yidish kontsert" featured a Rabbi Shumovitch, a Cantor Shteinberg, and a "guitar duet." *Der tog* did not mention the program. The concert proved successful enough to become a short-lived series, and each Wednesday evening for the next few weeks WHN treated listeners to fifteen minutes of Yiddish entertainment. Whether or not Shumovitch spoke Yiddish or the guitar players performed arrangements of music from the Yiddish folk or theater tradition, the broadcast marked the beginning of a new phase in Yiddish radio culture. Unlike the novelty of a multilingual announcer or an English-language High Holiday program, this represented something different: it was, according to the Yiddish newspaper, a "Yiddish concert."

Yiddish had become an adjective, not a noun. It was not a guest appearance or a onetime "song in Yiddish" or a gimmick. In this instance, Yiddish-as-adjective signaled the concretization of an aural culture that preceded Saul Birns and that would continue to evolve on America's airwaves throughout the remainder of the twentieth century and into the twenty-first. The culture had begun to take shape, and only now, after radio had thoroughly penetrated the everyday lives of Jewish immigrants, could something called a "Yiddish concert" appear. This concert hinted at a new cultural formulation that described something greater than content, a performer's ethnicity, or even the language used. It implied that the culture of radio that had taken form in English up to this point had begun to develop a Yiddish accent.

After the appearance of WHN's "Yidish kontsert," other Yiddish programs could be found around the radio dial. Just two weeks later, the Yiddish Art Theater purchased fifteen minutes on New York's WRNY to promote its production of the Yiddish writer and folklorist S. An-Ski's play, *The Dybbuk*.[28] In the weeks that followed, audiences in New York could have heard Cantor Dan Fuchs sing arias and folk songs, a lecture about Jews, an appearance by "well-known Jewish actors," another concert of unspecified "Yiddish music," and a performance by the "Jewish-English" actress and singer Bertha Kalish. During the next two years, audiences in Chicago, Boston, Philadelphia, and Los Angeles would also hear the first programs in Yiddish.[29]

Los Angeles heard its first Yiddish radio shows in January 1928, with ninety minutes of unspecified "Jewish programs" on KTBI. Although they did not survive the decade, they opened the door for others, such as *Negina,* which was sponsored by Abraham Brodies, a butcher, and the Chicago Drug Store, and debuted on KELW in 1931. The Los Angeles Anglo-Jewish press welcomed *Negina* into the city's multiethnic radio lineup: "To the broadcasting arts of different nationalities of the city of Los Angeles was added a rare novelty art. The lovers of radioland will have the pleasure to listen to the 'Nagenoh' [sic] hour; when pure and rare Jewish music which is so popular for the "Echo of the Jewish heart."[30] The article continued by inviting listeners to submit requests for music. *Negina* was joined soon after its debut by the *Jewish International*

Hour, which offered community announcements, music, and "Jewish news" and aired regularly through the late 1930s.[31]

In Chicago, Yiddish broadcasting began in April 1927 with the *Yiddish Hour* on WEDC.[32] The *Yiddish Hour* quickly disappeared, but shortly thereafter WMBI began carrying Friday night services every other week, and WCFL, the station of the Chicago Federation of Labor, added its own Yiddish programs.[33] Meanwhile, Philadelphia's Yiddish newspaper, the *Idishe velt,* launched its eponymous program on WCAU in January 1928 with a thirty-minute concert starring Cantor Moyshe Oysher and the cellist Samuel Geshikhter, who played Kol Nidre.[34] The newspaper supported its program with front-page articles that announced or reviewed the most recent shows. One such article mentioned a "report": "Hundreds of readers have written to us saying that they are anxiously waiting to tune in so that they can hear the program of modern Jewish music." In a prescient cross-promotional move, Shuman Brothers, a local radio dealer, took out an advertisement in conjunction with the program's debut that promised, "We guarantee to deliver and install any radio you buy from us in time to hear this wonderful concert."[35] These relationships between newspapers, radio stations, and radio dealers strengthened the material dimension of this aural culture and gave the structures of feeling routed through radio yet another manifestation.

As it emerged in Philadelphia, Los Angeles, and New York and, later, in cities such as Baltimore and Cleveland, Yiddish radio programming relied on delicate networks of relationships among Yiddish-speaking performers, Jewish-owned stores, the Yiddish press, and locally owned radio stations. The one exception to this rule made its debut in 1928, when *Der tog's Yiddish Program,* a weekly Sunday afternoon radio revue sponsored by the Yiddish newspaper, appeared on New York's WABC. At the time, Alfred Grebe, a local businessman, owned the station, which he hoped would anchor the burgeoning network that he called the Atlantic Broadcasting Company. Before Grebe could launch his ABC, however, William Paley, who had recently begun to organize his Columbia Broadcast System, bought WABC with the intention of turning it into his network's flagship station. Paley, more concerned at this point with signing up stations to participate in his network than with the quality or tone of his programming, simply transferred WABC's existing lineup to his new network and carried *Der tog's Yiddish Program* as part of his network's weekly programming until 1930, making this the only Yiddish program to be carried on a national network.[36]

A RACE FOR FIRST PLACE

In mid-1926, only a few months into the life of Yiddish-language radio programming, the *Forward* found itself behind in the race for a radio audience. Since Vladeck's failed attempt to secure permission for a radio tower for the Forward Building, the newspaper seemed resigned to play a supporting role in the development of radio by printing advertisements, schedules, and articles about the industry and its stars. Meanwhile, in spring 1926, just up the Lower East Side from the Forward Building, local businessman Max Bernstein completed construction on the Libby's Hotel and Turkish Baths.[37] Named after Bernstein's mother and featuring a portrait of her in the lobby, Libby's promised to become one of the most prominent buildings in the neighborhood, with a lavish ballroom, guest rooms, kitchen, and elaborately appointed baths. Bernstein celebrated the opening in grand fashion. He announced the hotel as "a step in 'the redemption of the ease [sic] side'" and hailed it as a "milestone in the history of New York Jewry."[38] *Der tog* and the *Forward* focused their coverage on the building and its facilities, but one week earlier, a small article in the *New York Times* had reported an aspect of the hotel that had escaped New York's Yiddish newspapers. The headline read simply, "To Broadcast in Yiddish."[39]

This news did not sit well with the people at the *Forward*. While Bernstein finished construction on his new building and broadcast facilities, the *Forward* hastily put together a "radio concert" to broadcast on New York City's municipal station, WNYC, on Friday, 2 May—a week *before* Libby's scheduled its inaugural broadcast. Courting a broad, not exclusively Jewish audience, the *Forward* bought a series of small advertisements in the *New York Times* to promote the program. But in its own pages, the Yiddish newspaper was a little less modest. A front-page headline urged readers, "Listen to it with a neighbor if you don't have a radio at home!"[40] The article that followed explained that the Stringwood

Ensemble would play one piece by Mozart and another by Tchaikovsky and that Isa Kramer, a star of the Yiddish stage, intended to sing one song each in Russian, English, and Yiddish, as Abe Cahan, editor of the *Forward*, presided over the evening's festivities.

On the Sunday following the *Forward radio kontzert*, the newspaper reported, "First 'Forwards' Radio Concert a Great Success." A front-page article observed, "Readers make parties in houses to hear the program," and reported that in Monticello, New York, a crowd gathered in the town square to hear the concert over a loudspeaker.[41] The remainder of the coverage paid lip service to the concert itself and offered faint praise for the evening's "moving performances," focusing instead on the sizable Jewish audience that the program managed to attract. Although not the first Yiddish program, the *Forward*'s account of listening parties and public gatherings represents the first report of an actual audience for them. The programs that preceded the *Forward*'s, despite the cultural shift they represented, may or may not have managed to actually attract listeners. While the *Forward* clearly had good reason to exaggerate the size of its audience, the report nonetheless captured a moment in which the audience proved more newsworthy than the program. And, perhaps more important, this moment saw the coalescence of a discrete audience for Yiddish programming.

Ironically, the *Forward*'s emphasis on its audience inadvertently sealed its own fate as a broadcaster. For all the fanfare in print, no *Forward radio kontsert* broadcast the next week or the week after, due to "arrangements (pending) with another station." The *Forward* finally returned to the air on Sunday, 13 June 1926, on WMCA, but not even a concerted promotional effort and the appearance of Tosha Seidel, "The Magician of the Fiddle," could save the series, and it quickly disappeared again. The *Forward* admitted that its primary problem lay in the fact that it committed to broadcasting on Friday evenings, noting that it received many requests from "*Forward* readers who are also radio listeners" to change the day and time of the program because Fridays still belonged to the Yiddish theater.[42] The *Forward*, for its part, bet that the allure of radio would be an alternative, and possibly even a challenge, to the dominance of the theater. However, the newspaper underestimated the power of that institution and overestimated the attraction of the still-new radio as a viable alternative. Yet its failure was a result not just of poor planning but of an emerging and still quite complex constellation of forces that the newspaper only barely understood. Its newfound radio audience represented a significant advance in the culture of Yiddish radio, but it misjudged the power and momentum of cultural practices that their audience, or the audience they hoped to carve out, also already participated in. People habituated to attending the theater or listening to English programs would not necessarily shift their attention and their behavior just because Yiddish programming became available. Just because people *could* hear programs in Yiddish did not meant that they *would*.

Even with the widespread popularity of radio, the relative acceptance of English as the language of radio, the comfort of immigrant Jews with English, and the availability of Yiddish programs, developing and attracting an audience remained a challenge. And for all the fanfare in print, the *Forward* understood that in order to cultivate an audience for Yiddish programs, the newspaper—or any broadcaster, for that matter—would have to rely on an existing base of listeners. This became clear when the *Forward* tried to relaunch its concert series later that year. In a full-page advertisement, the newspaper asked its readership:

> Do you already have a radio at home?
> Do you have the same pleasures as other people?
> Have no fear of radio—it is really a new invention
> Open your home to the wonderful invention of our time.[43]

The advertisement did not mention Yiddish but focused instead on selling radio to readers. It intimates the *Forward*'s understanding that Yiddish programming alone would not be enough to draw people away from phonographs or live performances, nor could it exist without the widespread acceptance of radio generally. Like Saul Birns, the *Forward* understood that there had to be listeners before an audience could be drawn from among them. If Yiddish-language broadcasting was going to succeed at all, the advertisement suggested, it would have to carve an audience of Jewish immigrants out of radio's general listenership.

While the *Forward* floundered, a few blocks away Libby's prepared itself for its radio debut. In a half-page advertisement in the *Forward*, electric letters splayed across an image of the hotel's facade exclaiming, "The First Yiddish Radio in the World in Libby's" (see figure 5).[44] A business-man, not a broadcaster, Bernstein did not buy his own radio station but rather made arrangements to broadcast over WFBH, a small New York station that broadcast from the top of the Hotel Majestic, an Upper West Side hotel. Bernstein spared no expense, hiring as his musical director Josef Cherniavsky, the former cello soloist of the Petrograd Imperial Opera House, leader of the Yiddish-American Jazz Band, and widely known as "the Jewish Paul Whiteman." Cherniavsky, coming off a successful national tour, brought a softer, smoother, "pop" sensibility to the music of Jewish immigrants by adding American-style orchestrations and more danceable rhythms than the typical Jewish wedding bands of the time. Blending American style and Jewish melodies, Cherniavsky promised to provide the perfect sound track for Libby's radio show.[45] Bernstein matched his Americanized musical pitch with a lineup of Jewish stars with crossover appeal in mainstream American entertainment and invited performers such as George Jessel and Molly Picon to appear on the program.

Unlike the *Forward radio kontsert,* which challenged the institution of the theater, the *Libby's Program* complemented it and thus managed to attract and sustain an audience. Airing on Sunday afternoons instead of Friday nights and featuring a more Americanized sound, *Libby's* supple-mented existing patterns of Yiddish entertainment and, in so doing, expanded them. More important, however, *Libby's* patterned itself on an already successful English-language protogenre: The hotel-hosted, star performer–oriented variety program. Though it aired in Yiddish, *Libby's* did not distance itself from emergent English-language musical vari-ety programs like *Goldie and Dusty, The Gold Dust Twins,* or the *Cliquot Club Eskimos* that also took their names from their sponsors, according to the advertising convention of the time. *Libby's* modeled itself on its English counterparts by presenting a variety program that featured a house band—Cherniavsky in place of the "Eskimos"—and supporting an eclectic roster of performers each week. On the strength of its suc-cessful combination of American and immigrant taste, the *Libby's radio program* became the first truly successful Yiddish program and eventu-ally expanded to two broadcasts each week for two seasons.

Ironically, Max Bernstein did not launch the *Libby's radio program* because of a passion for radio. Unlike Baruch Charney Vladeck or Saul Birns, both of whom shared a fascination with the new medium and understood its broader cultural and communal potential, Bernstein started his program in order to promote the facilities of his new hotel. But the program proved more successful than the hotel, and by June 1929, the building was in foreclosure, having fallen prey to the changing demographics of Jewish New York.[46]

Structurally, the early success of the *Libby's radio program* established the presence and interest of an audience of Jewish immigrants that realized the hopes of Birns, Vladeck, and Cahan. In terms of content, it set the rhythm for the aural culture that would come to characterize Yiddish radio during its development over the next twenty or so years. Modeling programs and performances after English-language shows and complementing Yiddish performances with arrangements drawn from American popular music would become two of the central aesthetic conventions of the medium. Its ability to fit Yiddish content into existing listening habits succeeded—accidentally or otherwise—where the *Forward* failed. By presenting a sound that suited Jewish immigrant ears both as members of the general radio audience and as immigrants, *Libby's* amplified the possibility that Yiddish-language radio programming could thrive. Both structurally and aesthetically, *Libby's* solidified the audience that the *Forward* identified but never developed.

Once the audience took shape, the airwaves opened up. In the wake of *Libby's,* programs began to appear more regularly, and Yiddish-speaking broadcasters wasted no time turning Jewish religious and cultural life into mass entertainment. Beginning in 1927, Yiddish radio programs celebrated practically every Jewish holiday on the calendar. Passover, Purim, Hanukkah, Shavuot, and especially the High Holidays elicited

Figure 5 (opposite).   Advertisement for the debut of the *Libby's Hotel Program*, the first successful Yiddish radio program. Note the radio towers to the left and right of the image and the "electric" lettering. Performers on the debut include Mashka and Cantor David Roitman. Note also pictures of Libby's owner, Max Bernstein; the hotel's musical director, Joseph Cherniavsky; and the building's facade. *Jewish Daily Forward,* 22 May 1926, 4. Courtesy of the Forward Association.

an outpouring of programming, including broadcasts described by the *Forward* with Yinglish adjectives—"Kol nidreish" (from Kol Nidre, the opening hymn of Yom Kippur) and "Yom toverdiker" (Holiday-like)— suggesting the evocation but not necessarily the observance of particular holidays.[47] In addition to holidays, Jewish religious and cultural life offered an almost endless array of opportunities for Yiddish speakers to adapt for broadcast. Following the successful formulas of Yiddish plays and musicals, which often included dramatizations of life-cycle events, Yiddish radio entrepreneurs found they were able to up the ante. Because radio broadcast "live," announcers did not have to limit themselves to dramatizations, and they eagerly began airing real ritual events and gravitated toward those with the greatest sentimental and communal resonance.

Weddings provided much popular fare for broadcasters during the late 1920s. The Yiddish-speaking radio star Rubin Goldberg broadcast his own nuptials on WABC in 1928, complete with the full sponsorship of Branfman's Kosher Sausages and supported by an advertisement featuring photos of Goldberg and his bride alongside Mr. Branfman.[48] On the *Libby's Program*, Max Bernstein hosted a contest that promised the winners "a million guests," a free "wedding with all the trimmings," and a set of furniture in exchange for the opportunity to broadcast their wedding. The winners, Ms. Mirl Treiber and Mr. Benjamin Alperovitch, happily aired their nuptials in June 1926.[49] Other ritual broadcasts served even deeper communal purposes, such as WRNY's broadcast of a bar mitzvah celebration, hosted by Rabbi J. Hopman and his choir, while Jewish orphans' homes from around the city broadcast their own *b'nai mitzvah*, inviting listeners to fill in for the orphans' absent families.

But the appearance of a virtual family of listeners, or the presence of "a million guests" at a wedding, could not replace the largely face-to-face interactions of a community. "Listening parties" could not fulfill the religious obligations of guests at Jewish life cycle events. Listening was one thing, but participating in ritual was another, and audiences, especially religious audiences, felt this tension keenly. While radio broadcasters frequently blurred the lines between audience and community for publicity purposes, the actual experience of listening to religious rituals on the radio often complicated or confused their meanings. While Yiddish-speaking broadcasters and American Progressives still invested radio with every manner of hope that it could ameliorate social ills and inequalities while strengthening a sense of national belonging, within the Jewish community radio occasionally seemed to raise more questions than it answered.

A month after the *Libby's* wedding broadcast, the *Forward* ran a cartoon depicting Reb Yankev Leib, an elderly Jew standing over a radio with the Hebrew words, "Borei Pri Hagafen"—the blessing over wine—emerging from the radio's horn. The cartoon's English caption read, "Reb Yankev Leib is torn between conflicting emotions. Should he say 'amen' or applaud the cantor's fine singing" (see figure 6).[50] Although the fictional rabbi heard the blessing over wine, he could not determine what he had heard; was it a performance or a ritual? What would be the proper response to a real blessing, spoken as part of a real ritual, heard over the radio by a man accustomed to sacralizing a blessing by responding to it in person? Just because radio broadcast religious content did not mean that the audience received the same, and just because the radio spoke Yiddish did not mean that its audience understood what it was saying or what it meant.

Though sometimes confusing, misunderstandings or mistranslations were part of the culture of Yiddish radio. Whereas more didactic venues like the answers to letters printed in the popular Yiddish advice column, the *Bintl briv*, newspaper editorials, or even advertisements tried to explain America to their immigrant audiences, radio programs invited listeners to translate both the languages and the cultures in which they were now living. English, Yiddish, American, and immigrant all combined to create radio's aural culture, where translation of both, rather than fluency in one, became a listener's most valuable skill. Already a historical fact of Jewish life, radio required Jewish immigrant listeners to recalibrate this skill with respect to a mass medium. By the end of 1926, radios carried programs in Yiddish and English, but although they were bilingual, radios could not translate. Making sense of these programs and the cultural changes they wrought lay in the hands, heads, and ears of their audience.

Broadcasting a Jewish Wedding

Reb Yankev Leib is torn between conflicting emotions: Should he say "Amen!" or applaud the cantor's fine singing?

Figure 6. Cartoon from the *Forward*'s English Page highlighting some of the contradictions between ritual and entertainment that the invention of radio fostered. *Jewish Daily Forward,* 4 July 1926, 4. Courtesy of the Forward Association.

The culture of Yiddish radio took root among Jewish immigrants well in advance of the first Yiddish programs. Novelty records, advertisements, and radio listings appeared before radio's first Yiddish word. When the first programs did appear, they both relied on and mobilized the broader apparatus of mainstream radio to support their endeavors. Meanwhile, Yiddish-speaking immigrants learned how to attend to radio through their experiences of the Yiddish theater and press and by becoming consumers of radio programs in English. As immigrant consumers of English-language programs, they seemed to fit the audience profile of radio's Progressive idealists, as well as that of Secretary Hoover, who hoped that radio would unify the nation and its interests. Radio, they argued, could teach English and American culture to its immigrant listeners. However, everyone underestimated the powerful affective allure of Yiddish programming and how bilingualism informed the creation of a listening audience and an ethnic community.

Always engaged in acts of cultural and linguistic translation, Yiddish radio listeners inadvertently challenged the subtle nationalist narratives that drove radio regulation during the 1920s. Instead of presenting American culture for immigrants to consume and assimilate wholesale, radio opened up avenues for expressions of immigrant American identities both outside of the audible mainstream and in conversation with it. This dynamic both reinforced and undermined the sense of a particular community of Yiddish speakers that participated in radio in both Yiddish and English. From behind the microphone, early Yiddish-speaking radio broadcasters worked within the structures and strictures of the emergent medium as they learned to extract an audience from one already tuned in to English-language programs. Audiences, meanwhile, grew comfortable with radio both any listening in English and by encountering it in other cultural areas as well. The emergence of programming in Yiddish relied on programming in English and on an audience of Jewish immigrants who had, by 1926, learned how to listen but were still trying to figure out the meanings of what they heard.

TWO Americanization, Audience, Community, Consumers, 1925–1936

The ether is a public medium, and its use must be for public benefit. The use of a radio channel is justified only if there is public benefit. The dominant element for consideration in the radio field is, and always will be, the great body of the listening public, millions in number, countrywide in distribution.

Secretary of Commerce Herbert Hoover, 1925

The typical listening audience for a radio program is a tired, bored, middle-aged man and woman whose lives are empty and who have exhausted their sources of outside amusement when they have taken a quick look at an evening paper. . . . Radio provides a vast source of delight and entertainment for the barren lives of millions.

Roy Durstine, "The Future of Radio Advertising in the United States," 1935

Just as radio transformed from a hobby into a near-necessity, a series of successively restrictive laws virtually closed the door on immigration from Eastern Europe. Encouraged by labor unrest, bolstered by popular pseudoscience, and supported by conservative Anglo-American members of government, a groundswell of nativist sentiment succeeded in influencing the passage of two anti-immigration bills in 1921 and 1924. The measures placed stringent quotas on the number of immigrants permitted to enter the United States and effectively ended the wave of immigration that began around 1880 and had seen the relocation of some 23 million people to the United States, including nearly 2.5 million Jews.[1] In his 1923 State of the Union address, President Calvin Coolidge infamously supported limiting immigration based on the perceived inability of immigrants to become proper citizens. "American institutions rest solely on good citizenship," he stated. "They were created by people who had a background of self-government. New arrivals should be limited to our capacity to absorb them into the ranks of good citizenship. America must be kept American. For this purpose, it is necessary to continue a policy of restricted immigration. It would be well to make such immigration of a selective nature with some inspection at the source, and based either on a prior census or upon the record of naturalization."[2] Coolidge's presidential remarks recapitulated comments he had made as vice president two years earlier, with more troubling and more overt racial overtones. In an article published in *Good Housekeeping* in 1921, Coolidge wrote, "America must be kept American. Biological laws show . . . that Nordics deteriorate when mixed with other races."[3] The mixture of civil and racial discourses suited American nativist sentiment, as it drew on both social and political fears that the sheer numbers of immigrants could neutralize the American "melting pot" and render it unable to alchemize undisciplined immigrants into American citizens.

From both ends of the political spectrum, Progressives and xenophobes considered immigrants a problem in need of a solution. Nativists believed that they could solve the problem by simply shutting immigrants out; Progressives tried to improve the situation of immigrants by strategically intervening in housing, health care, labor rights, family structures, and other areas of immigrant life.[4] Concerns about the assimilability of immigrants into the American mainstream persisted long after the imposition of strict immigration quotas and continued to reflect deep social concerns that policy alone could not solve. Immigrants were not only largely working class; they were foreign and thus stood twice removed from Victorian and American Progressive ideals of good, disciplined citizens. Many believed that immigrants could be turned into productive members of American society by learning English, acquiring appropriate social and cultural skills, and absorbing the civic values that defined American society as they understood it.

The idea that immigrants threatened the stability and character of the nation dovetailed with concurrent concerns about radio. Radio could teach immigrants English, inform them of American politics, culture, and life, and accelerate their absorption of American civic ideals. Many placed their faith in radio's perceived ability to lift immigrants out of their isolated communities and include them in debates on national issues. Journals such as *Popular Radio* and *Radio Broadcast* praised radio for its unique ability to "promote cultural unity" by servicing every small town and farm from coast to coast and putting all of America in touch.[5] One such article argued, "Perhaps no man could mould these one hundred and twenty millions of people into a harmonious whole, bound together by a strong national consciousness; but in place of a superhuman individual, the genius of the last decade has provided a force—and that force is radio."[6] As evidence for his argument about the power of radio, the author explained, "To-day we see it everywhere, in Little Italy, Chinatown, Slovakia, etc., each retaining, as far as possible, the customs, language, and traditions of its mother country. Each is a parasite living upon the natural resources and under the protection offered by America. . . . Our problem is evident. It is the problem of assimilation, not only of the foreign-speaking people but of millions of people who enjoy the privileges of American citizenship, yet who secretly cherish and adhere to the traditions and customs of their mother country."[7] His argument about the potential of radio to unify the country was thus rooted in concern not only for improving the lot of all Americans but also specifically in response to the presence of immigrants who seemed more significantly in need of "assimilation" than others. An article in *Collier's* magazine credited radio with "spreading mutual understanding to all sections of the country, unifying our thoughts, ideals and purposes, making us a strong and well-knit people."[8] Radio held the promise of a technological solution to social problems by bringing those marginalized by geography, class, race, nationality, or language within earshot of the American mainstream.

Ironically, instead of moving from a multilingual country of immigrants to a more ordered nation of English speakers, radio diversified during the 1920s and became more hospitable to non-English speakers on the airwaves, albeit accidentally. During the 1920s, radio grew rapidly, but the federal government balked at the prospect of instituting a formal governing or oversight body. Instead, beginning in 1922, Secretary Hoover organized a series of four national radio conferences that, he hoped, would empower the industry to organize and regulate itself. Encouraged by Hoover and agreed to (in practice) by the interested parties, self-regulation collapsed when Chicago's radio station WJAZ intentionally challenged the Commerce Department's ability to enforce the agreements that emerged from the conferences.[9] In his ruling on the case, Judge James Wilkerson determined that the Commerce Department had no power to regulate radio and that its authority extended only to the ability to grant—not deny—requests for broadcast licenses. As a result, the United States housed some 15,111 amateur stations, 1,902 shipboard stations, 553 land stations for maritime use, and 536 broadcasting stations but had no regulatory framework or vested authority to govern the behavior of broadcasters. Judge Wilkerson's decision forced Secretary Hoover's hand, but without congressional action, Hoover could not act. Wilkerson's decision pushed the industry into virtual chaos.

Small and large stations alike took advantage of the power vacuum to claim squatters' rights on wavelengths of their choosing. During the seven months following the WJAZ decision, nearly two hundred new stations applied for and received licenses to broadcast as already overcrowded airwaves became even more crowded. Small stations accounted for the majority of new licenses, and many of these would go on to host multilingual programs for their cities' immigrant populations. Los Angeles station KELW took advantage of the lapse in oversight, as did Chicago's WHFC. In New York, the nation's largest radio market, twenty new stations took to the air, nearly half of which went on to carry Yiddish radio programming, including WABC, WARD (which became WSGH), WBBC, WBKN, WBRS (which became WCDA), WCGU, WPCH, and WWRL. These stations often sounded as varied and multiethnic as the audiences and communities they served. On any given afternoon, listeners could hear programs in any number of languages in fifteen-minute segments.

Even as radio writers, politicians, and representatives of larger commercial interests voiced their hope that radio would both unify and serve an audience "millions in number, countrywide in distribution," independent radio interests began appealing to immigrant ears on the basis of linguistic difference rather than in spite of it. The debut of the NBC network in 1926 certainly buoyed fantasies of a national audience, but immigrant audiences, when given the chance, turned their attention to local programming on smaller stations with weaker broadcast signals. To be sure, immigrants continued to listen to radio programming in English, but during "radio chaos" the airwaves opened up and so did the audience. Thus the very audiences that Progressive and nativist interests tried to influence began to speak and to listen for themselves when the opportunity presented itself. New stations cultivated new audiences that were both a part of and apart from the broader American audience that had been imagined by Hoover and NBC. The differences between these discrete audiences, the communities they represented, and the popular notion of the broader American audience influenced the development of the radio industry as radio interests slowly made progress toward defining the people they were supposed to serve.

WHO IS AN AUDIENCE?

Between 1921 and 1927, Congress debated no fewer than fifteen regulatory schemes to replace the outdated Radio Acts of 1912 and 1922. Finally, Representative Wallace White (R-Maine) and Senator Clarence Dill (D-Washington), both of whom had participated in the radio conferences, introduced what would become the Radio Act of 1927. Effectively, this act accomplished two things. First, it established the Federal Radio Commission (FRC) as the governing body of radio. Second, it established "public interest, convenience, or necessity" as the standard by which radio stations and programs would be evaluated. The newly established FRC offered the following clarification of the "public interest" standard: "[It is] a matter of comparative and not an absolute standard when applied to broadcasting stations. . . . All of them give more or less service. Those who give the least, however, must be sacrificed for those who give the most. The emphasis must be first and foremost on the interest, the convenience, and the necessity of the listening public, and not on the interest, convenience, or necessity of the individual broadcaster or the advertiser."[10] The attention to protecting the public as a virtual audience set a powerful precedent for how radio regulators understood their relationship to American audiences and in whose name they were empowered to act.

Representative White explained further, "We [the participants in the radio conference of 1924] have reached the definite conclusion that the right of all of our people to enjoy this means of communication can be preserved only by the repudiation of the idea underlying the 1912 law that anyone who will may transmit and by the assertion in its stead of the doctrine that the right of the public to service is superior to the right of any individual to use the ether."[11] Essentially, White inverted the issue of free speech in the specific context of radio to protect reception rather than access. According to White, the First Amendment, applied in the context of radio, protected the "right of the public to service," not the rights of broadcasters to speak. By placing the audience at the legislative center and establishing its "right" to listen, the 1927 Radio Act reaffirmed the place of the audience at the center of radio, but it did little to reconcile the question of who, generally or precisely, counted as part of the American radio audience.

In his study of American audiences, Richard Butsch makes a compelling argument that the nature of audiences is inherently social. Grounding his study in the history of theater, Butsch argues that entertainments such as theatergoing and listening to the radio are embedded in existing social practices (going out to dinner, visiting with friends or family) and therefore borrow, rather than disconnect, from those social structures.[12] Though he does not address immigrant audiences in great depth, his overall argument applies here in a general way: in spite of the imagined unity and collectivity of American audiences, they grafted their approaches to entertainment onto existing habits and patterns of socialization. In other words, listening habits were going to develop according to extant social norms, not by the rule of law. Obviously, for immigrant audiences, this included a choice of language. That radio regulation, rhetorically at least, moved to protect the rights of listeners reinforced the idea of the sovereign listener and inadvertently lent some measure of protection to audiences that wanted to listen outside the mainstream.

For speakers of Yiddish, Italian, German, Russian, and other languages who aspired to get on the air, this created both an obstacle and an opportunity. By favoring the rights of listeners to hear over concern about what, specifically, they might hear, the Radio Act effectively guaranteed non-English speakers access to the air. As long as a given station did not pose a threat to other stations and, by extension, the right of the audience to hear those other stations, then the FRC could not keep it off the air, no matter what it said or in what language it said it. Though protected in the abstract, the measure of to what extent the programs actually served the "public interest," would remain the stations' Achilles' heel throughout the next few decades. Insofar as stations catered to different immigrant populations at the same time rather than serving one large audience, their very mission seemed to operate in general opposition to the preferred tendency of the industry and the implications of government legislation.

This question found further elaboration when the Radio Act came up for renewal in 1928. Although congressional debate focused on how radio broadcast licenses ought to be distributed, its subtext remained consistently attentive to the question of who counted as radio listeners and who did not. As it stood, the Radio Act used population to determine the number of broadcast licenses in a certain area; more people meant proportionally more licenses. Representative Erwin Davis (R-Tennessee) offered an amendment to the renewal bill that proposed to shift the allocation of radio licenses from a reflection of population to distribution based on geographic region. Essentially, Davis objected to what he understood to be the disproportionate representation given to the Northeast to the exclusion of the South, but congressional debate provoked discussion of a subtler set of concerns about not only how many people lived in a given area but also whether they owned radios and understood what they heard. Could you be considered an "audience" if you did not own a radio? What if you owned a radio but did not speak English? The overtones of the argument were clear: If radio is an English-speaking medium, then can non-English-speaking immigrants be considered part of the radio audience? And should they count when distributing broadcast licenses?

Davis implicitly questioned the place of immigrants in America. He explained, "New York is a great city and has a good as citizens as may be found anywhere." And, he continued, "the same is true with respect to the citizenship of the third zone [the South]. . . . It is true that we have a considerable number of negroes with us, but they all speak and understand the English language and they are all American citizens and loyal to their country."[13] Even though far fewer African Americans owned radio receivers than did European immigrants, supporters of the Davis Amendment returned again and again to the claim that language excluded immigrants from listening to radio and that counting immigrants artificially inflated the populations of northern cities.[14] Representative Emmanuel Celler, the outspoken Democrat from Brooklyn, vociferously defended his constituents.

MR. CELLER: Comparatively few of the negroes in the Gentleman's state have radio sets, and you cannot bunch the colored population together with the white population and base your demands upon the combined total. The gentleman knows that the negro in the South is the victim of great poverty and is unable to purchase radio sets. It is quite improper to use general population as a standard. The test is, what is the radio population?

MR. MCKEOWN: Will the gentleman give the committee information as to what per cent of the people own radio sets as compared with the North and also will the gentleman tell the house in counting radio population the difference between an unfortunate negro population who do not have receiving sets, and a lot of the foreign population that can not understand the English language?

MR. CELLER: Oh, that is beside the point.

MR. SCHAFER: Can not they understand music?[15]

Though Celler failed to produce the statistics that McKeown asked for, the exchange revealed more than numbers could. The debate over the allocation of radio broadcast licenses echoed a set of concerns similar to those that motivated the anti-immigration movement, which had culminated only four years before in the severe curtailment of immigration. Notably, Celler did not explicitly defend his primarily immigrant constituency but emphasized the fact that music could speak across languages and that anyone could enjoy it, regardless of the language they spoke. Though Celler and Schafer rightly argued that language was beside the point, the point of who did and did not count among the American radio audience remained deeply intertwined with questions of ethnicity, language, immigration, region, and race. According to Congress, immigrants could count among the radio audience as long as they listened like everyone else. But they did not.

SERVING A COMMUNITY AND AN AUDIENCE

With an implicit agreement that neither African Americans nor immigrants fully counted as audiences, Congress renewed the Radio Act with the Davis Amendment and reinstated the FRC. The newly empowered FRC acted quickly, issuing General Order 32, which slated 162 radio stations for deletion, claiming that they obstructed the signals of other stations, broadcast off frequency, or otherwise interfered with the rights of listeners. Not coincidentally, General Order 32 named practically every outlet of foreign-language programming in the country. The stations protested, and the FRC responded by holding a round of hearings in summer 1928, during which representatives from each station would have the opportunity to explain how they served the "public interest" and why the service they provided could not be replicated by other, larger stations.

Part of the strategy employed by these stations was to make a case for their unique relationship to the communities they served. In their defense, many of the stations sent community delegations as well as representatives; Brooklyn, for example, brought petitions and representatives from more than a hundred community groups to the hearing. Peter Testan, president of Brooklyn-based WBBC, argued that his station had recently undertaken a $25,000 improvement project and provided a "definite service" to its Brighton Beach community.[16] Oliver J. Amaducci, manager of the Italian Educational Broadcasting Association, which operated Brooklyn station WCDA, petitioned the FRC to permit his station to continue because it "serve[d] 4,000,000 Italians in the United States" and because it was primarily committed to "educating and Americanizing Italians in this country."[17] Philadelphia's WRAX sent the Reverend Herbert Hogg of the Becharah Church, Inc., who asserted that the FRC ought to encourage religious broadcasting because it would be difficult for churches to pay for time on commercial stations.[18] Emil Denemark, owner of Chicago's WEDC explained that his station attracted over "200,000 Bohemians and Jews every day" and ought to be spared for that reason alone.[19] G. August Gerber, secretary of the Socialist-owned New York station WEVD attempted a slightly different approach. "WEVD," he argued, "is the only civil liberty peace trade union and radical broadcasting forum in the eastern part of the country. To remove it from the radio channels would lead one to the conclusion that free speech in this country, as guaranteed by the Constitution, has no application to the dissident minority groups and opinion."[20]

The arguments presented throughout the hearings all emphasized the relationship between the stations and the communities they served, specifically with respect to immigrants. In every case except that of WEVD, station owners advocated on behalf of their communities as if every resident was a listener. Whether their communities were religious, geographic, ethnic, linguistic, or even political, station owners argued that their service to the "public interest" manifested locally rather than nationally. The confusion of community and audience echoed the conflation of nation and audience employed by writers and politicians previously and offered a similar argument on a smaller scale. At its core, though, the arguments remained quite similar: radio's service to a particular audience would strengthen the common bonds between audience members and effectively benefit all who listened. For American radio writ large, this fit firmly within its overall logic. For programming in languages other than English, however, the FRC viewed this strategy with some skepticism, as membership in an immigrant community seemed at odds with membership in the broader American nation. This theme would continue to play implicitly throughout the 1930s and 1940s with respect to non-English-language broadcasting as the FRC and the FCC routinely demanded that stations explain just how much of a community service they provided to their immigrant listeners.

By the end of summer 1928, the FRC agreed that rather than delete these stations, it would reorganize the airwaves to protect larger corporate interests from interference from smaller stations.[21] The agreement created a three-tiered structure that consisted of "clear channel" stations at the center of the dial, low-powered local stations on the margins, and mid-sized regional stations in between. The closer a station lay to the center of the dial, the higher its power allotment. Clear channel stations included those owned or operated by NBC and broadcast between 30,000 and 50,000 watts. The FRC granted regional stations about 5,000 watts of power and local stations 100 watts, a signal strength that covered a broadcast area with a radius of approximately thirty-five miles.

Most of the stations that carried Yiddish and other immigrant-language programs fell into the last classification. In New York, the commission banished WMBQ, WLBX, WCLB, and WWRL to the high end of the dial and ordered them to share time at 1,500 kilocycles (kc), and the Brooklyn-based stations WLTH, WCGU, WBBC, WSDA, and WSGH received the same treatment at 1,400 kc. The new arrangement also forced WEVD to share time with WBBR and WHAP at 1,300 kc. In Philadelphia, WRAX moved to the upper end of the dial, 1,440 kc; and WLIT found itself sharing time with WPI at the opposite end, at 560 kc. The commission moved WCFL, the radio station of the Chicago Federation of Labor, to 970 kc and limited it to 1,000 watts. Simply, New York crowded eleven stations within 200 kc at the high end of the dial. By comparison, NBC's radio stations had at least 100 kc of clearance between themselves and their closest stations (see figure 7).[22]

Despite the clear favoritism shown clear channel stations and the rather precarious position of local stations, the renewal of the Radio Act helped to ensure the continued presence of local broadcasting interests.

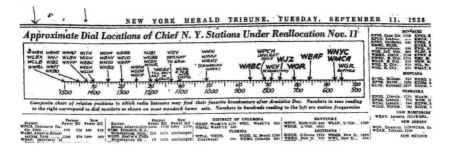

Figure 7. Diagram of New York's reorganized radio dial as outlined by the Federal Radio Commission's General Order 40. Note the density of stations at the lower end of the dial. *New York Herald Tribune,* 11 September 1928.

The creation of a distinct class of local broadcast stations meant that the FRC at least recognized that radio had become a national phenomenon and that broadcasters who catered to particular communities deserved a measure of protection within the law, however marginalized. Moreover, the adoption of this classification scheme tacitly affirmed the possibility that local stations, including those that broadcast in languages other than English, benefited the "public interest" and, by extension, that their smaller, localized audiences represented a public of a different scale.

THE AMERICANIZATION STANDARD

Protected by the letter of the law, smaller stations still had to serve the public interest, which meant maintaining the standards set by the FRC in terms of both technical operation and content. Technically, this meant maintaining a functioning broadcast facility, always having a licensed broadcaster on-site, and only operating on one's assigned frequency during one's assigned hours.[23] Defining or determining the bounds of content proved a more complicated matter. Obscene and profane material clearly fell beyond the pale of acceptable content, while commercial advertising became increasingly acceptable. Generally, for programming in English, the FRC could rely either on complaints from listeners or on the stations themselves to supply scripts or transcriptions (recordings) of programs, should questions about content arise. For programming in other languages, the FRC could neither reliably police nor control content, so when concerns arose, it found other ways to adjudicate matters. Effectively, this meant that the FRC evaluated the content of stations that broadcast in languages other than English in terms of how well or poorly they helped to educate immigrants about American culture and life. The FRC offered one of its clearest messages on this matter in 1931 in response to a broadcast license renewal request from WJKS in Gary, Indiana. In its report, the FRC "cited with approval the broadcast of foreign language programs where they were designed to educate and instruct the foreign populace among its listening public in the principles and ideals of our government and American institutions."[24] Echoing earlier questions about the differences and distance between immigrant communities and the American radio audience, the FRC advocated for programs that served immigrant communities but did so in the name of educating them in things American.

The FRC's "approval" still left a fairly wide berth for non-English-language programming. How didactic did a station have to be in order to earn the FRC's approval? Or would it be possible for members of the "foreign populace" to learn about America through magazines, movies, and advertisements, as Neil Cowan and Ruth Schwartz Cowan recalled: "To immigrant youths, the newspaper and the magazines, the movies and the radio program were primers, teaching them to become Americans by showing them how to walk and talk and dress and act like Americans: to drink Maxwell House Coffee out of a cup instead of tea out of a glass; to chew gum; to hold a cigarette between two fingers as movie stars did; to apply lipstick as Clara Bow did; to imitate the English pronunciation of radio announcers; to make up a bed not with one but with two sheets, as the advertisements suggested."[25]

Yet the FRC was not the only entity to express this concern. Clearly, immigrants learned about American culture in a variety of places and through a variety of media. Radio was only one such site, but because of its unprecedented power, its ability to influence and instruct immigrant audiences seemed more powerful than that of other media. Consequently, the FRC exercised its power to regulate and control radio in a way that reflected concerns about audiences, listeners, and communities, in terms of their relationship to an American audience, broadly conceived.

The ownership of some stations that hosted programs in languages other than English met the FRC's mandate with their own assertions about how they served their listeners by "Americanizing" them. Oliver J. Amaducci used this argument in defense of his station during the summer 1928 hearings. He emphasized that WBNY in New York established a "Jewish Department," dedicated to the "Americanization of foreign-born Jews and the education of Jews."[26] Established in 1927, the Jewish Department preempted the FRC's concern about immigrant audiences and thus illustrated the fact that the stations themselves were at least partially invested in a process similar to that advocated by the FRC.

Though the FRC generally favored stations that advocated "Americanization," the application of this standard proved inconsistent. As a result of the tension between its desire to Americanize immigrant audiences and its recognition of local broadcasters, the commission occasionally gave permission to radio stations that exhibited a particular connection to the community it served. In one such instance, in fall 1932, Arthur Faske, owner of the Long Beach, New York–based radio station WMIL petitioned the FRC for special permission to suspend broadcasting for the Jewish holiday of Yom Kippur. Citing the religious beliefs of his audience, he wrote, "As Radio Station WMIL is serving the greatest Jewish Community in the metropolitan area, we ask your honorable commission to allow this station to suspend operations for the following periods which falls on Yum Kipper [sic], the day of Atonement. Sunday Oct. 9th from 11P.M. to 1A.M. and on Monday Oct.10th from 2P.M. to 6 P.M. The suspension of operations will be in strict adherence to the traditional customs of the community which we serve."[27] The FRC honored his request and the following year praised the station for its effort among "foreign populations" to aid their integration into American society and life: "The program service of WMIL appears to be good. Educational, political, social and religious matters, as well as general entertainment, are broadcast. Regular periods are devoted to programs presented by recognized medical and dental societies; aid is rendered in unemployment and emergency relief activities, and features designed to assist in the Americanization of foreign populations are presented."[28] The Americanization standard, in this respect, was not absolute during the early 1930s but, more generally applied, could be shaped to suit the apparent needs and desires of particular communities. During this period, the desire for Americanization and the respect for local, community-based concerns did not stand in opposition to one another but operated in constant negotiation around the needs of listeners and broadcasters along national and locally ethnic lines.

This negotiation also meant that the FRC sometimes ruled harshly against stations that sponsored non-English-language programming and threatened them with deletion. In summer 1933, it recommended the removal of Brooklyn's four radio stations, WARD, WBBC, WLTH, and WVFW, from the air because they "suffered economic losses," failed to serve "as large an area as would reasonably be expected," and gave "excessive time for foreign language programs."[29] Immediately, G. August Gerber, secretary of the Debs Radio Trust and attorney for the owner of WBBC, filed an appeal defending the four radio stations precisely because they served a mostly immigrant population and aided their integration into American life. Gerber wrote:

> Exception is taken to the failure of the Examiner to find that the composition and the racial and national representation, the distribution by language and ethnic groups comprising the population in the Borough of Brooklyn, compels and requires that any service, in the public interest, convenience and/or necessity, present radio programs representative of the said peoples and population factors, and that it is in the interest of the American Government and the American People for the purpose of bringing these foreign elements, which are so large a part of the Brooklyn Population, into sympathy and consonance with the American scene, purposes and ideals; and that a powerful method to do so is for radio station to broadcast in the foreign languages as well as in English.[30]

In an echo of Abraham Cahan's vision for the *Forward*, Gerber successfully defended the stations by arguing that the best way to integrate immigrants into "the American scene" was to speak to them in their own languages.

This is one of the central ironies of Yiddish-language radio broadcasting during this period. Jewish immigrant audiences could have and often did listen to English-language programming, yet broadcasters of Yiddish programs defended their place on the air by arguing that they served the aims of Americanization. WMIL and WEVD argued that in serving their local audiences, they also served the broader public. These attitudes coexisted and illustrated the shifting boundaries between language, audience, and community on the air. Yiddish programming simultaneously reinforced the linguistic bounds of its immigrant community and claimed to be working toward its dissolution. Yiddish-speaking audiences—on whose behalf Yiddish-speaking broadcasters claimed to operate—listened to programs in both English and Yiddish and never chose one or the other exclusively. Finally, the FRC appeared partial to stations that strove to instruct immigrant listeners about America, even or especially when they did so in the languages of the immigrants themselves. Yet direct "instruction" was only one realm in which immigrant audiences learned how to behave like Americans. Equally important were the stylistic aspects of American life that could not be easily taught as such but which immigrants proved amenable to learning when they listened for them.

COMMERCE, COMMUNITY, AND AMERICANIZATION

As audiences learned how to hear cultural messages both implicit and explicit, the FRC began to weigh in on what kinds of messages would best serve immigrant listeners. One of the most contentious areas of radio's growth in this regard was commercialization. The development of sponsorship agreements, the eventual acceptance of indirect and direct advertising, and the economic agreements that came to define broadcasting occupied a great deal of public debate over how radio ought to sound and how it should serve its listeners.[31] While the process by which radio became a medium driven, in large part, by advertising dollars was certainly complicated by political expectations, the underlying economic rules remained quite simple: the larger the potential audience, the more money one could charge advertisers to support the program. Stations with higher power allotments, clearer signals, and network affiliation had access to a larger potential audience and could therefore attract larger and more lucrative sponsorship agreements. It follows that smaller stations had a more difficult time doing so and that those that further circumscribed their potential audience by broadcasting in immigrant languages limited both their listeners and their sponsors and had to make up the difference by selling more advertisements at lower costs. Although the FRC and the FCC understood these principles and generally accepted commercialization as necessary but unpleasant, they expressed particular concern that the commercialization of non-English-language radio was counterproductive to the "Americanization" of immigrant audiences.

The FRC and the FCC held that commercialization could inadvertently corrupt immigrant listeners, even while it inculcated them in American-style capitalism. In a 1933 report, the FRC criticized WLTH's "foreign language programs . . . [for being] almost entirely of a commercial nature, designed for the purpose of selling merchandise by direct advertising in foreign languages." The report concluded, "The foreign language programs of station WLTH were, for the most part, not designed to educate or to assist its large foreign populace to become better citizens, or to familiarize them with American principles and ideals, but were primarily advertising programs stressing the sale of merchandise. Hence this large proportion of its programs cannot be said to serve public interest merely because they are given in a foreign language."[32] Even though "foreign-language programs" represented only 40 percent of the station's total schedule (20 percent Yiddish, 10 percent Polish, 10 percent Italian), the FRC found its "commercial nature" too prominent and recommended denying its request to renew its broadcast license. Fortunately for WLTH, around the same time, President Franklin Roosevelt facilitated the formation of the FCC, which essentially suspended all the FRC's recommendations, leaving WLTH on the air but not out of trouble.

One year later, the FCC reaffirmed its preference for programs that instruct immigrants about America, adding a not-so-subtle criticism of commercial radio. Focusing this time on WBBC, which shared its frequency with WLTH, the FCC concluded, "The foreign language programs broadcast by this station appear to be of a kind calculated to assist the foreign population in that section to a better understanding of American ideals and principles, rather than seeking merely to advertise merchandise to these people."[33] Despite its acceptance of commercialization on radio generally, the FCC found commercialism and Americanization at odds, as if immigrant listeners needed some additional protection under the law. The opposition of Americanization and commercialization intimated not only that the FRC and the FCC advocated for the absorption of immigrant audiences into the broader American audience but also that there was a preferred course that immigrants ought to follow: American citizenship could be learned, but it should not be bought.

This logic extended to religious programming, which made for even an even more complicated calculus of measures with respect to the Yiddish-speaking radio world. Generally, the FRC and the FCC approved of religious programming, and the conventions of mainstream radio followed the lead of both CBS and NBC, which promoted religious broadcasting according to a policy that would "interpret religion at its highest and best." CBS even explicitly forbade the sale of time for religious programs.[34] This policy left Yiddish-speaking broadcasters, for whom religion, culture, and commerce could not easily be separated, in a delicate position. Did that mean that kosher butchers could not advertise? Or that programs that commemorated specific holidays could not seek sponsorship? What about sponsorship opportunities for Meyer Wolozin's ritual objects store? Or *Libby's* wedding broadcasts? What Yiddish-speaking audiences may have heard as cultural or religious, the FCC may have heard simply as overly commercial.

Essentially the question of commercialism in this context reduced to the issue of congruence between a station and its audience; where the FCC heard the former, Jewish immigrant listeners heard the latter. The FCC took a slightly less nuanced approach in its criticism of WLTH for being overly commercialized without attending to the ways in which commercialism in this context operated differently than it did on the national networks. The Lower East Side dentist Julius Luninfeld, the United Fish Dealers, and even the B. Manischewitz Company differed substantially from Colgate, Michelin, and Texaco in terms of their relationships to their customers. Consequently, in Yiddish, the relationship between sponsors, stations, and listeners took on a different resonance that raised questions of community, not only of commerce.

In one especially illustrative example from the early 1930s, Rabbi Bernard Levinthal, a leader of Philadelphia's Orthodox community, wrote a letter to a Jewish butcher who sold nonkosher meat, requesting that he stop advertising in Yiddish on station WRAX. The butcher apparently did not advertise his store as kosher, but Levinthal feared that listeners who heard a Yiddish advertisement would mistakenly conclude that the meat was kosher.[35] Although radio presented, essentially, an open market, Levinthal heard in the nonkosher butcher's advertisement a threat to the religious unity of his Jewish community. In contrast, the butcher heard in WRAX's Yiddish programming merely the sound of a new market. In this instance, the slippage between audience, community, and market became an opportunity for marking off one from the other while it also revealed the sometimes curious negotiations of those very boundaries. Levinthal did not object to commercials per se but only those that he believed threatened the community.

Yiddish radio was not necessarily less commercial than mainstream radio in absolute terms, but it certainly offered commercial relationships of a different scale and kind. In the mid-1930s on Yiddish radio, almost all the sponsors came from the communities to which they advertised and thus contributed to an ethnic economy in which radio and newspaper advertising played a large mediating part. Moreover, commercials for ritual objects, kosher food, and even cemeteries articulated a culture shared by advertisers and audiences alike, and they did so in a language that effectively set the conversation apart from the mainstream. Sometimes when mainstream advertisers appealed to Yiddish-speaking listeners, the results proved almost comic in their illustration of the cultural gaps between the two groups. In her memoir, Gertrude Berg, who would later become the writer and principal performer in the influential English-language program *The Rise of the Goldbergs,* recalled an early assignment that captured precisely this phenomenon. A Mr. Schwartz called her into his office to read a Christmas announcement for Consolidated Edison. After a successful reading in English, Schwartz informed Berg that she was to recite it on the air in Yiddish.

> A Christmas cookie in Yiddish for a public utility in America seemed a little odd, but it gave me my second lesson in radio: Be surprised at nothing. On my way home I got nervous. I suddenly remembered I couldn't read or write Yiddish, I could only speak it. Lew [her husband] . . . could read and write Yiddish and Hebrew, and he wrote out the commercial phonetically for me. . . . I practiced for hours and by the time I got to the studio I had it memorized. . . . I got my cue and the words from "Our sponsor" issued forth from my lips like a news bulletin from the Tower of Babel with its combinations of Yiddish and English. "Eire Freindliche gas and electrische company brengen alle menschen fun New York eine speciele recepie far cookies far dem yontevdiken seison . . . [Your friendly gas and electric company brings everyone in New York a special recipe for cookies for this holiday season . . .]."[36]

While Consolidated Edison believed that it could reach the Jewish audience by speaking Yiddish, the company underestimated the differences between community, commerce, and culture and invested instead in language that it hoped would suffice.

Other mainstream retailers had more success with Yiddish-speaking audiences during this period when they articulated a unique kind of relationship between the two parties that indicated a greater sensitivity to community formations. To take one example, Vim's, a large New York radio and phonograph retailer, printed a letter in the *Forward* to express its appreciation to its Yiddish-speaking customers. Published in both English and Yiddish, the letter read, "It is our earnest belief that with the growing interest in Radio evidenced by the vast Jewish public, that the Radio manufacturers could find no better media for advertising their product in New York than the *Jewish Daily Forward* and the other Jewish newspapers."[37] Vim's also hired popular Yiddish performers such as Aaron Lebedev, Molly Picon, Ludwig Satz, and Cantor Yossele Rosenblatt to appear in their advertisements in the Yiddish press.[38] Vim's became one of the first mainstream advertisers of radio receivers to speak directly to its Yiddish-speaking customers as a distinct bloc.

Instead of simply translating their English advertisements into Yiddish for the Yiddish press, Vim's tapped into the broader language of Yiddish entertainment, mass media, culture, and community. The nature of this interaction hinted at an intimate connection between advertiser and audience that took account of the particulars of Jewish immigrant life during the late 1920s.

The radio set manufacturer Zenith took a similar approach in a stunning series of full-page advertisements in the *Forward* that appeared weekly in fall 1929. Charcoal drawings of street scenes, wedding scenes, and holiday scenes featuring explicitly Jewish characters accompanied lengthy Yiddish texts explaining how radio—Zenith radios in particular—suited Jewish traditions and bridged the traditional and the technological. In one advertisement, Zenith announced radio as the "source of entertainment for the working masses" (see figure 8). The accompanying image included an opera singer, a jazz band, and a likeness of Al Jolson in his famous "mammy" pose, alongside an image of a cantor and his choir and two figures of boxers, one of whom wore a Star of David on his shorts. Despite the fact that Zenith, a national company, produced the advertisement, it spoke directly to the specific interests of the Jewish immigrant audience and represented that audience's desire to listen to both Jewish and mainstream programming.[39]

Both Vim's and Zenith tried to capitalize on the specific characteristics of the Jewish immigrant community. Both companies knew well that Jewish immigrants did not listen to Yiddish programs only, yet both understood that they had to appeal to the particularly Jewish character of this audience. By speaking to this audience in this way, advertisers suggested a very different relationship to their potential customers that took advantage of localized, culturally specific knowledge in which language was only one element. Both Vim's and Zenith were primarily interested in this community as a customer, but the cultural knowledge they displayed in these advertisements demonstrated a more nuanced understanding of this specific audience and of their respective relationships to it.

However, just knowing or belonging to the community was not necessarily sufficient for an interested sponsor. On at least one occasion,

Figure 8. Advertisement for Zenith Radio that reads, "Radio—the source of entertainment for the working masses." Note the side-by-side images of the cantor and the opera singer, the image of someone resembling Al Jolson and a jazz band, as well as the boxers, including one with a Star of David on his shorts. *Jewish Daily Forward*, 1 September 1929, 9. Courtesy of the Forward Association.

the sponsor himself proved too controversial for the community and captured the contradictions implicit in the negotiation of audience, community, commercialization, and custom. *Shadkhn rubin's yidish sho* (Rubin the Matchmaker's Yiddish Hour) debuted in 1929 on New York station WSGH and almost immediately raised objections from other Yiddish broadcasters. Hosted by Aaron Kronenberg, a Brooklyn-based rabbi and aspiring radio personality, the program featured testimonials about Rubin's matchmaking success and commercial announcements for his services. In 1930, WSGH folded and became WFOX; the following year, Peter Testan, owner of station WBBC, which shared broadcast frequency with WFOX/WSGH, wrote a letter to James Baldwin, secretary of the FRC, to express concern about Rubin's program. "We beg to inform you," he wrote, "that about a year ago we received an inquiry from Rubin's Matrimonial Bureau, 1575 Eastern Parkway, Brooklyn, New York, which stated that they wished to broadcast an advertising program for the purpose of promoting additional business for them." WBBC declined his request due to "the questionable nature of that particular type of business."[40]

Denied by WBBC, Rubin turned to WFOX, which agreed to carry his program. Fearing that listeners would confuse his station with WFOX, Testan petitioned Commissioner Baldwin for "some means of relief."[41] Baldwin, citing the relationship between the station and its large Jewish audience, permitted the station and the program to continue, explaining, "It further appears that the program in question would probably be distasteful to a large number of persons, but inasmuch as the custom of patronizing marriage brokers seems to be well established among the Jewish people, and that a large percentage of the listeners of this station are Jewish, it does not appear that the commission would be justified in finding that the operation of this station is contrary to public interest because of this program and refuse to renew the station license."[42] Although Baldwin agreed with the "distasteful" presentation of the program, he could not justify it as grounds for deleting the station because matchmaking was a Jewish custom. As in the case of WMIL earlier in the decade, commonalities between the program, its audience, and the community proved strong enough to convince Baldwin to permit the program to continue. Perhaps inadvertently, Baldwin's adherence to the broader goals of the FRC actually protected the rights of this community to listen to programs in Yiddish.

The program remained on the air until 1935, by which time it had migrated to Rabbi Kronenberg's WARD. In another round of petitions, the FRC again defended matchmaking but objected to the combination of commercialism and religious services in this context.

> Although the right of Aaron Kronenberg to style himself a "Jewish Rabbi" was questioned by considerable testimony, the record contains unrebutted proff [sic] that he was properly ordained, and, at the time of the hearing, cloaked with full authority to discharge all rabbinical duties. He is shown to have made use of the WARD facilities to advertise his availability for marriages (Rubens' [sic] Matrimonial Bureau), and, as well, his availability for circumcisions. In this connection, the president of the Jewish Ministers' Association characterized the announcements by Aaron Kronenberg, and particularly those concerning wedding ceremonies, as being in such form that they were desecrating to the Jewish people and were cheap and vulgar. . . . In any event, broadcast programs religious in character but commercialized as were these, are offensive to the sensibilities of the people generally, and are not in the public interest.[43]

Finding Kronenberg properly ordained but improperly commercial, the FCC had little choice but to place the station under investigation and deny its request for renewal of its broadcast license. Though Baldwin could allow that Rubin's commercialism sounded differently to Jewish audiences than to him, the FCC still connected commercialism and vulgarity and voted to delete Kronenberg and his station.

The episodes with WMIL, *shadkhn* Rubin, and Rabbi Kronenberg highlighted the ways in which the FRC and the FCC treated the culture of Yiddish radio differently according to whether the FCC was addressing an audience or a community. When the FRC or the FCC treated Yiddish-speaking broadcasters and their listeners like a community, it seemed far more permissive and allowed for more leeway in commercialism and religious content. Yet even these distinctions took on other resonances and sounded different depending on who was listening.

COMMUNITY AND COMPETITION

Though invested in community, radio remained a business, and competition, especially among those invested in a relatively narrow audience, remained fierce. The stations that catered to immigrant audiences vied for the attention of the same potential pool of listeners through ever flashier promotions and innovative programs. Sometimes they tried to leverage the FCC to delete their competition. Although the FRC and the FCC occasionally praised these stations for providing a service to their communities, the stations saw their listeners as a limited resource, themselves as businesses, and one another as competition. Working within an already crowded field, the stations did not behave in ways that demonstrated a sense of common cause or shared purpose. Instead, the familiarity of these stations with one another and with their audience bred contention and even contempt.

Audiences, however, heard things differently. As a result of the reorganization of the radio dial in 1928, the four Brooklyn-based stations found themselves sharing a single wavelength and consequently having to divide up the broadcast day four ways. This agreement fed the sense that the stations were interchangeable and therefore shared the same goals, because, to audiences, it sounded that way; listeners could tune in to WLTH and then to WARD without actually turning the dial. Moreover, it further limited each station's ability to earn income; unlike the clear channel and regional stations, they were only permitted to broadcast one quarter of the day. That listeners likely did not distinguish between the stations themselves—because they could not hear the differences between them—likely increased the antipathy between station owners, while the FCC evaluated each station's fitness independently and virtually regardless of what the programs actually sounded like.

Though the FCC criticized stations that hosted non-English-language programming for being too commercial, it also criticized them for not generating enough income. In 1936, the FCC recommended denying WARD's license renewal application on the following grounds: "It is quite manifest that the WARD station management is not in a financial position to conduct its affairs in such a manner as to render the service reasonably expected."[44] WVFW fared even worse, receiving criticism for its "decidedly mediocre" programming and the fact that "the transmitting equipment of the station is housed in one room [at 427 Fulton Street], and the basement of the building and the other rooms are occupied by the caretaker as living rooms for himself and his family."[45] Meanwhile, WLTH earned its share of criticism for keeping its transmitting equipment in a "disorderly manner." Somehow too commercial and not financially successful enough, the stations found themselves caught between the competing expectations of their listeners, their sponsors, and federal regulators.

So when Peter Testan of WBBC launched one of the first attacks against the other stations, he did not hesitate to call out other stations for deletion. In a letter to President Roosevelt, Testan emphasized that WBBC devoted only eight hours per week to "foreign language presentations" and highlighted his inclusion of "daily releases of governmental news [from the National Recovery Act Headquarters]" during his "foreign programs."[46] Simultaneously, Testan also sent a telegram to the FRC, objecting to the business practices of his frequency-mates, WARD and WLTH, on the grounds that they pandered to the basest interests of immigrants instead of aspiring to uphold the dignity of the radio industry.

> As a time sharing station we protest against the activities of stations WARD and WLTH. WARD is using tables at subway stations also in front of stores with a person calling to everybody passing by to sign a petition if they want the station and the Jewish programs to remain on the air. WLTH is using placards in stores and other places soliciting signatures both stations are using own facilities to broadcast long unwarranted statements. Signatures so obtained are misleading to the commission denotes nothing insofar as the popularity of station is concerned. Anyone probably could secure a million signatures by going through streets asking for them. [The] dignity and propriety of the broadcasting profession being dragged into the gutter by these tactics. We consider such procedures harmful.[47]

In order to compete, Testan mobilized his own listeners in a letter writing campaign. In response to more than two hundred letters received on behalf of WBBC, Representative George Lindsey wrote of his intention to forward them to the FCC, and Representative Stephen Rudd passed on more than one hundred additional letters. More letters of endorsement arrived at the FCC from the Gold Pen-Makers and Grinders Union, in addition to other testimonials from churches and Jewish organizations that supported the station.[48] Testan objected to the ways in which WARD and WLTH leveraged their community and explicitly objected to the equivalence of community and audience. The community, he suggested, would sign almost anything, and signatures did not adequately represent the real popularity of a station. Instead, Testan tried to capitalize on the soft distinctions between audience and community to suggest that only audience mattered. Radio, he argued, should not be in the business of community but in the business of audiences, and therein lay the difference between his station and his counterparts'. Testan's efforts succeeded. The FCC granted WBBC its license renewal but did not elect to delete the other stations.

However, this did not mean that the stations were safe. WEVD, which was sharing time on a different frequency, heard the fighting at 1,400 kc and made a play to take over the frequency from the beleaguered Brooklyn stations. In principle, the FCC strongly approved of WEVD's balance of commercial and noncommercial programming, as well as its commitment to broadcasting "educational and cultural broadcasts" every evening from six o'clock onward, except Sundays.[49] However, the FCC had to deny the station's request on technical grounds.

Spared deletion yet again, the Brooklyn stations' relationship to their primary audiences and to their community remained a source of ongoing contention. One year later, the *Brooklyn Daily Eagle,* an English-language daily newspaper, made a bid to take over broadcasting facilities at 1,400 kc. M. Preston Goodfellow, principal stockholder in the ninety-four-year-old newspaper, proposed converting the top floor of the Daily Eagle Building into a studio for the new Brooklyn station. The FCC reported with approval that Mr. Goodfellow "resides in Brooklyn, for many years has been identified with the newspaper and is recognized as a leading citizen of that city."[50] The differences between Goodfellow and Testan, Kronenberg, and D'Angelo could not have been clearer; although nearly two million immigrants called Brooklyn home, the commission thought the airwaves would be safer in the hands of a local businessman. "The station will be a Brooklyn station in every sense of the word," it stated in its order. "It is believed that the applicant, identified as it is with the business and civic life of Brooklyn, will be better enabled to serve the public interest than one not so closely identified therewith."[51] The stations, although they served the immigrant populations of Brooklyn, still could not convince the commission that they were sufficiently "Brooklyn stations" to deny Goodfellow's request. The commission still considered their audiences "immigrant," as opposed to "Brooklyn." The stations in question found themselves too closely identified with their limited audience-community and not identified enough with the borough at large.

In truth, Brooklyn's stations echoed the ethnic and linguistic makeup of their borough. The 1930 U.S. Census established Brooklyn as New York's most populous borough, with 2,560,401 residents, of whom 869,047—approximately one-third—were non-native white ethnics and 1,126,952 were native-born whites with mixed-heritage parents.[52] Although Brooklyn's radio stations were representative of the borough's diversity, the FCC still favored Goodfellow's request. But, once again on the verge of elimination, Brooklyn-based Yiddish radio celebrated a second reprieve in as many years. Under the law, granting another license to Brooklyn would have pushed the New York area further over its Davis Amendment quota, so the FCC, although it favored the *Eagle*'s request, was forced to deny it. However, the specter of Goodfellow's request and the FCC's decision about the compatibility of the stations and their city continued to hang heavily over the airwaves.

By 1936, the FCC had come to recognize that a significant immigrant population lived in Brooklyn and, more important, that "a definite need . . . exist[ed] for programs in foreign languages."[53] The FCC even praised WVFW for crafting a lineup "calculated to meet the needs peculiar to the populace within the Brooklyn area . . . [that serve] the public interest."[54] However, it continued to express skepticism about the operation of these stations and their ability to supervise content.

That these stations served diverse, multilingual audiences necessarily meant that they operated according to a different set of guidelines from their English-speaking and monolingual counterparts on the air. In order to capitalize on their ethnic economies, these stations relied on Yiddish-speaking sponsors for their Yiddish programs, Italian-speaking sponsors for their Italian programs, and so on. This meant that the stations largely employed members of each of these ethnic communities to broker advertising and sponsorship agreements, but it also meant that station ownership likely could neither understand nor vouch for the content of all the programming their stations carried. Though this business arrangement made sense on a local level, it proved too lax for the FCC. In the calculus of audience, community, commerce, and radio, the operation of the industry at large trumped the local relationships born of and fostered by radio. It was not the programs per se that the FCC objected to but the ways in which the stations conducted their business. Thus the FCC could appear to protect business interests without raising the question of censorship.

On this basis, the FCC criticized WBBC because "supervision [was] extremely lax in character." On WARD, Rabbi Kronenberg found himself under investigation for hiring a Mr. Capola on commission to arrange Italian programs when "neither the station licensee, nor any of its employees, appear to have had information with regard to the nature and character of the program." Similarly, Sam Gellard of WLTH hired a Mr. Witkowski on commission to arrange the broadcast of Polish-language programs. Although Gellard testified that he was familiar with the message and content of the program, he admitted that he "neither spoke nor understood the Polish language." Perhaps most interesting in the Jewish context, Gellard also had a similar agreement with Cantor Jacob Altman, a regular performer on his station.[55] That advertising brokers like Witkowski, Capola, and Altman typically worked on commission exacerbated the problem. According to the FCC, this meant that they did not have a stake in the station but only in the success of their own programs and that they would therefore be more likely to tolerate programming of a questionable nature. Thus the FCC concluded that, in general, "it does not appear that responsible representatives of the licensee corporations exercise complete supervision or control of the foreign language programs which are broadcast." Further, it said, there was the temptation to broadcast material "which, although lucrative, may not be of high quality and which might possibly be detrimental to the welfare of the listening public."[56] By emphasizing the question of supervision over audiences, the FCC put these stations in yet another double bind: It singled them out for the unique service they provided to immigrant audiences but held them to an absolute standard that did not acknowledge the peculiar relationships that defined these stations and their relationships with their audiences and sponsors.

Testan's objections to the contrary, these stations did provide a unique service on the air that connected them not just to their audiences but to their communities as well. Both the FRC and the FCC acted in the name of the broadest possible American radio audience, while stations that carried programs in languages other than English often appealed to their local communities. To be sure, there is no hard and fast distinction between audience and community in this context; members of a community constituted an audience, and an audience may, ultimately, constitute a community. But the uneven application and mobilization of the two concepts throughout the 1930s illustrates the challenges that multilingual stations like WBBC, WEVD and WPEN posed to the conception of an American radio audience and to prevailing notions of American radio in general.

While English-language and network-based radio in America certainly articulated a kind of national vision supported by the FRC and the FCC, the stations that catered to local audiences in languages other than English represented a powerful presence that allowed radio to propagate a different sense of identification. Along the local, Yiddish-speaking airwaves, commerce did not necessarily corrupt, religion was not held to a higher standard, and listeners could learn about America in Yiddish. Despite the Americanization standard articulated by the FRC and extended by the FCC, Yiddish radio cultivated a set of relationships and practices that did not oppose identifying as an immigrant and being an American and did not pit one language against another. Instead, the culture of Yiddish radio, structured in part by an ongoing conversation with federal regulations, took shape through its ongoing engagement with the local and the national, with the Yiddish-speaking community and the English-speaking industry, and with an audience that grew out of but was not entirely congruent with community.

THREE Listening to Themselves, 1929–1936

> Schmalz it: a command by the production director to
> the orchestra conductor to have the music played in a
> sentimental style.
>
> From a glossary of radio production terms, 1939

> The "radio" is already a factor in our lives. Very few houses
> do not have one. Every day and every evening, Yiddish
> programs reach millions of Jewish ears. Are the programs
> satisfying? Do people enjoy them? Or do they grate on
> people's ears? The *Theater and Radio World* will pay much
> attention to exactly these questions.
>
> Introduction to *Teater un radio velt*, 1935

By the end of the 1920s, radios had become quite common among immigrant families. The 1930 census revealed that 57.3 percent of families
with one immigrant head of household owned a radio, compared to 43.6
percent of families headed by two foreign-born parents and 39.9 percent with two "native born" white heads of household.[1] Accounting for
regional differences, the census found that in the Northeast, where the
majority of Jews settled, the percentage of "mixed parentage" families
that owned radios exceeded that of their "native born" counterparts, 65
percent to 59.9 percent, and 45.4 percent of "foreign-born white" families
owned radios. In New York and Chicago, which in 1930 had two of the
largest Jewish populations in the United States, nearly 75 percent of
mixed immigrant-native families owned radios.[2] A 1935 study of the
leisure activities of Lower East Side youth elaborated on these find-

ings. In a master's thesis for the Graduate School of Jewish Social Work, Harry Barron observed the near-ubiquity of radios, despite the generally impoverished conditions of the neighborhood: "It is interesting to learn that in an area such as this section of the Lower East Side where a large proportion of the population resides in squalid, dirty, decrepit tenement houses and where so many of the flats are sparsely and cheaply furnished, such a comparatively high percentage of the homes possess a radio."[3] Within his multiethnic sample, he highlighted the popularity of radio among Jews: "Among the three 'major' [immigrant] groups we find that the Jews have the highest percent of their number reporting this activity." "The Italians follow," he continued, "with approximately nine percentage points lower than the Jews; 61.6 percent of the Italian children reporting radio listening."[4] As Victor's *Talking Machine World* had observed a decade before, immigrants ranked among Americans most likely to own a radio, but what they listened to, how they listened, when they listened, and how they understood their relationship to radio generally were complicated questions.

Barron's youth probably listened to English programming, because it remained the primary language of broadcasting in America and the preferred language of immigrant youth. For their immigrant parents, the number of Yiddish broadcast hours and the number of stations that carried them continued to grow. By 1932, New York audiences could hear Yiddish on the air up to five hours a day, and in Philadelphia audiences could hear up to three hours of Yiddish. Chicago and Boston began carrying regular Yiddish programs, Detroit and Los Angeles featured occasional Yiddish shows, and in Baltimore Nathaniel Yongelson launched the city's first Yiddish program on WCBM. Thus early in the decade more Jewish immigrants could hear more Yiddish programming in more areas of the country than ever before.

Now that broadcasters began speaking Yiddish regularly and advertisers began courting the emerging Yiddish-speaking audience, the relationship between the audience and the medium began to change. The presence of Yiddish programming certainly changed listening habits, and though Yiddish speakers remained part of the audience for English programs, in the minds of broadcasters, regulators, and advertisers, they were becoming an independent audience with their own habits, desires, and regulatory demands. While the FRC and the FCC listened with special attention for programs that hoped to inculcate American values, Yiddish programs raised the volume on conversations and concerns particular to the needs and interests of their immigrant audience. In both form and content, Yiddish radio programs fit the desires of their listeners and broadcast back the voices of an audience that wanted to hear itself on the air.

THE STATUS OF YIDDISH

Though emerging as a cultural formation in its own right, the sounds and structures of Yiddish radio often resonated with the audience's comfort with English-language programs. Yiddish would never replace English on the radios of Jewish immigrants, because it simply could not compete in terms of number of hours, production values, broadcast power, or number of stations. Consequently, Yiddish-speaking radio announcers had to figure out ways to capitalize on their listeners' desire to hear Yiddish programming and fit in to the preferences and habits that their audience had already developed. This produced two distinct but related effects. First, Yiddish-speaking broadcasters actively looked to English programs for successful formulas, which they unabashedly copied, adapted, and translated into Yiddish. Second, audiences of Jewish immigrants tuned in to Yiddish programs almost entirely irrespective of the programs' perceived "quality." It became clear that audiences would tune in to Yiddish programs simply to hear Yiddish and that the precise nature or content hardly mattered. They tuned in to hear Yiddish itself, and thus to reinforce their community through sound.

As the 1920s drew to a close, Yiddish-language versions of popular English programs punctuated the airwaves. Every Rudy Vallee produced a Rubin Goldberg, and every *Uncle GeeBee's Stories* led to a *Kinder mayse-lakh mit mume polie* (Children's Little Stories with Aunt Polly). Programs with titles like *Al un sy's yidishe shtunde* (Al and Cy's Jewish Hour), *Yidish ortofonic sho* (Yiddish Orthophonic Hour), *Entins kinder sho* (Entin's

Children's Hour), and *Yidish art teater* (Yiddish Art Theater) appeared within earshot of English programs like *Playboy of the Air,* the *National Farm and Home Hour,* and *Roxy's Gang.* Yiddish-speaking performers even tried to copy the popularity of *Amos 'n' Andy,* the Chicago-based blackface duo who drew an audience of nearly forty million listeners, six nights a week.[5] Shortly after *Amos 'n' Andy's* network debut, a handful of Yiddish programs with names like *Herring and Potato, Max and Morris, Mr. Bernstein and Mr. Goldstein,* and *Berl and Shmerl* appeared, each vying to become the "next *Amos 'n' Andy*" (see figure 9).[6]

Less linguistic translations than cultural ones, these Yiddish programs used the English-language originals as, in the words of one Yiddish radio producer, "inspiration."[7] For example, when Rudy Vallee became a national sensation as the host of *Fleischman's Hour,* Rubin Goldberg responded with "a new funny feature" called *Di yidishe akhsanya* (The Jewish Inn).[8] *Fleischman's Hour* took place in a restaurant, so Goldberg's set his show at an inn, and both programs incorporated dialogue and musical performances. When Arthur Tracy, a popular singer, created a sensation as the mysterious "Street Singer" on New York's WABC, almost every station that catered to immigrant listeners responded with its own Yiddish version, including Der yidish vanderer, Der yidish vagabond, Der geto zinger, and Di yidishe mama. The most successful of these Yiddish "mystery" performers, Herman Yablokoff, made a name for himself as Der payatz (the Clown). In his memoirs, Yablokoff noted that by 1932 performing on the radio was "no novelty," since he had already been appearing in weekly promotional broadcasts with the Hopkinson theater company on WFOX.[9] Eager to expand his popularity and his income without compromising his cachet in theater, Yablokoff explained how he developed his on-air alter ego: "The program, I felt, must have an individual style that would intrigue listeners. The Street Singer flashed across my mind. Why couldn't I do the same? Why not come up with some sort of novel title, like . . . 'der Payatz,' for instance? Under such a pseudonym I could present a varied program: dramatic compositions of recitation and song, romantic ballads, light comedy. Above all, I'd guard against being connected with the actor, Yablokoff, now playing with Menashe Skulnik. I must be presented on the radio exclusively as the 'Phantom of the Air—Der Payatz.'"[10]

Figure 9. Cover of the second issue of *Teater un radio velt* (Theater and Radio World) featuring Berl and Shmerl, "the Jewish Amos 'n' Andy," October 1935. From the Archives of the YIVO Institute for Jewish Research, New York.

Producer Sidney Hart and Yablokoff managed to replicate the success of the Street Singer and his eponymously titled show, and with the help of Norman Furman, an "English-speaking agent," inked a thirteen-week contract with Klein and Zwerling's Department Store, where he settled in as the "Phantom of the Air." Yablokoff eventually became so well known as Der payatz that when he translated and published his Yiddish memoirs in English, the book took his pseudonym for its title.

Unlike the distance that Yiddish performers and programs tried to put between themselves and other Yiddish programs, when they turned to English shows, they tended to play on similarities. Instead of competing with Vallee or Tracy, Goldberg and Yablokoff capitalized on their audience's familiarity with their English-speaking counterparts and used it to promote their own programs. They relied on their audience's ability to hear the echo of English in the similarities as well as the differences. The prevailing logic held that the closer these Yiddish programs came to approximating the English originals, the better they would sound. In other words, Yiddish-speaking broadcasters needed their audiences to listen to English-language programs so as to turn that familiarity into fuel for their own programming. The audience for Yiddish radio programming, although distinct in some ways, still needed the mainstream, English-speaking industry for direction and for cues but not as a substitute.

Although it helped to create the audience for Yiddish radio, this dynamic meant that Yiddish radio always operated in the shadow of its English-speaking counterpart. And Yiddish newspapers did not hesitate to criticize radio for its low quality, especially when they were trying to promote their own programs. Philadelphia's *Idishe velt* offered its version of this strategy when it launched its own program in 1928. "Years ago," read one promotional article, Jewish programs featured "only prayers sung by cantors. But today, when many lovers of Jewish music attend the opera, symphonic concerts, or concerts of singers, fiddlers, cellists and pianists, [our program will] take all kinds [of music]."[11] Although the *Idishe velt* program's debut featured Moyshe Oysher, one of America's most famous cantors, it still tried to distance itself from other Jewish musical offerings. When *Der tog* launched its radio program later the same year, it published a front-page article that claimed, "*Der tog* was actually the first and only institution that initiated systematic and regular Yiddish programming on the radio during the past two years. There had been Yiddish radio programs previously, but these radio programs carried a religious overtone, or else they were sporadic and were not popular."[12]

Most notable about this strategy is not the base claim that the *Idishe velt* or *Der tog* program would be better than its predecessors' but rather the readiness to disparage all Yiddish radio programming. Although the hyperbole could be justified in terms of promotional strategy, the disparagement of Yiddish radio proved nearly ubiquitous. Each high-profile launch of a new Yiddish program promised to rescue Yiddish radio from itself and finally deliver the "quality" programming that audiences deserved. Unwilling to abandon the whole concept or provide Jewish programs in English, Yiddish-speaking radio producers continued to attack one another's contributions while highlighting their own as the only Yiddish program worthy of their audience's attention.

When the *Forward* launched its program in 1932, it used the same strategy but instead credited the taste of its audience, claiming that listeners were "happy that it is not like other radio hours. . . . Everyone longs for real Yiddish songs and Yiddish numbers. But real Yiddish, beautiful Yiddish and no crippling squeaking or rhyming advertising jingles."[13] Following the program's debut, one *Forward* writer continued to compliment his audience's American taste and boasted about how different the program sounded from its Yiddish-speaking counterparts. He wrote, "Most [American children] don't like the 'Yiddish' hours on the radio . . . but they like the *Forward Hour* just like their parents." In his review of the first *Forward Hour*, Cy Major, the newspaper's writer, also praised his audience's discerning taste, without sparing a harsh word for the other Yiddish programs: "The fans are not just 'patriotn' but intelligent, knowledgeable people, men and women. . . . [The *Forward* has heard] from many American-born children, high school and college students who had, for the first time, heard a Yiddish concert on the radio of which one must no longer be ashamed."[14] For Major and the *Forward*, the *Forward Hour* promised to save Yiddish-speaking Jewish immigrants and their children from Yiddish radio by presenting Yiddish radio.

Even those who succeeded on Yiddish radio felt self-conscious about their cultural status within the Yiddish-speaking cultural community. When the playwright Baruch Lumet began writing for radio in 1929, he did not publicize his name in connection with the new medium, believing radio the lowest form of Yiddish entertainment and holding that any association with it would diminish his stature as a serious dramatist.[15] Born in 1898 in Poland, Lumet performed throughout Europe with David Herman's vaudeville troupe before immigrating to America in order to avoid conscription in 1920.[16] After limited success in the theater, Lumet found himself in need of steady income to support his family. Though suspicious of radio, Lumet knew someone at WLTH who gave him a free fifteen-minute "audition" at ten o'clock on a weekday evening, outside the normal broadcast schedule. Finding himself with serious writer's block but in need of the money, Lumet recalled a famous Jewish folktale in which a boy who did not know how to pray offered the alphabet to God knowing that God would organize the letters correctly. "'All right, Dear God,'" Lumet began, "'I give you the *aleph-baiz* and you make up a sketch for the radio,' . . . and He made up a sketch."[17]

Lumet called the show *Der bronzviler zeyde* (The Grandfather from Brownsville), and the Coward Shoe Store paid him $20 per episode, making this the first Yiddish-language serial on the radio.[18] Operating on a slender budget, Lumet hired members of his own family, including his young son, Sidney, to perform the roles of the *zeyde*'s family, while he played the lead.[19] Dr. Julius Luninfeld, a dentist with an office on Delancy Street who had already purchased airtime for his own advertisements, approached Lumet with an offer to pay $25 for each fifteen-minute episode. The program became so popular that soon WLTH asked for two episodes weekly, earning Lumet a steady salary of $45 a week during the first few years of the depression. Despite the program's popular and financial success, Lumet always looked down on the show. Like Solomon Rabinowitz, who wrote Yiddish short stories under the pseudonym Sholom Aleichem because he feared punishment for writing fiction in a "jargon" considered unworthy of its own literature, Lumet considered writing for radio "below [his] dignity" and never attached his name to the program.[20] Audiences, however, did not particularly care, and their attention sustained *Der zeyde* for eight years as they listened to the title character travel to Japan and Palestine and even get married.[21]

Other performers also accepted Yiddish radio work but routinely downplayed its importance to their artistic lives. The actress and singer Molly Picon, who began her radio career in 1934, generally regarded radio as little more than a steady-paying job while she looked for her next theater gig. In one of her autobiographies, Picon routinely and casually dropped references to her radio career in between stories about benefit shows and theater tours without comment or elaboration.[22] At one point, she recalled, "[My husband] signed us for another twenty-six weeks for Maxwell House, and I was happy only because we were working together. Otherwise, I was plagued by the blues. . . . Europe was at war, earthquakes had devastated Turkey, Jews were being driven madly about, and the Yiddish theater had hit a new low. The world was in shambles and my career along with it."[23] Her "career" meant theater. The radio performer and actor Zvee Scooler expressed a similar sentiment. "It is art that counts," he said. "Radio is not enough for me. I've got to have a living audience in whose presence, I feel, I can create."[24]

The Yiddish radio audiences may not have disagreed with Picon's, Scooler's, and Lumet's characterization of radio entertainment as low-brow and of lesser quality than either Yiddish theater or English radio programming, but their behavior indicated that they did not really care. Listeners continued to tune in to Yiddish programs. Audiences wanted to listen to programs in Yiddish and understood, intuitively at least, that objective "quality" mattered less than the opportunity to listen in the first place. Moreover, the relative quality of the programs did not diminish the ability or desire of listeners to establish meaningful relationships with the programs and their characters. In one example, Lumet recalled a live performance of *Der zeyde* at a theater in Brownsville that took place in the mid-1930s in which the lead character got married. "The theater was packed," he said. "I'll never forget how many people came from New Jersey, from Newark, there the station hits very strong, in New Jersey. People, old men and women on crutches, they came and paid a dollar admission, and the wedding gave me several hundred dollars, of course I paid all the actors that participated in it. It was something unusual and that's how I realized that I have an audience for a play."[25] Although audiences undertook a significant effort to attend the performance and see their beloved radio stars in person, Lumet remained unable or unwilling to recognize the popularity and significance of radio. For him, the radio show's greatest contribution was its indication of the promise for future endeavors in "proper" theater, but his listeners seemed more than satisfied.

Yet the world of Yiddish entertainment was not divided only between theater and radio; there also existed a hierarchy within Yiddish radio itself, with smaller stations ranking below the larger stations in the minds and contracts of the performers. Freydele Oysher's career offers a good example. As a young girl, Oysher emigrated from Poland to Brooklyn via Canada with her family. Her career began when Al Entin, a New York businessman with a few Yiddish radio programs to his name, heard her performing on local stages and put her on variety shows, from which she quickly graduated to regular appearances on some of the Brooklyn-based stations. Soon she moved up from the small Brooklyn-based stations to WEVD, whose longer broadcast schedule and larger power allotment meant a bigger audience and a contract with Horowitz-Margareten, a matzo company. Although Oysher called WEVD "the mother and father" of Yiddish radio, she admitted that she did not feel like she had "made it" until she signed a thirteen-week contract with WMCA, a New York station with a reputation for high-quality talent and programming.[26] The station's English-language roster included the bandleaders Ozzie Nelson, Chick Webb, and Cab Callaway. Among its alumni, WMCA counted Rudy Vallee, "The Street Singer" Arthur Tracy, and the original "Radio Girl," Vaughn DeLeath. WMCA, which did not usually carry Yiddish programs, held its English-language Jewish programs to a similar standard and offered quasi-educational programs such as *Romances in the Bible* and *Great Jewish Composers and Their Work.* Because of the station's high-rofile English-language lineup and high-quality Jewish programs, WMCA established relationships with sponsors such as Maxwell House and Junket Milk Products, along with large Jewish-owned companies such as Rokeach and Horowitz-Margareten.

Oysher's recollection of her career trajectory emphasizes the fact that

Yiddish-speaking performers were well aware of the hierarchy of the radio business. Like Baruch Lumet, who believed radio to be so far below the "legitimate" theater that he refused to associate himself with his own radio program, Oysher evaluated her radio career on the relative size of her fame, income, and platform. In an industry where income was a function of fame, Oysher's recollection and Lumet's artistic snobbery made a certain amount of sense: Yiddish radio simply could not compete with mainstream English-language radio for either financial gain or cultural status.

And yet people continued to listen. The columnist Sam Brown, writing in the Brooklyn-based, English-language newspaper the *Jewish Examiner*, framed the contradictory feelings of audiences as they simultaneously rallied around Yiddish radio and expressed their distaste for its perceived low quality:

> As far as we're concerned, the average Jewish program is a
> McGee. . . . [A]s soon as they come on the air, we take our cue to
> tune off. The trouble isn't solely the blatant ballyhoo employed on
> these programs but the inferior quality of the entertainment as
> well. . . . And still, we would not like to see Jewish programs
> disappear from the air. . . . After all, they do offer some diversion to
> the older Jews. . . . It gives one satisfaction to observe the expression
> on their faces as they crowd around a radio when a Jewish program
> is on. . . . We have one more complaint to make, however—the policy
> recently has been to translate English songs into Yiddish. . . . With
> the wealth of Jewish talent available, why couldn't it be possible to
> compose original Jewish songs?[27]

Despite dismissals of the quality of Yiddish radio, its strength derived from the ways in which it wove itself into the habits and preferences of its listening audience. Brown, too, acknowledged the problem with quality; nevertheless, he did not wish to see Yiddish programs taken off the air.

Quality, it seemed, had little to do with the audience's desire to listen to programs in Yiddish. Rather, listeners were motivated by a slightly different desire—a desire to hear Yiddish and voices that sounded like theirs. The structures of feeling that defined Jewish immigrants' relationships to Yiddish radio meant that they did not act according to strict assessments of what made for "good" and "bad" radio. Instead, they acted according to a set of desires that were neither purely rational nor purely affective.[28] Despite the disparaging remarks of Yiddish-speaking radio performers, audiences tuned in regularly just to hear Yiddish, even when they could have been listening to programs in English. Or, more accurately, they tuned in to Yiddish programs in addition to English ones and heard different articulations of their lives in America in each.

WEVD

Even WEVD exhibited a less than appreciative attitude toward Yiddish programming throughout the 1930s, though the station would later become its premier outlet and would continue broadcasting a robust Yiddish schedule through the 1980s. Echoing the sentiments of performers like Lumet and Oysher, management at WEVD felt that the station ought to be committed to improving the civic life of the city, not simply entertaining immigrants. Thus the station, while more than happy to accept advertising income from sponsors of Yiddish shows, kept its Yiddish programs out of the spotlight, in favor of its more civic-minded English offerings. Ironically, this arrangement allowed Yiddish programming to flourish and for WEVD to become the most beloved outlet for Yiddish radio in America.

WEVD took its call letters from the initials of the Socialist leader Eugene V. Debs, who had died in 1926 and left a sum of money in his will to establish a broadcast venture that served his political vision. The Debs Radio Trust intended its station to become a "'militant voice of the American labor movement to give expression to the aspirations of the millions of men and women who toil for a living'" and hoped to be supported by contributions from the same millions.[29] Almost immediately after its establishment in 1927, WEVD found itself in financial trouble. In 1928, the station operated at a loss, a situation that its management hoped to rectify by selling broadcast time, despite the obvious conflict with its Socialist ideals. Two years later, the station faced obstacles significant enough to result in a handful of technical violations, including broad-casting off frequency, failing to post its broadcast license, broadcasting without a licensed individual on the premises, and an overall "lack of proper supervision." Despite its unique contributions to the civic and political life of New York and the venue it provided for political dissent, the FRC argued that these violations proved too serious: "A minority is not a thing apart and entitled to preferential treatment as of right. A minority has a proper place and being but its existence cannot justifiably be made an excuse to abuse the privileges granted to it by the govern-ment under which it so exists."[30] By 1931, the station was in danger of deletion.

In February 1932, the Forward Association, parent company of the *Forward* newspaper, rescued the station with a pledge of $200,000 for upkeep and maintenance, promising $70,000 to be used immediately for station improvements and the remaining $130,000 to be given if the FRC renewed the station's license. Norman Thomas, a Socialist leader, and Louis G. Caldwell, former general council of the FRC, argued the sta-tion's case to the FRC, claiming that WEVD actually represented main-stream rather than minority opinions. "WEVD is a public forum open to the presentation of all viewpoints in matters of public interest. It is a sure avenue of communication to the public for all schools of thought. It is available when other avenues are closed. WEVD is giving practi-cal application to the time-honored principle which forms part of the groundwork of our civilization, freedom of speech and of the press. The influence of this policy cannot be measured solely with reference to the advantages it offers to minorities."[31] No longer the voice of working men and women and a far cry from the "'militant voice of the American labor movement,'" the station now staked its future solidly in the American democratic tradition.

In a sense, Thomas and Caldwell had to kill the station in order to save it, and they hired Baruch Charney Vladeck to do the job. Vladeck, a Jewish immigrant, managing editor of the *Forward,* and a leader in the Socialist movement, helped to restructure the station in a way that would have a significant impact on its Yiddish-language programming. Dedicated to entertaining and informing the largely immigrant working

people of New York, in the late 1920s, WEVD developed a distinctly mul-
tiethnic lineup, including the shows *Seeing the Irish Cities, Hits and Bits of
Scotch,* and the *Nestle Club Colored Art Hour* featuring African American
performers.[32] Before 1932, WEVD carried very little Jewish programming.
Apart from the annual appearance of the English language comedy *Mrs.
Rabinowitz's Christmas Tree,* the only other Jewish programming was
Cantor Isidore Sheyn's weekly *Jewish Hour,* a program of the Jewish Art
Theater, and the regular appearances of a female impersonator named
Zalman about whom, sadly, little is known.[33]

In 1932, with the support of the Forward Association and under the
direction of Vladeck, the station moved into a new studio at the McAlpin
Hotel and inaugurated its new facilities with a program featuring the
philosopher John Dewey, the Socialist leader Morris Hilquit, and the
Forward editor, Abe Cahan, who spoke English for the occasion. Not
quite what the networks would have called a star-studded lineup, but the
dedication of WEVD's new studios clearly indicated the direction that
the station hoped to take. Eschewing flash and entertainment, WEVD
renewed its commitment to providing highbrow political and educational programming aimed at the working people of New York City.[34]
Gone were the entertaining ethnic programs in favor of a more serious,
more studious program schedule.

Vladeck hired Morris Novick, a twenty-nine-year-old, Russian-born
Jewish immigrant and graduate of a Lower East Side yeshiva, to serve
as the station's new program director. Novick had recently made a name
for himself in the Socialist movement as the director of educational programming at Unity House, the International Ladies' Garment Workers'
Union's (ILGWU's) summer resort in the Catskills. In that capacity,
Novick prided himself on constructing "links between the labor movement and the cultural organizations of artists and intellectuals" and
drew praise for turning Unity House into a coveted venue for liberal
and radical performers. In an interview, Novick recalled that before his
arrival WEVD "played absolutely no part in the life of New York, or
hardly any," and that "it wasn't worthy of the license in the first place."[35]
But, hopeful about the power of radio to reach larger audiences than
speeches and meetings, Novick built the station into a forum for intel-

lectual discussion and political debate. Soon after his arrival, the station began featuring lectures by Clarence Darrow and Bertrand Russell while also cultivating local programming such as *University of the Air* and *Talent Detective*, an amateur hour with an educational focus.

Strong-minded and independent, Novick feared that the *Forward* would try to exert some editorial control over the station and thus hamper his ability to make it as successful as it could be. Novick was so concerned that the Yiddish newspaper would curtail the effectiveness of the station that he took the position only after assurances that he would answer to Vladeck alone rather than to Abe Cahan or the newspaper's editorial board. Novick had proven his ability to create powerful and successful programming with a serious commitment to left and labor politics, and Vladeck understood that he would not stand for popular programming that simply entertained. Yet Vladeck, as the newspaper's managing editor, also understood the bottom line and rightly feared that lectures and discussions of labor issues could not compete with Eddie Cantor or Jack Benny. Thus Vladeck and Novick created, essentially, a two-tiered station that featured Yiddish programming primarily during the day and English programming in the evening. Because of the political and intellectual nature of the station's English-language programming, the responsibility for supporting the station fell to its Yiddish programs. Beginning with the debut of the *Forward Hour* in fall 1932, WEVD aggressively built up its Yiddish radio presence throughout the 1930s, securing more and larger sponsors so that it could keep up its important English programming. One FCC report found that "for the first six months of 1933, the station realized a total net income of $17,399.63, of which $16,294.63 was received from foreign language programs."[36] Aided by Sholom Rubenstein and Meyer Kielson, owners of a fledgling advertising agency that focused on Yiddish programming, WEVD's popular Yiddish programs earned enough income to allow the station's unsponsored English-language programs to earn awards for their contributions to the city's civic life and, according to the FCC, justify the otherwise overly commercialized Yiddish-language lineup (see figure 10).

Even under the ownership of the Forward Association, WEVD still

Figure 10. Photograph of Molly Picon and Sholom Rubenstein performing on the *Maxwell House Radio Program* (WHN). Courtesy of the American Jewish Historical Society of Newton Center, Massachusetts, and New York.

considered Yiddish a second-class language and hardly recognized either the growing creativity or contribution of Yiddish programming on the station. By mid-decade, WEVD had introduced Marc Schweid's radio adaptation of the popular newspaper column, the *Bintl briv* (Bundle of Letters), Nukhem Stutchkoff's first family dramas, dramatizations of Yiddish literature, and countless musical performances. It boasted a schedule of nearly twenty-five hours of Yiddish programming each week, supported by a healthy roster of sponsors. Yet when WEVD moved from the McAlpin Hotel to a new studio at the Claridge Hotel in Times Square in 1938, the division between the station's Yiddish and English programming became clearer than ever. At the dedication of the station's new home, guests celebrated its contributions to education, civic welfare, and politics, but none mentioned Yiddish.[37]

Although Yiddish programs attracted a significant audience and had begun to draw the attention of larger sponsors, they remained relegated to radio's second tier, even on WEVD. Compared to English radio, as Yiddish radio always was, it simply could not compete. Even its own performers saw it as a stepping-stone to larger stations, bigger audiences, and fatter paydays. Nevertheless, Yiddish radio thrived. More programs appeared on more stations each year, and the variety of programs continued to grow as performers branched out into dramas, advice programs, and even news. Productions became slightly more elaborate as larger sponsors took interest in mining the Jewish immigrant market, and a few advertising agencies emerged to broker contracts between sponsors and stations. Yet the FRC and the FCC continued to view the commercialization of Yiddish radio with skepticism, fearful that stations that catered to immigrant audiences would become overly commercial and would not support the ideals of Americanization on the air. Even with these limitations, however, the stations that carried Yiddish shows continued to expand their eclectic lineups, and though performers and stations ranked Yiddish below English, audiences eager to hear themselves on the air continued to tune in.

RELIGIOUS RHYTHMS

What audiences heard on Yiddish radio echoed the cultural contours of Jewish life generally and generated some of Yiddish radio's most audible convergences with the specifically Jewish culture of its audience. Most broadcasters focused on emulating English-language radio, but they also produced an aural culture that resonated with and echoed back the cultural preferences of their listeners and the communities they shared. These manifested not only in the kind and the content of programs that emerged but also in the development of a distinct broadcast structure. Most clearly, Yiddish radio developed broadcast schedules that drew on the cultural expectations and habits of its Jewish audience and echoed the sometimes subtle negotiations between the community, the audience, and radio. WMIL's request for permission to suspend broadcasting on Yom Kippur is the most obvious example, but throughout the 1930s, other stations adapted their schedules to suit the cultural contours of their audience's habits and tastes.

As the broadcast schedule took shape during the late 1920s and early 1930s, Yiddish radio developed a distinct rhythm that responded both to emergent listening habits and available airtime within the world of Jewish immigrants. In 1927, the networks were still feeling their way around the Radio Act and commercial broadcasting, and they had not yet developed a coherent strategy for appealing to sponsors or listeners. With the success of the serial programs *Amos 'n' Andy* and *The Rise of the Goldbergs* and the growing popularity of radio hosts such as Eddie Cantor, Jack Benny, and Fred Allen, evening hours became known as "prime time," attracting many of the wealthiest sponsors with programming that could entertain the whole family. Daytime hours, which most men spent at work and many women spent at home, hosted the new genre of dramatic serials that came to be known as "soap operas," in mocking tribute to their sponsors—Proctor and Gamble and other makers of household goods. Despite the derision, daytime broadcasting became a powerfully important source of income for the networks. In 1927, NBC's two networks offered 88 evening programs and only 45 minutes of daytime programming each month, but by 1934, new networks and growing interest from sponsors and advertising agencies increased the amount of daytime programming to include 311 shows each month.[38]

While mainstream sponsors and networks found gender an effective way to subdivide their audience and target their advertisements and the programs that supported them, sponsors of Yiddish programs found that gender did not have the same resonance within Yiddish radio. When Yiddish daytime programs did appear, they tried to appeal to the perceived interests of female listeners, but even then, they appealed specifically to Jewish women. More accurately, they spoke Yiddish to their female listeners' Jewish concerns. The first daytime program in Yiddish debuted in 1932, when WLTH launched the short-lived *Yidish heim sho* (Yiddish Home Hour).[39] The program addressed the perceived concerns of Jewish homemakers and provided a Jewish gendered imitation of mainstream English-language programs. The following year, WBNX unveiled its daily *Yidish froyen program* (Jewish Women's Program), a combination of talk, music, and advice.[40] This remained the only regularly broadcast daytime program in Yiddish until WFAB launched a competing program in April 1934.[41] Where these programs addressed gender explicitly, they generally framed gender within Jewishness. The remainder of Yiddish daytime programming also focused on Jewish issues or entertainments, for example, *Der freylikher khazen* (The Happy Cantor) and other light musically focused or talk-based programming. Yiddish radio's only proper serial drama did not debut until 1942, when *Mein muter un ikh* (My Mother and I) began a three-year run on WEVD. Because there was no particular genre or format that belonged to Yiddish daytime broadcasting, it bore greater similarities to the remainder of the Yiddish broadcast schedule than English daytime broadcasting did, despite its gendered address. This is not to suggest that gender did not matter but rather that the difference between Yiddish and English radio resonated more loudly than gender-based appeals within Yiddish radio itself.

In response, Yiddish programming developed a schedule that relied less on traditional differences between "family entertainment" and "women's serials" and more on the rhythms of the Jewish work and worship week, more broadly considered. This manifested in two primary ways. First, many Yiddish radio broadcasters took Saturday off, while Friday and Sunday emerged as the two days with the strongest Yiddish lineups. This likely was not because of religious reasons but because of cultural ones in which the Jewish Sabbath, from sundown on Friday through sundown on Saturday, retained its cultural cachet.

Second, Yiddish-speaking broadcasters took advantage of gaps in the English-language broadcast week to highlight their own best programs free of competition. By emphasizing the Jewishness of its audience, Yiddish-speaking broadcasters hoped to capitalize on convergences between audience and community as they turned cultural commonalities into broadcast conventions during the 1930s. Yet speaking Yiddish to Yiddish speakers proved only part of the story, as this dynamic created characteristics of its own that gave Yiddish radio a different rhythm from English radio.

This became especially clear on Sundays, when many stations dedicated their broadcast hours to unsponsored, civic-minded programs in service to the "public interest" and in line with the FCC's requirements. Generally unwilling to cede valuable evening and daytime hours to these programs, station owners looked for a vacant space on their schedules to carry the burden of their sustaining programs. Explicit commerce seemed at odds with Sunday's religious overtones, and, augmented by a fear that radio would keep people out of church, broadcasters opted against airing popular programs, leaving the day to house sustaining programs committed to politics and social issues. Typically, English language-programming on Sundays featured broadcasts connected to churches, universities, and other social welfare institutions, as well as roundtables, lectures, and the like. This full but relatively unattractive lineup, which drew neither large sponsors nor large audiences, earned the nickname the "Sunday ghetto."

Absent religious overtones and not concerned that attractive programming would keep listeners out of church, Yiddish-speaking broadcasters turned the "Sunday ghetto" into the most popular venue for Yiddish programming by attracting parents and children at home from work and school without competition from popular English programs. Virtually every station that carried Yiddish programming contributed at least one program to Sunday's Yiddish lineup, and most stations used the day to highlight their most elaborate and expensive productions. When WEVD introduced its *Forward Hour* at eleven o'clock on Sunday morning in fall 1932, it quickly became the anchor of the Yiddish broadcast week. The debut program followed the format of a fairly typical variety show, including a few songs, a short speech by Abe Cahan, a "dramatization sketch," a selection of folk and theater songs called "Melodies from the Ghetto," and the "Forward Hour Theme," which recalled the "sounds of revolutionary songs."[42] More precisely, the theme song was a medley of popular melodies evocative of the station's roots in the labor movement. It opened to a Russian-sounding march, punctuated with a chorus of voices shouting, "Forward!" in time with the music, before segueing into the first few bars of the "Internationale" and concluding with the opening refrain of "La Marseilles."[43]

The following year, the station added Nukhem Stutchkoff's first family drama, *Annie and Bennie,* along with a series of afternoon concerts. Later in the afternoon, Stutchkoff returned to the air as the host of *Feter nukhem's kleynvarg,* after which WEVD returned to its evening English programming. On Sundays, Dave Tarras, Sholom Secunda, and Naftule Brandwein and other popular musicians appeared alongside stars of the stage such as Lucy Levin, Molly Picon, Menashe Skulnik, Anshel Shorr, and Maurice Schwartz. Writers such as Mendel Osherovitch supplied dramatizations of popular literature, and the Jewish Little Symphony broadcast weekly concerts.[44] In Philadelphia, WRAX and WDAS offered a whole afternoon of Yiddish programming on Sundays, including children's programs, musical concerts, commentary, poetry, and news.

Whereas network stations used Sundays to fulfill scheduling responsibilities, Yiddish broadcasters used Sundays to take care of business. Although radio stations were beholden to federal radio regulations requiring a certain percentage of unsponsored programs, the sponsors themselves were not, so many turned to Yiddish broadcasting to create opportunities where none otherwise existed. Non-Jewish, English-speaking sponsors like Ralston, Edelstein's Tuxedo Brand Cream Cheese, Postum, and Planter's, in addition to Jewish sponsors like Manischewitz, Sachs Clothiers, the Roland Theater, the Liberty Theater, and the Wonderland Café, all supported Sunday programs. In Philadelphia, H. Kandel and Co. and Kolster International Radio sponsored the *Kandel-Kolster Hour,* and Philadelphia's biggest Yiddish theater, the Yiddish-speaking Arch Street Theater, also sponsored programs in support of its latest production. Jewish sponsors approached Sunday like any other day and sank their resources into the day that promised the largest Jewish audiences and the least competition.

Saturday presented a different story. Jewish law prohibits work of any kind on the Sabbath, as well as the use of electricity, which includes lights and radios. Observant Jews would have honored the Sabbath by not listening to the radio, going to work, or spending money. But most Jews did not observe the Sabbath with such rigor. Since the 1910s, theater audiences far outnumbered synagogue attendees on an average Friday night. One frustrated rabbi noted, "The most visible sign of Sabbath observance, perhaps, is the stream of hundreds of Jews entering a synagogue, with a ticket of admission, the price of which was probably paid on a Saturday."[45] Attendance at the Yiddish theater on Friday night at least achieved parity with synagogues and likely exceeded it, and many people attended both. If audiences went to the theater on Friday night, then the performers had to as well, leaving nobody behind in the broadcast booth. In fact, one of the factors that contributed to the failure of the *Forward*'s concert series in 1926 was that it scheduled the performances for Friday night, when observant Jews could not listen and performers were onstage and audiences sat in their seats. Though most Jews did not strictly observe the laws of Sabbath, Yiddish radio broadcasters still typically took the day off, leaving Saturdays a fairly quiet day in Yiddish broadcasting and the stations that carried Yiddish programs to fill in with programs in other languages. Although not for explicitly religious reasons, the silence of Yiddish radio echoed the religious observance of the day, before broadcasters again took to the air on Saturday nights, once the Sabbath had ended.

The schedule of Yiddish radio developed a cultural rhythm that echoed conventions of Jewish religious and cultural life. The relative quiet of Saturdays did not necessarily mean that audiences would be more likely to observe the Sabbath according to the law but rather that religious law continued to exert a force on the cultural lives of Jewish immigrants and on the weekly Yiddish radio schedule. This reflected the congruence between the Yiddish-speaking community and the Yiddish radio audience. If, by cultural convention, people did not listen to the radio on a Friday night, then Yiddish-speaking broadcasters wouldn't bother to broadcast. In March 1931, Rokeach moved its high-profile Tuesday night broadcast featuring Joseph Rumshinsky to Monday because the first night of Passover fell on Tuesday.[46] Again, Rokeach probably moved the program in recognition of its audience, not because of religious observance. These trends emphasized the cultural formation of radio in dialogue with its audience and illustrated the mutual acknowledgment of communal similarities and support.

Following this pattern, Friday became the most popular day of the week for broadcasting, most of which took on religious overtones, as it provided accompaniment to Jews preparing for the Sabbath. Rabbi Samuel Rubin, Cantor Jacob Altman, and Rabbi Joseph Leibowitz each offered their wisdom, while theater performers like Jacob Mason ("The Happy Cantor"), Jennie Goldstein, and Menashe Skulnik accompanied Sholom Secunda to contribute to the festive mood. Most of the programs advertised *Shabesdike melodies* (Music in the Spirit of the Sabbath), cantorial music drawn from Sabbath liturgy, sermons, or, occasionally, all three. Programs like *Erev shabes kontsertn* (Sabbath Eve Concerts) and *Khazn altmans shabes melodien* (Cantor Altman's Sabbath Melodies) entertained listeners in anticipation of the Sabbath. In Chicago, *The Jewish People's Hour* under the direction of Jacob Ellenhorn aired Friday nights at nine o'clock, in violation of the laws of Sabbath but in keeping with the spirit of the law that left Saturday as the day of rest.[47]

Radio offered a cultural sound track that echoed the spirit of Jewish tradition even as it violated Jewish law. It provided a Yiddish sound track to both the sacred and the secular as mutually supporting areas of Jewish life. The poet Kadya Molodowsky captured this phenomenon in "Sabbath Arrives in Brownsville," which described the ways in which the sounds of radio, prayer, and popular music intermingled and accompanied the arrival of the Sabbath.

> Chopping knives knock out an old, old melody
> From Berditshev, from Berezne, from Demir,
> And the radio sings: "Oh come already, my sweet life,
> Your true Tsipele awaits you, dear."

. . . .

"Ah, Lekho dodi likras kale [a prayer from the service for welcoming
   the Sabbath],"
An old man sings with a sorrowful beard,
"Forgive, my children profane the Sabbath,
And sorrow lies upon the whole wide world."

. . . .

The young folks near the candy store
In honor of the Sabbath all "campaign."
They sing loudly, with pure voices,
"Oy, bay mir bistu sheyn, Oh, let me explain."[48]

Mixing the sounds of the radio with the strains of the approaching
Sabbath and juxtaposing popular lyrics with liturgy, Molodowsky captured the aural culture of Fridays in Jewish neighborhoods, where the
sounds of popular music blended with prayer and where, at the end of
the day, the Sabbath still arrived.

THE AESTHETIC OF INTIMACY

Set to the cadence of an evolving Jewish culture in America, Yiddish
radio expanded throughout the 1930s and developed both a sound and a
sensibility that drew on and reinforced the cultural concerns of the community it served. Jewish immigrants listened to Yiddish programming
regardless of what the performers thought of it, and Yiddish programs
succeeded in carving out a unique space and a unique sound that resonated with the experiences and interests of their listeners. In this way,
Yiddish programs performed a version of Americanization that likely
did not quite sound like the FCC would have preferred but that came
out of first-person encounters with the lives and concerns of listeners.
The informal trade in sympathy and sensibility between the audience,
the community, and the broadcasters took shape along the contours of
an audience that liked to listen to itself.

In terms of content, music still represented the lion's share of Yiddish
broadcast hours. Programs that promoted Americanization—*Yidish*

college fun der luft (Jewish College of the Air), the *Jewish Program for Unemployment Aid*, or *Mein greiz* (My Mistake), a prime-time program that promised to "teach how to speak English without mistakes"—continued to populate the airwaves, but the majority of Yiddish radio tried primarily to entertain.[49] At least one program tried explicitly to combine entertainment and community. The noted theatrical producer Maurice Schwartz launched *Lomir ale zingen* (Let's All Sing), a show that hoped to lead its listeners in sing-alongs, which it encouraged by publishing booklets of lyrics so listeners could participate.[50]

When other programs began to appear in the mid-1930s, they assumed an almost exclusive focus on the lives of Jewish immigrant families. Despite the popularity of soap operas, westerns, science fiction, and spy/detective programs in English, not a single Yiddish program could qualify for any of those genres. Instead, Yiddish programming rarely strayed beyond the boundaries of Jewish neighborhoods and communities. Concerts focused largely on music from the Jewish folk and theater traditions, adaptations of literature drew almost exclusively on Yiddish literature, and original dramatic programs told and retold stories about the trials and tribulations of Jewish families who had immigrated to America. In short, Yiddish-speaking broadcasters spoke to their audiences about their own communities, and their audiences responded eagerly. Although Yiddish radio broadcasters imitated their English-speaking counterparts in form and content, they developed an aesthetic of intimacy that did not easily translate.

Radio historian Jason Loviglio has addressed the phenomenon of radio's intimacy during the 1930s as it operated on network radio.[51] For Loviglio, Roosevelt's fireside chats and programs, like the man-in-the-street interviews of *Vox Pop*, helped radio to cultivate an audible sense of intimacy among listeners who knew that they were but one of millions listening at any given moment. As a result, radio became a powerful political tool: it strengthened the sense of the American nation in the relatively atomized experiences of a listening audience. Loviglio's notion of the "intimate public" illuminates the relationship between interpersonal and mass communication and exposes some of the dynamics by which that relationship was both challenged and maintained. On Yiddish radio, acoustic intimacy served a related but different purpose.

Yiddish radio always operated within a community of Jewish immigrants, even as it relied on mainstream radio. Both on the air and off it, Jewish immigrants tended to live and socialize with one another, and the line between Jewish and non-Jewish, though certainly transgressed, remained symbolically and socially significant. During the 1930s and into the 1940s, Jews typically lived in Jewish neighborhoods, patronized Jewish-owned shops and restaurants, and worked, studied, and vacationed among other Jews. They belonged to Jewish organizations, both religious and not, and although struggling to become Americans, they traveled in circles populated primarily by other Jewish immigrants.[52] Among the immigrant generation in particular, Yiddish remained the common language of socializing and business, and practically nobody other than Jewish immigrants listened to Yiddish radio, read the Yiddish newspapers, or attended the Yiddish theater. Thus Yiddish radio's "intimate public" proved both more intimate and less public than its English-speaking counterpart, even while listeners to Yiddish radio tuned in to English programs, too. In Yiddish, the aesthetic of intimacy produced and reproduced common narratives for a community that already shared many experiences in common. Thus, instead of forging a sense of commonality among a diverse and dispersed listenership, Yiddish radio spoke to audiences proscribed by language, ethnicity, and region. Therefore, it required a different set of strategies for producing acoustic intimacy. According to Loviglio, participation in radio's "intimate public" gave disparate listeners entrée into an American audience, but Yiddish radio reversed this process. In Yiddish, the aesthetic of intimacy turned listeners inward and provided increased access to stories that amplified shared genealogies and social contexts. The public of Yiddish radio was exclusively Jewish, and the medium's intimacy amplified that sense.

This became audible first on advice programs that flourished during the mid-1930s. Building on the popularity of advice columns like the *Bintl briv* in the *Forward* and *Mener un froyen* (Men and Women) in *Der tog*, Yiddish radio broadcasters began mining the trials and the experiences of everyday people for broadcast material. When the Forward

Association took control of WEVD, Vladeck hired Marc Schweid, a modestly successful Yiddish playwright and translator, to adapt the *Bintl briv* for radio as the station's first regular Yiddish feature. The program, like the newspaper column on which it was based, quickly proved popular, and in a few months WEVD expanded the program to two shows per week.

The *Bintl briv* quickly spawned a host of imitators—*Der veg vayser* (The Knower of the Way), *Der familyen fraynt* (The Family Friend), *Der yidisher filosof* (The Jewish Philosopher), and *Der hoyz fraynt* (The Friend of the Home)—each offering its version of the popular formula. The shows followed a fairly simple format: the hosts read letters and then extemporaneously offered advice, criticism, and commentary for the benefit of listeners (see figure 11). One print advertisement for *Der hoyz fraynt* captured this desire perfectly. It pictured the partially obscured face of the mysterious host hovering above a cartoon cityscape, eagerly awaiting the word of a troubled listener. "Is something stressful in your heart?" asked the advertising copy. "Do you know about something that you can't share? Can you not speak with your wife? Do you have trouble with your children? Do you not understand your husband?"[53] Although the programs supposedly featured the letters and lives of real people, it is likely, as with the *Bintl briv*, that the program's hosts wrote their own letters to answer. Fictional or not, the programs attracted sponsors and audiences, and many of these programs enjoyed a good amount of success, as measured by their longevity.

C. Yisroel Lutzky, the man behind *Der yidisher filosof* and the most successful of these radio hosts, kept his program on the air into the mid-1960s, when he moved to Florida and continued his distinct brand of wisdom, criticism, and snake-oil salesmanship for Jewish audiences in Miami. In his heyday, Lutzky hoped to use the radio to build a modest empire of advice that included a regular advice column in Philadelphia's *Idishe velt* and leadership of the Jewish Philosopher's League, "an organization that

Figure 11 (opposite).   Newspaper advertisement for *Der hoyz fraynt* (The Friend of the Home). Note the mysterious appearance of the program's wise host, partially obscured by a microphone. Sponsored by Coward Shoes, "The friend of human feet." *Jewish Daily Forward*, 8 March 1937, 8. Courtesy of the Forward Association.

is truly a cultural and spiritual cult" that existed "to fill a much wanted need on behalf of the lonely and friendless men and women of all ages and in every walk of life."[54] In perhaps the most obvious, if odd, example of the dynamic between audience and community, Lutzky hoped to spin a social movement out of his radio shows and turn the medium from a source of entertainment to one capable of social organizing.

Although the Philosopher's League faded into obscurity, surviving recordings of *Der yidisher filosof* capture the passion of Lutzky's performance and the drama of his conviction and indicate that he provided more than mere entertainment. Letters told the stories of a man who was tired of being dragged into shady and unsuccessful business ventures by his wife's brother, a mother who loved her troubled son too much to punish him, and a husband who insisted that his wife hates all men, including him.[55] Typically, the letters went into great detail about the specific nature of the troubles. One letter read:

> My son[,] . . . who is 36 years old, was left a widower three years ago with a young child of five years. Last year he married an old maid who is about a year younger than him. And it seems to me that he has not made a very good move. Firstly, she knows nothing about how to prepare a good meal. Furthermore, when she comes to visit, she always holds his hand from the minute they both sit down until the minute they go home. Truth be told, my son doesn't look so bad that I can complain that she doesn't cook as well as me or his first wife. Nu? My husband says not to mix in so much, but what does he know about what a real mother feels who wants to see her son only happy and content.[56]

The letters, fictional and otherwise, presented familial conflicts, and "der filosof" offered his best impassioned advice. Certainly the most flamboyant and ambitious of the on-air advisers, Lutzky captured a vital acoustic sensibility central to Yiddish radio: the allure of eavesdropping on intimate details of others listeners uncertain about themselves, their families, and their place in America. Though not quite a "cultural and spiritual cult," *Der yidisher filosof* presented tales of Jewish immigrant life for an audience who seemed eager to listen.

Yiddish advice programs showed the power of these interests as an organizational principle not of social movements but of entertainment.

The pleasure of listening to these stories in Yiddish fostered a sense of intimacy in their promise of opportunities not only to hear Yiddish but also to hear Yiddish speakers talk about the lives that they all lived. Sponsors followed audiences, but what drew an audience to listen to *Der hoyz fraynt* and neglect *Herring and Potato?* Why did advice programs proliferate while only one or two weekly serials succeeded during this period? In part, the popularity of these programs lay in listeners' desire to hear voices that sounded like their own. Choosing to listen to Yiddish programming illustrated that they wanted to hear broadcasts that expressed the world they knew. They wanted not only linguistic familiarity but cultural familiarity as well. These programs promised an excess of familiarity, a sonic sense of intimacy, framed by their dramatizations of people's "real life" troubles. Most people did not read the *Bintl briv* or listen to *Der yidisher filosof* for advice as much as entertainment value and perhaps even the familiar comfort of the conflicts they presented. Both played on the desire to eavesdrop, once limited to open windows and airshafts, now both broader and more discreet on the radio.

Network radio during this period hosted the expansion of the soap opera and the serial drama. These English-language programs typically revolved around families in small towns, an important market for the rapidly expanding networks and a powerful mythological location in the United States. Meanwhile, Yiddish advice programs focused exclusively on the everyday troubles of Jewish immigrants in urban America: death, love, divorce, crime, poverty, children, and the occasional religious question. As America's "intimate public" listened in on unfamiliar towns and neighborhoods, Yiddish-speaking listeners tuned in to hear their friends, neighbors, and relatives. Loviglio, following Benedict Anderson, suggests that radio provided a vehicle for overcoming unfamiliarity between members of the American polity and thus succeeded in fostering a sense of national unity. Yiddish radio succeeded similarly, albeit in a different register. It fostered a greater sense of intimacy among people who by and large shared a common language and a relatively similar set of experiences of immigration and resettlement. Whether or not listeners actually wrote the letters read on the air did not matter as much as the opportunity they shared to hear Yiddish-speaking voices describe troubles that listeners already knew. Instead of transporting listeners to faraway places,

Yiddish radio programs drew them deeper into their own communities. Whether these programs drew on "real life troubles" or created fictional characters, as Yiddish serial dramas would do later in the decade, the effect remained virtually the same: Jewish immigrant listeners tuned in to hear the sounds of their own world reenacted for their entertainment.

When other writers began creating original content for Yiddish radio programs in mid-decade, they used techniques similar to those pioneered by advice programs. A survey of some of the titles of these programs illustrates the emphasis on family-based drama: *A muters layden* (A Mother's Family), *Dem khazens tokhter* (The Cantor's Daughter), *Di ervakhenung* (The Awakening), *Di seltser mishpokhe* (The Seltzer Family—sponsored by the Good Health Seltzer Company), *Hayntige kinder* (Today's Children), *Eltern un kinder* (Parents and Children), and *Das familyen vinkl* (The Family Nook). Even comedies like *Di karps, Mr. un Mrs. pumpernickel, Das freilikhe porl* (The Happy Pair), and the peculiarly named *Di yidishe shikse* (The Jewish Gentile Woman) took Jewish families as their inspiration and setting.

The popularity and longevity of *Der yidisher filosof* notwithstanding, the master of this genre was Nukhem Stutchkoff, who made his radio debut in 1932, just as advice programs were beginning to take hold. Stutchkoff, a modestly successful playwright and translator, began his radio career as the host of *Feter nukhem's kleynvarg* (Uncle Nukhem's Kiddies), where he worked alongside composer Sholom Secunda and led a troupe of talented Jewish children performing every manner of Yiddish song on the radio. However, he did not find his true calling until he began writing original fifteen-minute family dramas. Over the next twenty-five years, Stutchkoff contributed no less than ten original programs, beginning with *Annie and Bennie* in 1932 and concluding with *Tsuris bay layden* (Other People's Troubles) in 1957. Over the same period, Stutchkoff also dedicated himself to collecting and editing a Yiddish thesaurus, the only one of its kind, which the YIVO Institute for Jewish Research published in 1950.

Like his colleagues, Stutchkoff focused on the Jewish family as the source of dramatic tension. His first Yiddish radio drama, *Annie and Bennie,*

Figure 12. Newspaper advertisement for Nukhem Stutchkoff's
Bay tate mames tish ('Round the Family Table). *Jewish Daily
Forward,* 22 November 1936, 11. Courtesy of the Forward
Association.

followed the marriage of an American-born woman and her husband, a
German refugee.[57] The program did not last long, and Stutchkoff followed
his debut with another family-centered program, *In a yidishe groseray* (In
a Jewish Grocery).[58] This program focused on a grandfather, played by
Stutchkoff, who owned a grocery store and whose daily interactions with
customers and family members delivered him an ever-changing cast
and plenty of chances to mention his sponsor, Planter's Hi-Hat Peanut
Oil. In 1936, Stutchkoff launched his most successful program, *Bay tate
mames tish* ('Round the Family Table) (see figure 12). Structurally, *Bay
tate mames tish* represented a slight departure for Stutchkoff. His first

two offerings followed the same characters from episode to episode, in a manner similar to *Amos 'n' Andy*, *The Goldbergs*, or *Der bronzviler zayde*. As soap operas and serial dramas began experimenting with longer, more involved story lines, *Bay tate mames tish* moved in a different direction by introducing new characters and new stories in each episode. Either to distinguish his program from or to capitalize on the success of Yiddish advice programs—or perhaps both—Stutchkoff frequently opened episodes of *Bay tate mames tish* with an announcement that the stories he told were fictional and that his performers were, in fact, actors. Thus he cannily acknowledged and disavowed the aesthetic of intimacy to which his programs contributed and on which they relied.

Others, too, capitalized on the popularity of family drama. In December 1936, soon after the appearance of *Bay tate mames tish*, WMCA debuted *Uptown-Downtown*, a new episodic drama to compete with and capitalize on the popularity of Stutchkoff's program (see figure 13). The program's transliterated title referred to the social stratification of Jewish New York and staged the struggle for Americanization between wealthier uptown Jews and their poorer downtown cousins. While Stutchkoff delicately downplayed overt appeals to the aesthetic of intimacy, the producers of *Uptown-Downtown* made it plainly audible.

> The history of *Uptown-Downtown* is the history of nearly every Jewish immigrant. It is a history of sorrow and joy, of tears and laughter; a history of aspirations of Jewish immigrants who sought a living that will express honor to their children, and that would exalt in some accomplishments in this land of possibility. . . . In this radio comedy you'll find the quiet or serious struggle between "European" parents and their "American" children, this struggle goes on in thousands of Jewish homes, and you'll surely recognize many of the scenes that you have played out more than once in your own home.[59]

Uptown-Downtown spelled out the connection between the show and its audience even more explicitly than Stutchkoff did, assuring listeners that they could hear both the universal story of Jewish immigrants and their own particular stories.

Still attending to the concerns of Jewish families, WEVD employed

Figure 13.   Newspaper advertisement for Zion National's *Uptown-Downtown*. *Jewish Daily Forward*, 8 March 1937, 8. Courtesy of the Forward Association.

a similar strategy in January 1942, when it launched *Mein mutter un ikh* (My Mother and I), the first and only Yiddish soap opera. The program's introduction echoed almost exactly the intention of *Uptown-Downtown*. "Just like a mirror," read the narrator," you'll be able to see, through the mother with the daughter, a reflection of the life of a Jewish family in America. . . . It's possible that these are your neighbors from *next door* [in English], your friend, your acquaintances, or even your own family, yours alone."[60] Written by Marc Schweid and starring Celia Budkin as Mrs. Levine and Miriam Kressyn as her daughter, Shirley, the program spun its story lines around the characters' immigrant roots and their American desires. Not simply an American soap opera translated into Yiddish, the program spoke explicitly about Jewish immigrant life by employing elements of the popular American genre in a Jewish immigrant milieu. The show's very first scene set the tone, as it opened on Shirley and Mrs. Levine setting their dining table for a party.

MRS. LEVINE: Now give me the napkin rings . . . they go on the left.

SHIRLEY: Here they are. (sound like from silver) They're so pretty, Mama.

MRS. LEVINE: I brought them from Europe. A souvenir from my mother, may her memory be a blessing. And do you see the silverware? Also brought from Europe. The silver has been in our family for four generations as an inheritance.[61]

The show left no doubt about the Levines' immigrant roots, which strengthened during the program's first significant story line about

Shirley's brother Irving, who married Bela, daughter of another immigrant family that had made a lot of money in furs. Against her parents'
wishes, Irving and Bela, "as they say in America, 'eloped.'"[62] Over the
remainder of its two-year run, the program followed story lines that
would have sounded at home on most English-language soap operas:
Irving and Bela's forbidden love, Shirley's tumultuous relationship
with her longtime "friend" Sidney, Mr. Levine's surgery for which Bela
secretly lent Mrs. Levine money, and so on.

However, the cultural references and popular idiom of the characters
could not have been heard in any of the small towns favored by English-
language soap operas. Whereas English programs like *Clara, Lu and Em*
featured the folksy wisdom of the American heartland, *Mein mutter un
ikh* thrived on melodrama tempered by Jewish wisdom and fragments
of immigrant life. In practically every episode, Mrs. Levine shared a
nugget of insight: "The most important thing is the beginning. . . . Even
the Torah begins 'in the beginning'"; or, "Only God can help, because on
Him alone hangs the help of humans." Forbidden love and family feuds
had long been the stock-in-trade of English-language soap operas, and
by translating them into Yiddish and relocating them in a Jewish context,
Mein mutter un ikh amplified both the program's American sound and its
Yiddish voice, capitalizing on the aesthetic of intimacy that its audience
preferred.

One of the few originally scripted programs that did not focus on
contemporary Jewish domestic life, Marc Schweid's dramatization of
American Jewish history, concentrated exclusively on the experience of
Jews in America, albeit from a historical perspective. Even so, its content
did not stray far from the convention, giving a generation of Jewish
immigrants their own American histories. *Yidn in der geshikhte fun america*
(Jews in American History) debuted in WEVD's Sunday lineup in 1934
with the story of the "Jewish Mayflower" arriving in New Amsterdam
from Brazil in 1654 and followed it with episodes about the first Jewish
landowner in the New World, the founding of the Mill Street Synagogue,
and an unpleasant run-in with Peter Stuyvesant. Behind each episode
lay a lesson designed for an audience whose own history began not in
New Amsterdam but in the "old country."[63]

In an episode that captured the desire for the audience to hear itself on the air, Schweid seized on the popular myth that Native Americans descended from one of the lost tribes of Judea. Beginning with the narrator's lengthy explanation of that myth, the story opened on a "little Indian house, a Wigwam," where Mingo "the peaceful Indian" helped his wife, Puhatami, prepare food for their holiday "that is similar to Sukos," the Jewish fall harvest holiday. Mingo announced his presence with a "traditional Indian chant," "Hal-hal-hal, le-le-le, lu-lu-lu, yah-yah-yah." The episode followed Aaron Levi, Columbus's Jewish navigator, as he stumbled upon Mingo and Puhatami, only to discover that Native Americans spoke a version of Hebrew, worshiped a God named "Yoheyvah," and shared the memory of the ancient Temple in Jerusalem, which was destroyed in 70 C.E. By turning Native Americans into Jews, Schweid imagined Jewish immigration as a kind of American homecoming. At one point, Schweid even had Levi exclaim in English, "I already feel at home." For a new generation of immigrants, this could sound tremendously reassuring—that somehow they, too, had come home to America and that America, too, had Jewish roots.[64]

As with the advice programs and Stutchkoff's family dramas, the intentional blurring of "real" and "fictional" stories parlayed the tantalizing allure of listening in on one's neighbors or the comforting possibility of hearing one's own story into an aesthetic of intimacy that highlighted the acoustic parameters of the Jewish audience. And, despite the disparaging comments of journalists and critics, the audience tuned in and heard programs that resonated with them personally, as Jews in America.

Letters written in response to the debut of the *Forward Hour* captured the almost personal sense of satisfaction and pleasure that listeners found in Yiddish programming. S. Trakoff of Brooklyn wrote, "I had tears in my eyes from the excitement as if it was our own child who was performing." The tenants at 1876 Bay Parkway collectively wrote, "In our 45 family apartment house, 38 of the tenants have radios. . . . Sunday, at eleven o'clock, you will not see any tenants on the stoop." Another listener testified that she burned dinner while listening too intently; yet another complained that the time went too fast and wished the program could last longer. Itche Feigenboym of the Bronx declared Sunday a "yom tov" (a holiday) in honor of the *Forward Hour.* Feygele Ratner wrote, "I am an American-born 14-year-old Jewish girl who heard the Yiddish music from your program and cried from pride." For another listener, the *Forward Hour* became a lifeline to his Jewish past: "The wise dialogue and compositions and fine sketches, and also to hear the always pleasant B. Vladeck it is doubly enjoyable when one lives in a country between goyim, where one hears not one Yiddish word. And Sunday morning one can go and open the radio and hear a good Yiddish program. . . . I love hearing a Yiddish voice in the house and it awakens in us a feeling of the olden days."[65]

Letters to other broadcasters bear out this sentiment. Listeners often wrote to their favorite hosts with requests for copies of particular programs or poems that had been read on the air. Others offered words of praise, criticism, unsolicited submissions of their own poetry, and advice about what listeners believed would attract other listeners. Often, these letters expressed the feelings of younger listeners about Yiddish programming One letter to Scooler explained, "You see, my mother is an ardent follower of your series and and [sic] it is almost a rite with her each Sunday. We children, as we go about our duties cannot but pause in our work to listen sometimes, too. However, today was something that brought a sigh to our lips and a tear to our eyes."[66] Another letter, addressed to Victor Packer at WLTH, complained halfheartedly about one of the station's featured singers: "I've been married for a year, and someone is disturbing my *sholom bais* [serenity of my home]. Miriam Weiser. When she starts singing on Monday nights, my heart starts beating fast, and, what can I say, I'm in love."[67] Packer later turned the letter into a skit, echoing back the cultural conversations characteristic of Yiddish radio.

The listeners' letters echoed the intentions of the broadcasters and expressed a sentimental connection to the material they heard. To be sure, the *Forward* likely published the most effusive letters, and listeners wrote similar letters to English-speaking broadcasters frequently enough. But what is different here is the familiar—and often familial—tone that these communications assumed. The aesthetic of intimacy, then, not only existed in the intentions and promotional material of radio broadcasters but also in the preferences of listeners. The ways in which the broadcasters understood their audience and the ways in which the audience heard them reinforced the sense of intimacy that advice programs and family dramas made audible. The aesthetic of intimacy that emerged out of this engagement captured the sounds and desires of a community that knew how to listen to itself on the air.

THE SOUNDS OF RELIGION

Yiddish radio developed a cadence that matched the culture of the Jewish immigrant workweek, and much of the original dramatic programming focused almost obsessively on Jewish domestic life. When the programmatic focus broadened to the community more generally, religious life emerged as a popular source of content. Yet, as with the development of the Yiddish broadcast schedule, the presence of programming that sounded religious did not necessarily mean that the programs or the audiences who listened to them adhered to religious law or practice. In fact, some of the most popular programs with religious content indicate that audiences wanted programs that included aspects of the religious tradition but did not advocate religion per se. In other words, they wanted programs that *sounded* religious but that were not necessarily religious.

If the proliferation of performers with religious titles is any indication, audiences loved listening to them. Cantors Jacob Altman, Pinchas Levanda, Isadore Sheyn, Abraham Sokolow, Moyshe Oysher, Leibele Glanz and Rabbis Aaron Kronenberg, J. J. Margolis, and Joseph Leibowitz all appeared regularly to sing or sermonize. WEVD featured a performer known as "Der yeshiva bokhur" (The Seminary Student), and WFAB carried a daily program hosted by a character named "Der freylikher khazn" (The Happy Cantor), both of whom sang popular songs interspersed with talk. Cantors frequently included popular songs alongside performances of sacred music, while rabbis used their new pulpit to offer blends of social commentary, moral teaching, and Jewish law.[68]

Despite the promise that broadcasting held for spreading the religious word, broadcasts neither replaced nor became synagogues, and, like Reb

Yankev Leib in the *Forward* cartoon from 1926, the relationship between broadcast content and what audiences actually heard sometimes created more questions than answers. One prominent example emerged from the popularity of cantorial music when a handful of women began performing sacred music on the radio. Beginning in the late nineteenth century and accelerated by the advent of the phonograph, cantorial music became one of the most popular styles of music among Jewish audiences. "Superstar" cantors, such as Yossele Rosenblatt, Zavel Kwartin, and Gershon Sirota, made hundreds of recordings and performed regularly to sold-out audiences not just in synagogues but in secular venues as well.[69] The popularity of cantorial music proved so widespread and lucrative that by the 1920s a small but notable group of women also began performing cantorial music. Traditional Jewish law forbids women from taking a leadership role in religious rituals, a statute that even the progressive Reform movement honored until the 1970s. These women, who fit the traditional Yiddish term for cantor, *khazen,* with a feminine ending to dub themselves *khazente,* began appearing on radio during the mid-1930s, and used their popularity to cultivate audiences for their live performances. Freydele Oysher, whose career highlighted the hierarchy of radio and who performed as "Freydele di khazente," recalled getting her start singing folk music, but she always knew that she could bring the house down by imitating the cantorial style of her older brother, the well-known cantor Moyshe Oysher.[70]

Oysher considered cantorial music kind of a novelty, and she took advantage of her diminutive stature to thrill and surprise audiences with her ability to sing sacred music. Other *khazentes,* however, approached their craft with a bit more devotion. Many followed an older tradition of cantors taking their names from their Eastern European hometowns; Liviya Taykhl performed twice a week as "Di odesser khazente" (The Lady Cantor from Odessa), Sabina Kurtzweil worked as "Di berliner khazente" (The Lady Cantor from Berlin) and Perele Feyg sang as "Di ungarisher khazente" (The Lady Cantor from Hungary). Prohibited from working in synagogues, these women turned to radio as their primary stage and often performed with as much fervor as their male counterparts. In this regard, perhaps the most remarkable and the best known was Jean Gornish, who performed all over the country as "Sheindele die Chazente." According to her promotional material, "After being gradu-ated from high school, Miss Gornish (Sheindele die Chazente even to her classmates) received many flattering offers to appear in swanky nightclubs, and as soloist with outstanding bands, but all of these offers could not lure her away from her Chazonoth [sic]. Her mind was already made up—to launch out on a professional career as a Woman Cantor—and she loves to be called 'Sheindele die Chazente.'"[71] Born and raised in Philadelphia, Gornish began appearing locally in 1936 and eventually earned a contract with Planters Hi-Hat Peanut Oil, which sponsored her appearance on stations in New York, Philadelphia, and Chicago. In both press photos and performances, Sheindele always appeared in full cantorial garb, including a long black gown and black cap, and she often stood behind a podium draped in black satin in order to emphasize the religious gravity of her performances (see figure 14). Eventually, Gornish became so popular that she had fan clubs in both Chicago and Philadelphia, and when her contracts ended in those cities, her fans organized lavish dinners in her honor.[72]

The popularity of religious programs, however, did not mean that audiences heard or related to them as properly "religious." Insofar as they appeared on the radio, and audiences had long since grown accus-tomed to listening to recordings of cantorial music in their leisure time, Jewish religious radio programs fit an aesthetic and a listening style defined primarily by popular entertainment. This gave some of the per-formers license to be a bit more creative than their pulpits would have permitted. One such rabbi, Samuel Rubin, brought his rabbinic authority to bear on the aesthetic of intimacy pioneered by advice programs to build one of the more intriguing careers of any Yiddish radio performer. Rabbi Rubin began his career on radio during the early 1930s, appearing as "Der morey derekh" (The Guide) and "Der veg vayser" (The Knower of the Way), on one of the many advice programs at the time. Rubin eventually established one of the most rigorous schedules of the 1930s, appearing a few times each week on different stations while also writing short sermons that he published in the *Forward* to complement advertise-ments for his programs. Meanwhile, concerned about the treatment of

Figure 14. Promotional photograph of Jean Gornish, who performed as Sheindele the Chazente (Sheindele the Lady Cantor) from the 1930s through the 1960s. Note her formal cantorial attire and the sponsorship of Planters. Courtesy of National Museum of American Jewish History, Philadelphia.

elderly members of the clergy, Rabbi Rubin established the House of the Sages, a synagogue and house of study for retired rabbis located on the Lower East Side. Eventually, the House of the Sages became the home of Rabbi Rubin's popular and long-running radio program, the *American bord sholom v'tzedek* (American Board of Peace and Justice).[73] For more than twenty years, the program invited listeners to present their small claims and family squabbles to Rubin's rabbinic court for adjudication. Rubin served as the court's rabbinic authority, but in accordance with a loose interpretation of Jewish law, he rounded out the court with invited guests to assist him in weighing the merit of arguments and meting out his version of justice.

Typically, people fought over money, but his guests brought claims about everything: Wives complained about their husbands, children squabbled over who should take care of aging parents, tenants complained about landlords, employees fought their bosses, and, in one case, a family objected to the location of their son's burial plot in a local cemetery, arguing that it did not suit the honor they felt he deserved. Sometimes in English, sometimes in Yiddish, and often in a mixture of both, Rubin's guests would explain themselves, criticize their opposition, and plead their cases before Rubin and his court. The performances themselves vacillate from histrionic to overwrought, as everyone believed himself or herself to be correct and fully expected Rabbi Rubin to rule in his or her favor. The arguments themselves often became quite heated, and Rubin often intervened with as much legal acumen as folk wisdom. Once, he admonished a female guest, "You can buy a refrigerator and you can buy a house, but you can't buy a father."[74]

Rubin's court programs proved popular enough to keep him on the air until 1956, and after a short hiatus, the House of Sages returned with a program of its own that remained on the air through the 1980s. The endless stream of real-life family dramas and the promise of fair, rabbinically informed resolutions proved more popular and entertaining than sponsors could have imagined. And better still, Rubin did not need to hire writers. As radio entertainment, it followed the pattern of other Yiddish programs; Rubin modeled his program on the *Goodwill Court,* an English-language program that debuted in 1935 on WMCA and became so popular that it moved to NBC for a short time. Recognizing, as they had with advice programs, the popularity and promise of court programs, every station that carried Yiddish programming in the 1930s offered its own version of Rubin's formula show.[75]

Despite his popularity, Rubin's decisions carried little or no legal weight. Unlike the *Goodwill Court*, which hired lawyers and judges who were recognized by the New York State Bar, Rabbi Rubin did not posses the civic authority necessary to adjudicate cases, and even his rabbinical authority bore no power to enforce itself. For all the formalities of his rabbinic court, complainants were not bound to honor its ruling. Nevertheless, people lined up to have Rabbi Rubin's symbolic authority weigh in on what—and more important who—was right and wrong. At times, his guests seemed more interested in bragging rights than legal ones. Yet this was still a religious court, and while Jewish law does contain structures for restitution, Rubin's authority remained primarily moral, chiding disrespectful children or dishonest spouses for their behavior. Rubin's rabbinic stature played a central role in the program and gave him the authority to "hold court," as opposed to only solicit letters. This, amplified by its setting at the House of Sages, endowed the program with an echo of religious authority that other programs could not quite manage and likely contributed to its lengthy success. The aura of religious authority conveyed by the elderly rabbi contributed to the program's appeal and upped the ante on the histrionics of *Der yidisher filosof*. Measured rather than ostentatious and rabbinic instead of showy, Rubin brought the symbolic authority of the rabbinate to both his complainants and his audience and, in the process, addressed his audience's desire to hear religion, even if they did not adhere to it.

As the decade came to a close and as the culture of Yiddish radio took shape around the desire of audiences to hear themselves on the air, Yiddish radio reached more people than ever before. Yiddish-language broadcasting in New York continued to expand, and new stations took to the airwaves in Baltimore, Philadelphia, Los Angeles, Cleveland, Milwaukee, and even Tuscaloosa and Birmingham. In New York, Yiddish broadcasting reached approximately forty-three hours of original content each week, and more interest from larger sponsors buoyed everyone's dreams of a Yiddish radio culture that could be both self-sustaining and a gateway to the English-speaking mainstream.[76] The journalist Ben Rothman recognized the national growth of Yiddish radio programming and launched *Teater un radio velt* (Theater and Radio World), the only Yiddish-language publication dedicated explicitly to radio news. As radio could not have survived without the theater, Rothman covered both, offering news, advertisements, profiles of performers, and listings of radio programs. Although it ceased production after only four sporadic issues, the magazine's appearance illustrated the potential for Yiddish radio during the 1930s. More important, the magazine's mission statement, which serves as the epigraph to this chapter, clearly captures the sense that the audience listened intently to itself.

Throughout the 1930s, Yiddish radio broadcasters engaged in conversations with the FRC and the FCC, with mainstream English-language radio, and with their audience. These simultaneous conversations shaped both the content and the structure of Yiddish radio, as it came to speak to Jewish immigrants about Jewish immigrant life. Alongside English-language radio, which gave listeners of all kinds access to worlds beyond their own, Yiddish radio did not have to duplicate this effort but could give Jewish immigrant audiences a chance to hear their own voices on the air. The structure of feeling constructed around Yiddish radio gave audiences a framework for articulating cultural choices that reverberated with sometimes contradictory cultural preferences. Even as broadcasters tried to emulate English programs and Yiddish-speaking performers acknowledged the inferiority of Yiddish programs, audiences tuned in, and their choices reflected their desires to listen in on their own communities.

FOUR An Acoustic Community, 1936–1941

Q: [In English] You speak Jewish?
A: Yes.
Q: [In Yiddish] Answer in Yiddish. What's "yes" in Yiddish.
A: *Yo.* I don't know.

Victor Packer, interviewing Mildred Schwartz in preparation
for her appearance on his *Amateur Hour,* 1935

Manischewitz American Matzos sure are good! They're good
with milk or beverages. . . . They're swell in sandwiches. . . .
And for a special bright treat at mealtime, you can't beat the
crisp friendly flavor of Manischewitz American Matzos.

Advertisement, *American Jewish Hour,* 1940

In the late 1930s, Yiddish radio appeared in nearly every major city
with a Jewish population and more stations carried more Yiddish programs than ever before. Yet the stakes on the broadcast of Yiddish rose.
Audiences liked it, stations and sponsors recognized its potential, and
performers continued to produce engaging, clever entertainments. As
people heard more Yiddish programming, its meaning became more
resonant and its perceived differences from non-Yiddish programming
grew more distinct. Despite the popularity and perceived superiority of
English programming, people who wanted to hear Yiddish had more to
choose from than ever before, and the presence of this audience attracted
increasing attention from people interested in capitalizing on them.

To each of the interested parties, Yiddish radio sounded slightly
different. Sponsors saw a captive market. Performers saw a lowbrow

but lucrative outlet for their art. Listeners heard connections to other Jews, and the FCC heard a segment of the industry in need of supervision. These competing claims reflected two important characteristics of Yiddish radio at the end of the 1930s. First, it had become reified in the minds of some. Advertisers, in particular, came to understand that if they could speak Yiddish, then this rather sizable market could open up to them. In response, the owners of stations began promoting themselves as gatekeepers of this audience and potential market. Second, in conjunction with this trend, Yiddish radio programs themselves continued to voice complex and creative versions of the community that comprised their primary audience. Performing Yiddish adaptations of English-language shows, offering Jewish visions and versions of life in the United States, and pitching Jewish products that sounded as American as possible, Yiddish radio facilitated a conversation between its audience and its industry. The audience wanted to hear a version of itself, and sponsors wanted access to this untapped market. As a result, each developed an approach to and an idea of what Yiddish radio was and what it meant. Although clearly an acoustic community by Truax's definition, the meaning of both the sound and the community remained a source of some debate.

For Jewish immigrants, radio had become nearly ubiquitous, though this was not always considered a good thing. "We already have," wrote the columnist Herman Baer in the *Forward,* "thank God, radios even in baby carriages, in prison cells—where aren't they? Radios in homes are already commonplace, like a mistake in a Yiddish newspaper, like a nose in this influenza season and as a popular opera-motif in a musical comedy in Yiddish Theater."[1] Radio's popularity and success notwithstanding, cultural critiques still echoed with skepticism about the medium's place in the lives of Jewish immigrants. Another articulation of this skepticism was voiced in the 1937 Yiddish film, *Dem khazns zundl* (The Cantor's Son), starring Moyshe Oysher, which told the story of a cantor's son who migrates to America and becomes a popular nightclub singer. When the owner of a radio station offers him a contract to sing secular music, the cantor's son rejects him to return home to Eastern Europe, to his family, and to his childhood sweetheart. The film ends with the entire cast singing "(Mein shtetele) Belz" (My Little Town of Belz), a romantic paean to the young man's beloved hometown.[2]

Despite the persistence of such skepticism about radio in Yiddish-speaking communities, the radio remained as popular as ever. Anxieties surrounding Americanization—like those expressed in Oysher's film—were silenced by the sheer popularity of the medium in both English and Yiddish. In 1938, the Yiddish Writers' Union published its two Works Progress Administration–funded studies of Jewish mutual benefit societies in New York, which found that Jewish audiences often did not express a preference for entertainment based on language alone. Every family in the WPA study owned a radio, and every respondent replied that he or she listened to radio programs. One-half of the older generation enjoyed "light entertainment," while one-third reported their preference for "classical music."[3] Sixteen percent of the older generation preferred English programs, while 40 percent favored Yiddish-language programs. The remaining 44 percent expressed no language preference when it came to radio.

This pattern repeated itself with respect to other entertainments. Sixty-five percent of the older generation expressed their patronage of "cheaper" Yiddish theaters, 35 percent attended "better" ones, and 20 percent attended theater in English. By contrast, only 3 percent of the younger generation attended the Yiddish theater, while 20 percent enjoyed English-language stage productions. The remainder did not attend theater regularly enough to reply.[4] With respect to film, over 90 percent of respondents from both generations reported going to the movies regularly, and both groups preferred English-language films to Yiddish ones. Only 8 percent of the older generation favored Yiddish film; 30 percent preferred English-language films. "Almost everyone of the younger generation is a movie fan," concluded the study's author, but he added that the younger generation did not attend Yiddish films in any great number, and the vast majority of older respondents chose "films that strike their fancy" rather than those in a particular language.[5]

The omnivorous approach of Jewish immigrant audiences toward mass entertainment meant that the listening habits that took root in the 1920s persisted in the late 1930s. It also meant that the reasons for tuning in to Yiddish programs persisted and that Yiddish radio, despite its perceived lower quality, continued to resonate with audiences. As sponsors and stations began advertising and reifying Yiddish, almost as a product in itself, audiences, too, emphasized their attachments to the language. Letters, man-in-the-street interview programs, and amateur contests all echoed the sense that Yiddish radio's primary audience held a rather conservative attitude toward Yiddish radio. Their approach to repertoire, to the prospect of speaking Yiddish, and to the sounds that they wanted to hear indicated that they, more than Yiddish radio professionals, believed that Yiddish ought to exclude most things American or English. In this way, ironically, audiences and advertisers developed a more rigid approach to the performance of Yiddish on radio than did Yiddish-speaking radio announcers, station owners, or performers. When audiences invested their time in Yiddish radio, they wanted to hear Yiddish exclusively, even as performers frequently played with those expectations.

THE SALE OF SOUNDING JEWISH

In 1938, New York radio stations carried between forty and fifty hours of Yiddish programming each week.[6] In Philadelphia, audiences could hear Yiddish almost every day of the week on WRAX and WPEN, and when Chicago's WCFL stopped carrying programs in Yiddish, WGES and WHFC filled in. Meanwhile, stations in Boston, Philadelphia, Los Angeles, Detroit, East St. Louis, Daytona Beach, Birmingham, and Tuscaloosa hosted at least one Yiddish program each week.[7] Havana, Cuba, also hosted a number of Yiddish programs during the late 1930s, mostly sponsored by the Havana Jewish Center or by Havana's Yiddish newspaper, *Havana leben* (Havana Life).[8] Because of the local nature of Yiddish radio, each of these audiences represented a pool of potential customers to any sponsor who could break into it.

Consequently, increased programming translated into increased attention from sponsors eager to reach these audiences, alongside the nearly 30 million immigrant listeners nationwide. The *Radio Annual,* the yearbook of *Radio Digest,* reported in 1940 that 76 percent of the foreign-language market lived in urban areas and that about 55 percent of residents in urban areas speak languages other than English. The study also found that these communities spent $1.5 billion in 1939, although advertisers spent only $2.5 million on radio advertising. The most popular non-English broadcast languages were German, "Jewish," Italian, Polish, and Scandinavian, which together represented 65 percent of the total foreign-language output.[9] With numbers like these, the immigrant markets promised a tremendous return on investment. But the stations, as noted in chapter 2, did not have a systematic method for selling airtime to sponsors.

At a time when many stations boasted that they would "not accept wine, liquor or foreign language accounts," those that did tried to capitalize on their niches. Jersey City's WHOM, "The Little Station with Big Audiences," advertised a potential audience of 2 million Jews, 1.25 million Italians, 650,000 Germans, and 450,000 Poles, "all wanting to listen to their mother tongue programs."[10] Not to be outdone, the Bronx's WBNX, "The Station That Speaks Your Language," boasted that their 5,000 watts would "exert an even more powerful influence upon the listening and buying habits of [the] 6,982,675 foreign citizens of Metropolitan New York City."[11] Even little Brooklyn-based WLTH produced an English-language circular to promote its 1935 season to potential sponsors.[12] Chicago's WSBC boasted about its "Great Market . . . [o]f over 3 million" immigrants, and even provided potential clients with a map of the city's ethnic neighborhoods (see figure 15). In the *Radio Annual,* WEVD advertised that it excelled in "features in English, Jewish Italian, Polish." Detroit's WJBK publicized its "extensive foreign hours," and Chicago's WEDC dubbed its management the "pioneers of foreign language programs."[13] In Philadelphia, WPEN explained, "The kernel of every Advertising campaign is Sales! That's why more and more National Advertisers, in addition to their English shows, are also using our ITALIAN, JEWISH and POLISH programs. They know that specialized advertising in these important foreign language markets bears fruit" (see figure 16).[14] Meanwhile, Philadelphia's other main outlet for non-English-language programming, WDAS, tried a slightly more innovative

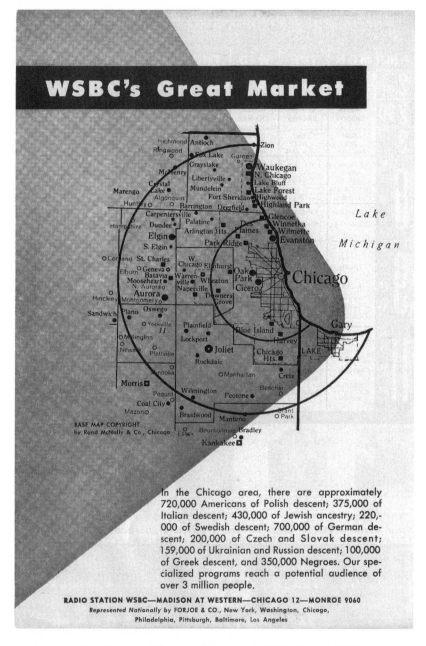

In the Chicago area, there are approximately 720,000 Americans of Polish descent; 375,000 of Italian descent; 430,000 of Jewish ancestry; 220,-000 of Swedish descent; 700,000 of German descent; 200,000 of Czech and Slovak descent; 159,000 of Ukrainian and Russian descent; 100,000 of Greek descent, and 350,000 Negroes. Our specialized programs reach a potential audience of over 3 million people.

RADIO STATION WSBC—MADISON AT WESTERN—CHICAGO 12—MONROE 9060
Represented Nationally by FORJOE & CO., New York, Washington, Chicago,
Philadelphia, Pittsburgh, Baltimore, Los Angeles

Figure 15. Advertising circular for radio station WSBC, Chicago. Note the emphasis on immigrant populations and the mapping of immigrant communities around the city. Ca. 1943. Courtesy of the Chicago Historical Society.

Figure 16. Print advertisement for radio station WPEN, Philadelphia. From the *Radio Annual*, 1940.

approach. The station claimed that it alone could deliver immigrant audiences because it spoke English just like its audience: "All our programs and all our ideals are focussed [sic] toward one aim—neighborliness. No Oxford English, no Cambridge accent, yet every one of our announcers does a good job."[15]

To be sure, some sponsors had been courting immigrant audiences as consumers since the mid-1920s. What sounded different by the late 1930s was the robust presence of programming in the languages of these immigrant audiences. When Victor and Vim's started this trend in the mid-1920s, English reigned as the language of radio, and although radio found audiences in immigrant communities, it had only just begun to speak other languages and these markets were anything but certain. More important, these early advertisers approached immigrants as consumers of radio receivers, not radio programming; neither company especially cared what audiences listened to, as long as they bought the hardware. By the mid-1930s, commercialism had become the norm and non-English-language broadcasting had become both popular and lucrative enough to encourage station owners to use their audiences as lures for potential sponsors.

Stations like WHOM and WBNX were, in effect, selling their audiences in addition to the perception that they had unique access to these audiences because they spoke their languages. This perception fueled the notion that the immigrant audiences stood apart from the radio mainstream and that they could not be courted in languages other than their native tongues. This, of course, did not reflect the real listening patterns and preferences of immigrants, but the perception translated into capital and cachet for the stations claiming to corner that market. But the stations, whose advertising arrangements relied on the often-haphazard efforts of time brokers, often found themselves in trouble with the FRC and the FCC because of associated problems of oversight and supervision. The development of a proper "foreign language market," one that could turn communities into commodities, would require a more formal structure for advertising and contracts.

Enter the Joseph Jacobs Company and the Advertisers Broadcast Company (ABC), the first advertising agencies dedicated to selling Yiddish programming. The Joseph Jacobs Company focused on advertising within the Jewish immigrant community and worked primarily in print; ABC positioned itself as the first advertising agency dedicated to packaging and selling Yiddish radio programs. Modeled on the advertising agencies that had come to account for up to 75 percent of content on mainstream radio stations, ABC and Joseph Jacobs hoped to deliver a similar service to the stations that carried Yiddish programs.[16] This would entail not only selling airtime and managing contracts but also producing and transcribing programs that it could distribute to stations that signed up for their service. ABC found early success during the late 1920s by promoting Yiddish-speaking stars such as Molly Picon and Jennie Goldstein on English-language programs on WMCA.[17] Later, it expanded its market to include "Jewish programs in English on WMCA and Yiddish language programs on WEVD."[18] In an advertisement in the 1938 *Radio Annual*, ABC followed the lead of stations that promised to deliver their own immigrant audiences by positioning themselves as interlocutors between their market and the mainstream: "As the Jewish Market Goes—SO GOES NEW YORK 2,225,000 Jews living in Greater New York—a market within a market that's the biggest and most vital factor in the Metropolitan trading area. . . . You can reach ALL of these people— young and old—by RADIO—the direct means of approach to the whole family. . . . Our programs, prepared and directed by experts who know technique and who know the Jewish field thoroughly, cater not only to the Yiddish-speaking Jews, but to the English-speaking ones as well."[19] Advertising in the *Radio Annual* opened up ABC to sponsors and contracts that time brokers could only hope to attain. ABC quickly compiled an impressive roster of clients, ranging from Horowitz-Margareten to Ralston-Purina and the Colgate-Palmolive-Peet Company.

Companies like Rokeach and Manischewitz, which produced kosher food and relied on Jewish customers, had been behind Yiddish radio almost since the beginning, and by the late 1920s, a few mainstream companies, for example, Beech-Nut, Ralston-Purina, and Chase and Sanborn, invested in advertising on Yiddish radio, too. A decade later, ABC and Joseph Jacobs opened up New York's Yiddish airwaves to interests well beyond the Jewish community. In fall 1935, New York's Yiddish stations carried approximately forty-two hours of weekly Yiddish programming, of which only about two hours attracted sponsors from outside Jewish communities. By the end of 1941, New York radio stations carried approximately sixty-nine hours of Yiddish radio each week, sixteen of which relied on support from mainstream companies.[20]

Even with the assistance of Joseph Jacobs and ABC, mainstream companies had to overcome the symbolic boundary of the Jewish immigrant community. If the community was a commodity, then the advertising interlocutors played an important role in speaking for the audience to sponsors and speaking to the audience on their behalf. ABC happily stepped into that role. Its success in this market relied on its ability to sound consistent with the needs, habits, and desires of potential Jewish customers. In other words, it had to make its products sound as "Jewish" as possible. This had been a popular strategy since print advertisements from the late nineteenth century, when advertisements emphasized the ways in which their products suited certain holidays or festivals.[21] This trend continued on radio when Planter's Hi-Hat Peanut Oil earned its kosher certification and the company published a large advertisement in *Teater un radio velt* boasting that its product had become "kosher under the supervision of Rabbi Hirsh Kahn," in support of Nukhem Stutchkoff's *In a yidishe groseray*. Meanwhile, Molly Picon, who began her radio career working for ABC but later signed with the Benton and Bowes agency, proudly promoted Diamond crystal salt as "specially prepared under strict Rabbinical Supervision for salting meat in accordance with the laws of kashruth! Not too coarse and not too fine, it sprinkles easily, spreads evenly, washes of [sic] quickly."[22] In an echo of Rabbi Levinthal's concern for *kashruth* in his community, Campbell's Soup, a longtime sponsor of the singer and actress Miriam Kressyn, took a subtler approach to advertising one of its soups. Instead of saying definitively that it was kosher according to rabbinical authority, Kressyn explained that the soup was "acceptable in the Jewish home" and led her audience to make its own decision.[23] By the end of the 1930s, Maxwell House, Carnation Milk, Best Foods, and Crisco joined the ranks of radio sponsors who promoted their products by emphasizing their *kashruth*.

Just as mainstream marketers emphasized their *kashruth*, producers of explicitly Jewish products that relied on an almost exclusively Jewish customer base downplayed the Jewishness of their products and instead highlighted the ways in which they suited their audience's modern, American Jewish palates. ABC, which represented Manischewitz, hired Stutchkoff to compose and read advertisements for his program, *Bay tate mames tish*. Stutchkoff, who did not shy away from melodrama and hyperbole, plumbed the depths of his thesaurus-sized vocabulary to deliver his sponsor's message that they not only produced the "finest, tastiest, most kosher" matzo products in their "most modern" baking facility; their matzos suited the desired eating and entertaining habits of American Jews. "Matzos," Stutchkoff half-reminded and half-instructed his listeners, make wonderful "canapés and daisy sandwiches" suitable for serving at "teas, bridge parties and at the dinner table."[24]

Traditionally, Jews ate matzo only on Passover, and even then, only because it was commanded in the Bible. By suggesting that matzo fit perfectly at bridge parties and afternoon teas, Manischewitz tried to turn matzo into a festive and fast food. Stutchkoff hailed his sponsor's matzo as the "second national Jewish food in America" (after gefilte fish) and boasted that the "finest restaurants" used Manischewitz matzo meal in their matzo balls.[25] Making canapés out of the traditional "bread of affliction," or finding matzo balls in the finest restaurants, gave audiences ways to imagine traditional Jewish fare fitting in to American eating habits. Just as ABC imagined Yiddish radio in the mold of the mainstream, Stutchkoff's Manischewitz matzo commercials imagined that even the blandest Jewish food could become American if listeners ate it like Americans. Insofar as they sold matzo in an imaginary American setting, Stutchkoff's advertisements echoed aspects of immigrant fantasies about that setting; "fine restaurants," "canapés," and "bridge parties" captured an image of middle-class leisure to which immigrant Jews aspired.

Manischewitz exploited every aspect of this approach to advertising and turned it toward product development, introducing what it claimed was the perfect synthesis of American and Jewish food. Traditional Jewish culinary culture specialized in large meals but fell short on snacks. Manischewitz's solution: the Tam Tam, a bite-sized six-sided matzo-like cracker that it sold on the radio as "the perfect, real Jewish cracker for the Jewish home."[26] Taking its name from the Yiddish word for "taste," the Tam Tam was supposed to be the first Jewish cracker in America, but really it was just matzo produced in bite-sized pieces and marketed aggressively to its audience's American aspirations. One advertisement affirmed, "America is a land of crackers, so it needs a Jewish cracker with Jewish taste."[27] Now, thanks to Manischewitz, "American Jews [had] their own cracker." Perhaps more important, Tam Tams filled a critical gap in the menu of American Jewish socializing. "When you're at a party and you see Jewish cookies, it's also good to see Tam Tams," one commercial pointed out.[28] The Tam Tam took matzo a step further by replacing American crackers on the Jewish table. The advertisements urged their customers in Yiddish to throw "Jewish celebrations with Jewish hors d'oeuvres," using the French-English word rather than the Yiddish "forshpeiz" to emphasize the American nature of Jewish celebrations. Together with ABC, Manischewitz promoted itself as the finest in

American Jewish food, highlighting Tam Tams as the American icing on its kosher cake

Selling to a radio audience of immigrant Jews during the late 1930s reinforced the sense that they were a captive audience, even though it betrayed the fact that from the very beginning immigrants listened to both English programming and programming in their native tongues. With immigrant audiences in place, station owners appealed to potential sponsors on the basis that they alone had the immigrants' ear, while advertising agencies promised to stabilize uneasy business arrangements. Mainstream advertisers who wanted access to Jewish audiences amplified their congruence with Jewish culture; Jewish advertisers emphasized the American sound of their products. In this way, advertising interests shaped the creation of a Yiddish radio audience that reinforced the contours of its community of listeners as it undermined them. These competing desires were most poignantly evident in advertisements, but they could be found everywhere in the culture of Yiddish radio.

THE SCOPE OF THE AUDIENCE

Advertisers still faced the challenge of how to maximize audience size while minimizing cost. Networks grew their audiences exponentially and kept costs low by signing on more and more affiliates without having to produce more programs. Yiddish radio, despite its growth, remained a local phenomenon, and each station had to produce its own programs, find its own talent, and make its own sponsorship agreements. This kept costs high, stations independent, and advertising agents angling for ways to reach larger audiences and sell them to ever-bigger sponsors.

This did not mean that the stations that carried Yiddish programming did not share talent. In fact, when possible, stations relied on touring performers to make guest appearances and occasionally even arranged long-term contracts for them. Jean Gornish, who performed as Sheindele die Chazente, had stints in New York, Philadelphia, and Chicago. Herman Yablokoff took his character Der payatz on the road to Philadelphia. And the comedy duo Beryl and Shmeryl had fan clubs in both New York and Chicago. Molly Picon and Maurice Schwartz used radio to promote their live performances when they went on national tours, but these shows were basically onetime advertisements and did not constitute a fully developed industry. Though popular among stations, performers, and audiences, these agreements were rather cumbersome and did not alleviate the financial strain on the stations or the sponsors, which, if they wanted, had to underwrite programs in multiple cities.

Another technology existed, however, that could easily and inexpensively link stations to one another and allow them to broadcast the same program. Essentially, it involved recording programs and commercials and selling the recordings for rebroadcast. Championed by advertising agencies, this process, called "transcription," created de facto networks, sometimes referred to as the "chainless chain," and made programs and advertisements widely available at relatively low costs. At the close of the 1930s, more than 575 stations subscribed to transcription services, and almost one-half of all stations employed the services of two or more. Transcribed programs accounted for only 10 to 15 percent of broadcast time on network affiliates, but some independent stations relied on transcription services to supply nearly 80 percent of their broadcast programming.[29]

Moses Asch, the son of Yiddish writer, playwright, and journalist Sholom Asch, had become WEVD's in-house radio and recording technician during the mid-1930s and heard in transcriptions the possibility for a national market for Yiddish programs. Before Asch, only one Yiddish program—*Der tog's Radio Hour*—found its way onto a national network, where it aired between 1928 and 1930. A transcription distribution system based at WEVD promised to take advantage of the deep wells of talent already on the air while also generating additional income for the station and for Asch himself. Asch recalled, "I built the [sound] equipment for WEVD, and they needed recordings to play on the air, since I was in electronics, since I knew Jewish actors and actresses from my father . . . I recorded them for the station to play and I realized that here was something."[30]

Asch was not the only non-English speaker to recognize the potential for a broader market for immigrant audiences. During the second half of the 1930s, Italian-speaking broadcasters organized a network that stretched from Philadelphia to Boston. Behind the strength of Italian-language programming on New York's WOV, a woman named Hyla Kiczales organized the International Broadcasting Corporation, a regional network of fifteen stations that carried Italian-language programming to an audience of nearly three million people and boasted a 90 percent renewal rate for sponsors.[31] At the same time, members of other ethnic groups began exploring the possibilities of transcriptions. In Los Angeles, the Hispano Broadcasting Company began producing programs in Spanish, and Italradio, Inc., produced and promoted Italian transcriptions in Boston. Asch was not even the only person to try to capitalize on the Jewish market. A man named Samuel Fisher formed the Judea Broadcasting Studio, a short-lived firm specializing in Jewish programming, in Roxbury, Massachusetts.

What Asch had that Fisher did not was easy access to technology and content. Having already recorded a handful of Yiddish performers, including the Bagelman Sisters (who would later become famous as the Barry Sisters) and Cantor Leibele Waldman, all of whom had become regulars on radio, Asch had only to develop a way to package and distribute his recordings. In the 1941 *Radio Annual,* he announced the establishment of the Asch Recording Studios as "leaders in the specialized field of foreign language electrical transcriptions." He described his studios as a full-service production company—"We do everything from the writing of the script, direction of dialogue, music and sound effects to the distributing of your records"—adding that his services were not limited to commercial transcriptions but could also create "unusual home record albums." Asch registered his company as a transcription service providing "off-the-air and off-the-line transcriptions, commercial records, transcriptions, recordings and production."[32]

Although Asch correctly assessed the market for Yiddish recordings nationwide, he misjudged the fundamentally local nature of Yiddish radio in America. Asch observed the national market for Yiddish entertainment and noted that the "demand for Jewish phonograph records is far greater than the production." "Since there is no live talent available out of town," he wrote, "the demand for Jewish phonograph records has increased ten-fold."[33] "Out of town" meant anywhere but New York, and Asch hoped that the dynamics of supply and demand would apply to radio as well as phonograph recordings. His ability to read the market did not quite pay off, however, as only a few Yiddish programs found secondary audiences through the distribution and sales of Yiddish transcription discs. The first program to do so, Nukhem Stutchkoff's *In a yidishe groseray*, was picked up by Philadelphia's WRAX in 1936 and rebroadcast on Sunday afternoons at 4:30—just enough time to bring the transcribed program by train from station to station. Soon thereafter, Esther Feld's *Di yidishe shikse* also found a buyer in Philadelphia.[34] Six years later, Chicago's WGES purchased a subscription to the *American Jewish Hour*, which it carried in its transcribed form.[35] Apart from these few examples, Yiddish radio transcriptions never managed to reach listeners on the scale that Asch had intended, and a national Jewish audience never quite coalesced.

Not easily deterred, Asch continued to pursue the national Yiddish market as late as 1943, when he wrote a letter to T. J. Slowie, secretary of the FCC, requesting a listing of all stations "carrying Jewish programs." The FCC replied with a list of 21 stations nationwide, including 2 each in Los Angeles, Philadelphia, Boston and Detroit; 3 in the greater Chicago area; 7 in the New York City area; and 1 each in Rochester, Baltimore, and Milwaukee. Yet, by this time, Asch had begun to turn his attention elsewhere. He had already made his first recordings of Leadbelly, along with a handful of other blues musicians that would eventually become the core of the important Folkways record label.[36] But other performers continued to use the transcription process, as evidenced by this letter of agreement between Zvee Scooler and his Philadelphia sponsor: "As arranged, you will appear in person for several initial broadcasts and supplement the remainder of the broadcasts with transcriptions of your features. However, I believe that it would be of mutual benefit to make personal appearances as frequently as possible. . . . Of course, as agreed, you are to broadcast in Philadelphia exclusively for L. Dubrow and Sons, and your transcriptions and records are not to be played on any other stations in the vicinity."[37] Scooler's agreement reveals a key characteristic of Yiddish-language radio. Although the letter effectively lays out the rights to the transcriptions, they are clearly intended only to supplement Scooler's live performances.

For a time, it seemed that transcriptions would alleviate the financial pressures of Yiddish radio, which, although part of a common cultural formation, always operated through independent stations. Transcriptions promised to make Yiddish broadcasting more affordable for each station and more lucrative for the sponsors. However, they never quite caught on, as each station continued to carry its own lineup of performers and its own roster of sponsors. Paradoxically, for audiences, the ability to hear Yiddish programming fostered the impression of connection to other Jewish communities around the United States, even as their radio schedules remained independent of one another.

PERFORMING THE JEW-S-A

What Jewish audiences actually heard, particularly during the heyday of the late 1930s and early 1940s, was a chorus of voices that spoke about Jewish life in America in Yiddish. Familial tension, communal concerns, politics, current events, and the very status of Yiddish all became grounds for commentary and dramatization. With sensitivity to changes and concerns that generally characterized the immigrant experience—conflict surrounding family roles, the place of religion, poverty, American culture, and so on—Yiddish-language radio echoed the sounds of Jews at home but as people not entirely comfortable there. Jewish audiences relished the sounds of Yiddish even, or especially, when they did not sound terribly harmonious. Neither the model Americanizing minority that the FCC had hoped for nor a self-contained ethnic enclave, Yiddish radio audiences listened attentively to hear disharmonious representations of their own communities and lives.

Elaborating on the aesthetic of intimacy established by advice programs of the mid-1930s, Stutchkoff drew on the kinds of conflicts born of immigrant life in America. Everything from child-rearing to the treatment of elderly grandparents to moving to a new neighborhood to infidelity found expression on his radio shows. A writer of seemingly infinite attention to Jewish detail, Stutchkoff specialized in fifteen-minute dramas that typically featured familial strife, and he mined the format for all its emotional worth. He turned every possible relationship into a source of conflict: parents against their children, children against their parents, husbands against wives, mothers-in-law against daughters-in-law, grandparents and grandchildren against parents, children against their siblings, children and mothers against fathers. Stutchkoff made his authorial debut on the radio in 1934 and two years later introduced his most popular program, *Bay tate mames tish*. Generally, the program specialized in broad caricatures of recognizable Jewish types and turned on the delivery of swift and severe Jewish justice. No other genre on Yiddish radio captured the listeners' attention like this one, and the extreme melodrama of *Bay tate mames tish* represented perhaps the finest example of the form.

Fueled by the drama of Jewish life in America, Stutchkoff's programs amounted to a kind of Yiddish fantasy that reinscribed a connection to Jewish community even as it described in sometimes excruciating detail the difficulties of maintaining it. Stutchkoff spared no emotional expense and made perfectly clear who was at fault in every episode, even if it was not always clear who was in the right. One typical episode revolved around a family in which the mother and children labored in a candy store to support their ne'er-do-well father. The father absconded with the family nest egg to move in with his mistress, and then, when his abandoned wife fell ill, he refused to pay for her medical treatment. Eventually, he finds himself bankrupt. When he turned to his children for support, they refused to help him. Stutchkoff concluded this episode by asking his audience to decide for themselves if the children had behaved properly.[38] His programs were infused with a deep sense of Jewish morality, such that the audience could share its outrage at the father's behavior and sympathize with the children but still wonder if they should have aided the impoverished old man. Stutchkoff's morality, however, did not translate directly into rewards for the righteous or punishment for the wicked. In the world of *Bay tate mames tish*, nobody stood above the Jewish justice that resolved all conflicts but only rarely allowed for peaceful resolution. In a deeply and peculiarly Jewish way,

Bay tate mames tish offered the fantasy of resolution without the promise of a fresh start. And audiences loved it, as long as it happened to someone else.

More often than not, the program concluded with a pang of guilt or a harsh sacrifice to drive home Stutchkoff's moral message. In one three-part episode, a young married couple tricked the husband's mother, Zisl, into moving into an old age home. Zisl escaped and found refuge as a maid for a "well dressed" elderly Jewish man, Mr. Horowitz. After discovering her secret, Mr. Horowitz arranged a meeting between Zisl and her son, which Zisl brought to a fitting conclusion with a curse that sounded like a blessing: "May your children be better to you than you were to me."[39] Though Zisl was clearly the protagonist, the poignancy of the final scene and the bitterness of her accusation resolved the story without a happy ending. Even the happiest stories of reconciliation relied on heartbreak or sacrifice, as in the episode in which a Jewish woman who married a non-Jewish man returned to her family on Yom Kippur, only to reveal that her son was struck and killed by a car on Rosh Hashana, the Jewish New Year.[40]

Although occasionally unsettling due to its graphic nature, *Bay tate mames tish* always presented the possibility that wayward children would return home, that abusive fathers would get their due, or that selfish children would have to live with the guilt of their parents. Somehow, within the generic structure of the program, conflicts would resolve and the general borders of the community would be maintained, albeit never without some strain. This, much more than the kind of Americanization favored by the FCC or the smooth synthesis of advertisers and sponsors, echoed the lives and processes of Jewish immigrants seeking to construct Jewish lives in America. Families struggled to fit conventions born in Eastern Europe into the context of American culture. Communities adapted to new neighborhoods, and new organizations and cultural forms arose to address communal needs and concerns.[41] Though *Bay tate mames tish* specialized in depicting the strain these changes effected in Jewish families, it never imagined that these strains would collapse or destroy them. Jewish communities, the program seemed to suggest, would survive regardless of strain, pressure, guilt, or conflict. Strain

seemed inherent rather than threatening to the conversation about community. Thus, although *Bay tate mames tish* did not trade in happy endings,
the overall message was one of survival rather than loss. Symbolically,
then, Yiddish continued to resonate as the language of both community
and conflict. And for audiences, listening remained an important way
to remain involved.

By and large, Yiddish radio performances did not peddle nostalgia.
Programs certainly featured some nostalgic elements, but performances
of Yiddish by Packer, Stutchkoff, Jewish amateurs, advertisers, and actors
did not constitute a broad yearning for a return to a time gone by. In fact,
unlike Yiddish stage plays and German and Italian radio dramas, which
often took place in the cities and towns of the old countries, Yiddish
radio programs were set almost exclusively in the United States.[42]
Generally, Yiddish programs tended to evoke the sounds of Jewish life
in America by performing representations of struggle and conflict. If
Yiddish radio represented Jewish communities, then the communities
often sounded cacophonous, uneven, rife with conflict, and bilingual.
Whereas audiences and advertisers invested heavily in constructing
communal boundaries with Yiddish at the center, radio professionals
proved a bit more nuanced, subverting their listeners' expectations of
what they might hear on a Yiddish program. Paradoxically, the more
they did so, the louder the affective power of Yiddish sounded to its
listeners.

When *Zayn vaybs yidine* (His Wife's Wife), one of the most unusual
of all Yiddish radio sketches, debuted in fall 1939, it offered a style of
humor that required audiences to understand precisely these kinds of
cultural tensions in order to laugh along with the performers. From its
first episode, the program's sense of humor became patently audible
in its confusions of gender and ethnicity. The program's introduction
explained, "And now, our newest women's matinee idol—the brave
fighter for women's causes. . . . Who, in his homey Polish shtetl, was
called 'Michael Meyer Galagan.' Here, his wife's Irish police family [calls
him] 'McMichael Gallagher.' Only his wife calls him 'honey bunch.' . . .
His children call him 'the old lady' . . . we shouldn't call him at all—he'll
come by himself . . . He, whom the whole world calls 'his wife's wife.'"[43]

The sketch, which aired on Chana Spector's *Alka seltzer froyen matiney* (Alka Seltzer Women's Matinee), revolved around a cross-dressing, Jewish Irish character played by the comedian Benjamin Fishbein. The program followed the well-established vaudeville-radio format, with Fishbein playing the comic lead and Spector the straight man.

Over the course of the program, Fishbein joined and became president of the Ladies' Auxiliary of the Young Men's and Young Ladies' of Beetchum Benevolent Society and Educational Association. In one episode, he organized a sit-down strike when he learned that he would not be permitted to be buried in the cemetery plots purchased by the Ladies' Auxiliary. He refused to wear a tie on Father's Day and started his own WPA—Women for President of America—with himself as the primary candidate. He even earned himself a black eye when he tried to explain to a census taker that he was a housewife. In some respects a fairly standard fish-out-of water comedy, *Zayn vaybs yidine* worked on the radio because its audience understood all his American references and could laugh along with his misapplication of them. The program played on audience's expectations of gender and ethnic roles as much as it used popular references like Eddie Cantor, Eleanor Roosevelt, the power of makeup, and the Dionne Quintuplets as both story lines and punch lines. When Fishbein compared St. Patrick's Day to Purim, tried to celebrate Mother's Day, or attempted to turn Passover into a version of May Day for women, the humor worked because he knew his audience would understand both sets of references and the futility of his efforts.

Like Rubin Goldberg and Herman Yablokoff, who understood that their listeners' familiarity with Rudy Vallee and the Street Singer would translate into their own success, Spector and Fishbein used their listeners' knowledge of popular culture as leverage for their own program. By referencing American popular culture, they used comedy the way Stutchkoff used melodrama—to present American Jewish life without resorting to nostalgia by allowing Yiddish to both speak to contemporary events and evoke active conflicts in the lives of listeners. They spoke Yiddish and troubled it through parody and outright conflict. They captured inconsistencies in Jewish communal sentiment by amplifying tensions between Jewish and American life. Finally, by speaking about America in Yiddish, they made America sound Yiddish and Yiddish sound American, but neither sounded totally at home.

By attending to these issues—either comically or dramatically—Yiddish radio performers offered their own versions of Jewish life in America, which often sounded out of phase with their audience's expectations. Zvee Scooler, who appeared weekly on radio from the mid-1930s until 1983, possessed perhaps the subtlest sense of how to play on his audience's expectations of how Yiddish radio should sound. Born in Ukraine in 1899, Scooler immigrated to the United States in 1912 and began his career working with Maurice Schwartz at the Yiddish Art Theater. During the mid-1930s, Scooler teamed up with the comedian Yehuda Bleich, and after some success on the stage, the two performers found their way to radio performing as "Kibbitzers Incorporated." Bleich and Scooler became masters of comic dialogue and a popular weekly fixture on the *Forward Hour.* In 1939, Scooler and Bleich parted ways, but Scooler remained at the *Forward Hour* and continued to develop his skills as a rhyming commentator, earning himself the moniker "Der grammeister" (the Rhyme-master) (see figure 17).

Each week, Scooler would write and deliver a ten- to fifteen-minute rhyming monologue that tied together his knowledge of Jewish tradition and his audience's familiarity with popular culture, whether he was speaking about World's Fairs, the weekly Torah portion, or current events. He compared the Levitical instructions for building the Tabernacle to "interior decorating" and made jokes about the Fuller Brush Man approaching the gates of heaven that parodied the traditional High Holiday liturgy.[44] He took the familiar format of the radio interview and applied it to famous characters from history, conducting interviews with everyone from the biblical Adam to Christopher Columbus, who observed, "To me, everyone is a greenhorn."[45] Fluent in both Jewish tradition and contemporary American culture, Scooler's audience heard in his presentations references that spanned their common experiences and drew on their familiarity with both Hollywood and history. As a commentator, Scooler spoke to his audience about what they knew, tying Jewish themes into American events (the "interview" with Columbus

Figure 17. Promotional photograph of "der grammeister" (the Rhyme-master),
Zvee Scooler, in the studio of WEVD, New York. From the Archives of the YIVO
Institute for Jewish Research, New York.

coincided with Columbus Day) and American themes into Jewish events and humorously highlighting the tensions that arose.

Scooler and Bleich celebrated American holidays like Mother's Day, Thanksgiving, Presidents' Day, and Father's Day alongside other days that had attained a place of honor in the American Jewish calendar and life cycle. In a monologue celebrating Graduation Day, Scooler and Bleich offered their Yiddish version of a commencement speech to mark this most Jewish of American rites of passage.

And so go the processions.
By each a profession.
Doctor, lawyer, engineer
There are no more places for you.[46]

Despite their cynicism about the job market in 1936, school graduations, from kindergarten to City College, had become important events in the lives of Jewish immigrants, who tended to stay in school longer than other immigrant groups.[47] By the mid-1930s, public school had become one of the most influential institutions in the lives of Jewish immigrants: it provided socialization, in addition to education that American Jews used to obtain white-collar jobs and, ultimately, access to middle-class stability.[48] Scooler and Bleich's on-air celebrations of Graduation Day and other American Jewish rites both informal and formal allowed listeners to both identify with and laugh at the less humorous ways in which Jewish dreams did not always square with American realities.

Yet, Scooler also turned his keen sense of satire at Jewish life. In 1936, Scooler and Bleich began an ambitious yearlong series that followed one entire annual cycle of Torah portions, presenting each Sunday a comic commentary on the portion read in synagogue the day before. They did not so much retell or sermonize about the week's portion as recontextualize it in terms of contemporary American culture. In one episode, they dubbed one of Moses' addresses "the state of the union of the Jewish people," and in another they compared the story of Jacob and his brothers to a Hollywood movie. In an episode about Purim, they substituted a "Bronx cheer" for the traditional sound of the noisemaker, and in another they explained the ancient Israelite system of governance:

A government system
Just like ours here at home.
With three parts
Under the name
Eretz Yisroel—*Jew S A.*[49]

In an echo of Marc Schweid's series earlier in the decade, Scooler and Bleich told immigrant Jews a story of immigration that sounded like a homecoming. America, in their humorous vision, became both Jewish and familiar, while the Bible still needed explaining.

Scooler, Fishbein, Spector, and Stutchkoff each gave a slightly different version of Jewish life in America from the one listeners typically imagined. Though rooted firmly in the lives of Jewish immigrants, each of these programs from the late 1930s presented Jewishness as unavoidably invested and involved in American culture while continuing to speak and listen to Yiddish. While audiences who tuned in seemed to respond most powerfully to the opportunity to hear Yiddish on the air and to hear people speak about Jewish topics and issues, the Yiddish that they heard often articulated a more fluid relationship between itself and the surrounding culture. Audiences hoped to hear their communities sonically represented, but by its nature, radio could never deliver such fidelity. In fact, toward the end of the 1930s, Yiddish itself, while still the spoken vernacular for a large segment of the immigrant generation, had begun to take on a meaning of its own.

"REDT ENGLISH, REDT ENGLISH" OR "REDT ENGLISH, REDT ENGLISH"

While advertisers and station owners maneuvered to establish the best and most lucrative positions with respect to the sale and purchase of Yiddish, listeners, too, began to articulate notions of what Yiddish radio was and what it ought to be. Although audiences would listen to just about anything in almost any language, by the late 1930s they developed a sense of what did and did not belong in Yiddish radio programming, based primarily on their own distinctions between what was and what was not Jewish. These were not hard-and-fast distinctions, but they did reflect the significance of Yiddish and what the audiences understood Yiddish radio to be. Despite the fact that many Yiddish programs copied English ones and that Jews numbered among the most popular performers, musicians, and songwriters in the United States, the audience for Yiddish-language radio demanded and desired a much narrower definition of Yiddish than Eddie Cantor or Irving Berlin offered. Despite the fact that the announcers on Yiddish radio programs often peppered their patter with English words, phrases, and references to American popular culture, their audiences held that Yiddish radio ought to remain monolingual, that is, Yiddish. Thus, realities of content and their own listening habits to the contrary, audiences offered up a rather conservative definition of Yiddish-language radio when given the chance to speak.

Audiences tended to consider Yiddish radio as a single entity and paid little attention to the animosity between the different stations. In an echo of the communities they served, the stations comprised a single cultural bloc defined primarily by the fact that they carried Yiddish programs. Listeners often sent their letters to Yiddish radio's most popular personalities to the wrong stations. Victor Packer, who for the majority of his career worked exclusively at WLTH, received letters addressed to him at WEVD, and Zvee Scooler, who worked at WEVD, received letters addressed to him at WLTH. Moreover, confusion between the stations that shared time at 1,400 kc and carried programming in Yiddish became practically unavoidable. Listeners would scarcely have noticed when WLTH took over from WARD, for example, as their schedules sounded similar. Thus, although the stations sought to distance themselves from one another, the audiences did not draw such fine distinctions, focusing instead on the differences between Yiddish and non-Yiddish programming.[50] This amplified the communal sense of the Yiddish radio audience. Choosing to listen to Yiddish radio programs meant also choosing not to listen to English programs (for that moment anyway).

Perhaps more powerfully, fan letters often expressed a deep connection with stations and announcers. Frequently, the listeners wrote to the stations asking for help, as if the stations served as Jewish mutual aid societies. In part an effect of the aesthetic of intimacy and in part owing to the sense that this radio arena was populated only by Jews, listeners' letters expressed identifications with the stations that generally exceeded those of mainstream radio. Packer and Scooler both received letters from people who claimed to be dying in hospitals, asking them to say their name on the air. People who fell on hard times or were not able to find jobs or obtain public assistance turned to radio personalities because, in the words of one listener, "I understand that often you aid people who are in dire need."[51] Another letter explained one family's particular hardship: "I am here only a few weeks after having fled the hell of Nazi oppression. Yet I am a regular listener in your amateur hours. Now, and I have been Chief Cantor in my home town, I would be glad if you would give me a chance to show what I can do. I was a chairman of the Chasonim [cantors'] organization of Germany, and I feel sure I could do my share to make your program attractive. Besides that I could use the money very urgently, as I do not yet have a position."[52] Packer granted the struggling cantor an audition. The letters demonstrated that some in the audience saw Packer and Scooler as both members of the media and de facto representatives of the Jewish community.

Like the Philadelphia rabbi who objected to a nonkosher butcher advertising in Yiddish, listeners, too, invested themselves in defining and protecting the boundaries that they felt defined Yiddish radio. On at least one occasion, a listener wrote in to Packer expressing his displeasure that Packer permitted a non-Jew to perform on his amateur hour. "I expect better of you," the author wrote with great disappointment.[53] Others used their letters to criticize programs that they felt represented different kinds of transgressions. One listener complained to Scooler, "Your broadcast from Thursday, July 31 [1942] was a shame and a crime. It would have fit a Nazi organization better than Jewish groups."[54] Still others offered their appreciation of the same programs. During the early 1940s, Rose Kaross wrote, "I just got thru listening to the recitation of 'God Bless America' and I think it was the most beautiful thing I ever heard. I am writing this letter to you with tears in my eyes." And another listener praised Scooler's "contribution to Americanism."[55] Others took offense at his presentations, as happened in response to a dramatization of the life of the German Jewish writer Heinrich Heine's life: "I cannot see much difference in the defamation in Heine in Naziville and on the Forward program."[56]

Even younger listeners expressed their appreciation for Yiddish programs, despite acknowledging that it belonged, primarily, to their parents. Writing in English to Scooler, one listener explained, "You see, my mother is an ardent follower of your series and and [sic] it is almost a rite with her each Sunday. We children, as we go about our duties cannot but pause in our work to listen sometimes, too. However, today was something that brought a sigh to our lips and a tear to our eyes."[57] For another listener who immigrated to the United States in 1940, WEVD offered a way to connect to her parents, whose fate in Europe remained uncertain: "Many times I think how much more yet my mother and father who are somewhere in a Jewish Ghetto in Poland—if they are still there—would have enjoyed your wonderful 'grams' [rhymes] and I wish the day would come that they might be able to listen in a quarter to twelve to WEVD and have the deep pleasure I feel on listening to your rhymes."[58]

For older listeners, too, the *Forward Hour* provided an avenue for relating to their children or, in the case of Max Flagler, his grandson: "This past Sunday my grandson Larry invited me to come visit. At 11 o'clock I turned on the radio to hear the *Forward Hour*. And truth be told, my grandson would slide back and count the passing minutes. Only out of honor for his grandfather did he not do it aloud. But when he heard the national anthem he sprung up from the couch and stood straight up. He's six feet one inch tall! And with tears in my eyes I saw him. And with my heart I felt thanks to you and to Abe Cahan."[59] Although Flagler did not explain which anthem they heard that morning—the Jewish or the American—and Larry likely did not understand all the program's Yiddish, Flagler felt that both Scooler and Cahan deserved credit for stirring his grandson's patriotism. And, more important, it gave him an opportunity to find common ground with his grandson through Yiddish.

Implicit in these letters were judgments about which kinds of messages suited Jewish listeners and which did not. The letters captured an important if informal conversation not only about the nature of Jewish communities in America but also about the visions and desires of that community for itself. Listeners addressed announcers as if they played communal roles beyond those proscribed by their profession, and they criticized and praised programs based on the feelings of connection they elicited. This echoes the findings of the historian Lizabeth Cohen in her work on the role of radio in the development of working-class consciousness among immigrant communities in Chicago in the 1930s.[60] Though among the letters of the Yiddish-speaking audience almost no evidence exists to suggest the sense of class consciousness for which Cohen argues, nearly every letter with any detail evoked a connection to Jewish life and a strong relationship to other Jews. Yiddish radio strengthened a sense of ethnic connection among its listeners. The cultural formation of Yiddish radio meant more than just what its Yiddish words conveyed, which meant, in turn, that when audiences expressed their hopes and definitions of Yiddish radio, they captured more than simply a desire to hear Yiddish spoken on the air.

When Victor Packer turned his announcer's microphone on his audience, they extended the conversation begun in their letters and provided a richer record of this sensibility. One of Packer's first successes on radio was a Yiddish amateur hour modeled on the *Major Bowes' Amateur Hour*, which had created a national craze for amateur shows just one year earlier.[61] Schoolteachers, pharmacists, shipping clerks, garment workers, students, and the unemployed turned to Packer's *Amator shtunde* for entertainment and the possibility of modest fame. One typical episode featured twelve-year-old Claire Kolker reading a poem and housewife Ida Shapses, butcher Hyman Goldberg, and "home girl" Mildred Schwartz singing Yiddish songs.[62] Norman Sanders auditioned with an accordion solo, and Max Lionoff, a cantor, so impressed Packer that he earned a regular spot on the program. Hal B. Rich, a traffic manager from Brooklyn, auditioned but failed to impress with his rendition of the Hebrew lament *Haben yakir li ephraim* (My Dear Son, Ephraim). The program entertained but did not produce any performers of note, save one. In September 1936, a young Fyvush Finkel sang a Russian folk song called "Proshtza" but lost that week's contest to a Mrs. M. Spector, a twenty-four-year-old housewife who sang the immensely popular Alexander Oleshanetzky ballad, "Ikh hob dikh tsufil lieb" (I Love You Much Too Much).[63]

Packer's amateurs came from virtually every neighborhood, age group, Jewish walk of life, and range of talent, yet they exhibited a remarkably similar sense of what performances belonged on Yiddish radio. Occasionally, musicians, most of whom played the violin or the accordion, offered renditions of "Russian mazurkas" or other folk melodies, but the vast majority selected songs from the Yiddish theater and folk music traditions; folk songs like "Oyfn pripetchik" (At the Hearth), the popular quasi-religious lament "Eli eli" (Oh God, My God), and the classic lullaby "Rozhinkes mit mandeln" (Raisins and Almonds) all received more than their fair share of attention. Not a single performer presented something beyond the pale of Yiddish or Eastern European music. Nobody attempted a song in English, and nobody offered up a Yiddish translation of a popular English number, despite the popularity of that form, too. Even American Jewish composers such as George Gershwin or Irving Berlin lay too far outside what the amateurs considered appropriate for Yiddish radio. Though professional Yiddish performers frequently used English in their programs and the children of Jewish immigrants spoke English, their repertoire choices revealed their tacit agreement that Yiddish radio ought to be presented in Yiddish. Had these same amateurs auditioned for Major Bowes, their selections would certainly have been different. In the similarity of their selections, they participated in the fantasy of Yiddish radio by reproducing a language barrier that did not in fact exist, even though it remained audibly and affectively meaningful for its audience.

In spite of these choices, very few of Packer's younger amateur hopefuls spoke Yiddish at all, and when interviewed by him for the program, they always admitted to speaking English. When asked if they spoke Yiddish, the majority of his younger applicants answered, sheepishly, "A little bit" or "I understand," as if they *ought* to be able to speak Yiddish in order to perform on the radio. Even those who attended Yiddish *schule*, the Yiddish equivalent of religious school, reverted to speaking English during their auditions.[64] The fantasies of Yiddish in America in which Packer's amateur hour perhaps unwittingly traded contributed to the aesthetic of intimacy that characterized the culture of Yiddish radio by maintaining a veneer of Yiddish even when neither the audience's own homes nor the majority of Yiddish programs spoke Yiddish exclusively. But the presence of Yiddish remained important, powerful, and symbolically evocative. Even more evocatively, they helped to raise the stakes of Yiddish radio by reinforcing the symbolic, if not the practical, presence of Yiddish on the air.

This sensibility persisted when Packer, who served as the time broker, announcer, performer, host, and program director on Brooklyn's WLTH, offered yet another venue for members of his audience to speak for themselves—his man-in-the-street interview programs.[65] Packer took a bulky transcription machine out of the studio and into grocery stores, butcher shops, and street corners where he asked passersby their opinions on "issues that interest everyone": Who is a better friend, a man or a woman? What was the most memorable day of your life? What kinds of recreational activities do you enjoy? Should women wear makeup? What makes a good husband? Would you rather work at home or for your husband? How do you spend your free time? What is your favorite Jewish holiday? In Jewish-owned stores around New York—Borenstein Brothers Butcher Market, Mr. Edelsteins Dairy, Mr. Tannenbaum's Public Market—and in Jewish neighborhoods like East Flatbush and Boro Park, Packer interviewed anybody who agreed to stop when he held out the microphone, transcribing the interviews for a later broadcast in the studio (but not distributed).

Packer always played the welcoming host, flirting, cajoling, provoking, and, when necessary, pushing his guests to share more of themselves than they often set out to, coaxing even the most reluctant guests into singing songs, sharing stories, opinions, complaints, advice, and family recipes for everything from chocolate cake to *ptcha*, an Eastern European jelly made with calves' feet, and, in honor of his sponsor, Sterling Brand salt. Encouraged by Packer, his guests expounded on the role of the *balebosta* (Jewish homemaker) and told tender and sometimes heartwarming stories about the men and women in their lives. They explained why Passover was their favorite holiday and why they thought women looked more beautiful without makeup. On one occasion, even Packer was taken by surprise when a woman recalled the death of her husband in response to the question, "What was the most memorable day of your life?" Packer joked and flirted with his listeners-cum-guests, congratulated them on the birth of their children and on their weddings, and wished others good luck finding a mate. Charming, gregarious, and witty, Packer interviewed as many as five or six people during each episode, expressing the sponsors' gratitude with two bottles of Foremost Milk or four pounds of Sterling Brand salt.

When he was stationed in grocery stores in largely Jewish neighborhoods, Packer attracted primarily middle-aged Jewish women but also a handful of men and younger people, all of whom willingly offered their opinions on his questions. Favorite recipes reflected Jewish tastes, and almost everyone's favorite holiday came from the Jewish tradition. And, most significantly, everyone who could answered Packer in Yiddish. This, again, was less strictly representative of the audience's attitudes in general and more indicative of their expectations of what did and did not suit Yiddish radio.

As with his amateur hour, Packer's younger guests shyly admitted that they could not speak Yiddish. Packer charmed them into speaking English. One guest, Edith Feigenbaum, who appeared on the *Sterling Salt Program* said that she could speak Yiddish, but when asked to explain why women made better friends than men, she stumbled and explained that she could not "talk Jewish." Packer, eager to keep the interview moving, encouraged her in his own bilingual way, "S'allright, s'allright, *redt* English, *redt* English [speak English, speak English]."⁶⁶ Though Packer appeared more comfortable in Yiddish than in English, it did not matter to him which language his subjects spoke, so long as they spoke. But both by speaking and by failing to do so, his subjects revealed how important Yiddish remained to them.

Packer's own work from this period captures his symbolic investment in the sound of Yiddish, even when he ventured into onomatopoeia. He was a prolific poet and a tireless performer and kept detailed if chaotic records of his performances, complete with the names of bits he performed on a given night for a particular audience, and his daily diary entries often covered the pages from top to bottom in miniscule, barely legible scrawl. A descendant of "di Yinge," a Yiddish poetry movement dedicated to a "shared concern for the individual voice that expressed personal feeling and the perception of beauty," Packer composed and broadcast epic ethnic poems that captured the rhythm and pace of New York City in onomatopoetic Yiddish.[67] *Subway, Coney Island, Sports,* and *Jazz* all tried to capture the sights, smells, and sounds of the city in action.[68] Packer's gift for impressionistic and occasionally nonsensical performances served up the sounds, if not always the words, of Yiddish culture in America. Thus, in order to enjoy Packer's radio poems, one did not have to speak or understand Yiddish fluently, as his onomatopoesis stood in for proper grammar and vocabulary. Yet, on Yiddish radio, the poems loudly expressed in nonsense syllables as much or more than proper diction could. In this way, Packer echoed back the symbolic resonance of Yiddish by breaking down the perceived barrier of language even as he remained committed to working solely in Yiddish. Even when his audience could not answer back in proper Yiddish, they liked their radio to sound that way.

Although performers frequently transgressed linguistic and generic barriers (Packer's imitations of *Major Bowes* and *Vox Pop* are only two examples), audiences came to Yiddish radio programming with the sense that it represented something greater than simply entertainment and more than a linguistic necessity. On Packer's programs and in his fan mail, the Yiddish radio audience revealed their own biases about what Yiddish radio programming meant to them and what stakes they held in it. Beyond parting gifts and the vague hope that a Yiddish amateur hour could launch a performing career, radio voiced a vibrant if rarely explicit conversation about the meaning of Yiddish culture in America. Despite the actual bilingualism of Yiddish radio and its frequent translations, audiences and sponsors contributed to the reification of Yiddish on the air. Audiences, in particular, did not feel compelled to push the sonic boundaries of their communities on the air but rather to reinforce them.

PERFORMING YIDDISH

Performers, for their part, wanted to keep their audiences tuned in but offered more complicated renditions of the commodity that their community wanted to hear. Bilingualism and cultural fluidity aside, on the radio, Yiddish still resonated loudly with audiences and supplied a sonic dimension to the lived community of Jewish listeners. As shown above, Yiddish itself had become a commodity during the later 1930s, as station owners tried to sell airtime based on their ability to speak to Jewish immigrant audiences and advertisers mentioned that they, too, spoke Yiddish.[69] Audiences exhibited in their self-representation on the air a desire for a more exclusively Yiddish-speaking radio culture. Yet performers, who had long been in conversation with English-language programming, with the FCC, and with one another, never offered this. Instead, they responded with performances of Yiddish that reframed and reinforced the language's cultural and market values while maintaining their traditions of bilingualism and translation. These characteristics had been part of Yiddish radio practically since the beginning. In fact, one of the first programs to call attention to the fact that it spoke Yiddish at all was a program of translations.

Robert birns yidish sho (Robert Birns's Yiddish Hour) debuted in 1929 under the direction of Rubin Goldberg, the first bona fide star of Yiddish radio, and presented condensed productions of popular operas translated into Yiddish. The debut program, appropriately, featured a version of the French composer Jacques Halevi's *La juif* (The Jew), and subsequent weeks carried performances of Bizet's *Carmen* and Verdi's *Aida*.[70] At least a part of Goldberg's audience knew the music and the story lines because of their familiarity with the originals through phonograph recordings and plot summaries published in the *Forward* and in books such as A. Muzikant's *Dos naye opera bukh* (The New Opera Book), which covered twenty well-known operas.[71] If audiences wanted to hear opera, they could have turned to the numerous other broadcast opportunities, including broadcasts from New York's Metropolitan Opera, which began in 1931. Goldberg's audiences did not need his Yiddish translations in order to understand and enjoy the operas, but many chose to listen anyway.[72] In this context, the program presented operas-in-translation, but even more prominently, it offered them for Jewish audiences who wanted to hear Yiddish on the air. What, precisely, the Yiddish translation contributed either to the originals or to the audience's experience of them is uncertain, but performances of Yiddish whose very appearance called attention to language through translation became central to the culture of Yiddish radio.

An outstanding example of this involved Paul Muni's visit to WEVD for a live interview during the *Forward Hour*. The station chose the well-known Yiddish theater actor Meshulam Weisenfreund to conduct the interview, in which Weisenfreund would speak Yiddish and Muni would respond in English.[73] The big joke of the interview was that the two men were in fact the same person and that when Weisenfreund turned his success in Yiddish theater into a career in Hollywood, he changed his name. Such overt performances of bilingualism were rare, but more regularly, Scooler, Fishbein, and others sprinkled their performances with English phrases or American popular cultural references. Even Stutchkoff, whose programs so thoroughly mined the aesthetic of intimacy, used a mixture of English and Yiddish to capture the textures of familial tension. In one episode, a young boy promised his grandfather, "*Mir dikh* teach*en* English, *un dir mikh* Jewish teach*en*" (I'll teach you English, and you teach me Yiddish).[74]

In the interplay of Yiddish and English on the air could be found echoes of the conversations in Yiddish immigrant homes, where bilingualism and translation were not special skills but ways of life. Families that consisted of an older generation born in Eastern Europe and a younger generation born or raised in the United States understood both languages at home, even if each generation spoke its own. Bilingualism and translation worked in tandem and tension among those people whom linguists call "heritage speakers," or people who understand a language but do not speak it.[75] Yiddish radio, then, echoed these practices back to their listeners and took their performances of Yiddish and translation to new heights.

Victor Packer's *Hammer's Beverage Program* regularly provided some of the most audible performances of translation. Packer hosted a variety program with the "Freylikhen tzviling" (Happy Twins), twin girls named Raisele and Shaindele, who spoke and sang in English and Yiddish, with the occasional foray into Hebrew (see figure 18).[76] As the program's host and writer, Packer created a casual and comfortable atmosphere

RAISELE and SHAINDELE
VICTOR PACKER
Sponsored by HAMMER'S BEVERAGES
WLTH - 1400 Kilocycles Mon. 9:00 P.M.
Tune in Thurs. 11:45 A.M. for JONAH BINDER

Figure 18. Promotional postcard for Victor Packer and the Freilikhe tzviling (Happy Twins), Raisele and Shaindele, enjoying a glass of Hammer's double-flavored fruit beverages. From the Archives of the YIVO Institute for Jewish Research, New York.

and invited listeners and members of the live studio audience to make requests for the girls to sing. Once, a listener asked to hear "Raisins and Almonds," an English translation of Avrum Goldfadn's popular Yiddish lullaby, "Rozhinkes mit Mandeln." Any Yiddish singer of the time would have known the song by either title, yet when Packer read the request, the Twins acted like they did not understand him. In Yiddish, Packer tried to explain, "[It is] a Yiddish song that is very popular in English," and the Twins, again, feigned ignorance until Raisele concluded in English, "I suppose he means 'Sleep My Baby Sleep,'" referring to a popular translation of the chorus's last line. Having settled the matter, the Twins promptly performed the song in English.[77] On another episode, the Twins required a translation back into Yiddish; when a listener requested that the girls sing "Like the Moon Above You," the Twins replied with a version of the song in the original Yiddish.[78]

Unlike Stutchkoff and Scooler, who performed bilingualism without translation, Packer used the program to perform translation over and over, as the Twins asked Packer to translate other words and phrases, such as "problem" or "zeit frage," from English to Yiddish and from Yiddish to English. Most of the time, they asked about words and songs their audience surely would have known; as with Packer's amateur program, nobody requested anything too far from the Yiddish musical mainstream. Yet Packer and the Twins frequently played up the translations, stopping their banter to ask about and then explain the words, or using a brief conversation about a song's title to introduce the song itself. In the case of "Raisins and Almonds," the Twins asked for a double translation—first from Yiddish to English and then from literal English to a popular vernacular. Charming and casual as these moments sounded, they were, in reality, performances that had been scripted and sometimes even rehearsed. This meant that the whole performance—from the singing to the commercial announcements to the light conversation—was an act. Neither Packer nor the Twins really needed translations or prompting; they only acted *as if* they did. On the Yiddish airwaves, translation, not just bilingualism, had become a performance in its own right.

Behind the microphone, performers were involved in other practices that reinforced this effect. Frequently, especially when working with younger performers and heritage speakers who may have learned to speak Yiddish from their parents but never learned to read or write it, radio producers drafted Yiddish scripts transliterated into English letters.[79] These were full scripts of whole programs or single episodes, which was something different from the occasional line or idiom that appeared in transliteration, which happened almost everywhere. The practice of transliterating full scripts allowed Yiddish-speaking performers who were not literate in the language to perform it as if they were. And their performances relied almost exclusively on their sense of the aurality of Yiddish. They knew how it sounded and could therefore mimic its inflections and intentions without full fluency.

To listeners, this may not have mattered at all. Those choosing to hear programs in Yiddish may have noticed little difference between

Goldberg's operas-in-translation, Packer's performances of translation, and heritage speakers' performances of Yiddish. Ultimately, they all sounded alike. To people for whom listening mattered, it still sounded like Yiddish, even when it was performed in English. Each performance produced similar effects and reproduced distinctions between Yiddish and English radio, allowing the presence of Yiddish on the air to articulate a host of communal concerns and identifications, even when spoken in translation.

YIDDISH IN ENGLISH

Still other radio programs during the late 1930s shaped the culture of Yiddish radio even though they primarily aired in English. English-language programs like *Uncle Abe's Children's Hour* or *Quiz Master*, which pitted teams from various schools and organizations, including the Menorah Society of New York University and the Junior Hadassah of Far Rockaway, against one another for the day's "*kovid* [honor] of cash," began appearing during the late 1930s. Featuring the English-speaking children of immigrants, the shows advertised heavily in the Yiddish press and thus remained firmly within the cultural sphere of Yiddish that many listeners desired. Choosing not to advertise in English newspapers and relying instead on Yiddish media for publicity meant limiting a program's appeal and maintaining the communal sense that moved Jewish immigrant audiences to tune in. In a preview of what was to come, these programs aired in English but still operated within the cultural orbit of Yiddish radio.

Molly Picon starred in a number of English-language programs, including *Nancy from Delancy*, a comedy set in a Romanian restaurant, and *I Give You My Life*, which dramatized her life in serialized form. Picon, a client of Rubenstein and Kielson, launched her semiautobiographical program in 1938 on the mostly English-language station WMCA in New York. The show aired Friday evenings at 7:30, and Picon, aware of the cultural consonance, took the opportunity to accompany her audience as they welcomed the Sabbath. She began, "Hello everybody. Good Shabos.

This is Molly Picon speaking. As I stand here before the microphone, I can see you all seated around your Shabos tables. Some of you are smiling and some of you are leaning closer to your radios. May I at this time introduce you to the Happy Maxwell family who, in a pinch, may be good entertainment. Here is Max." After acknowledging Maxwell House, her sponsor, and performing a version of "Yidishe Mame," Picon continued, "And now, Ladies and Gentlemen, it's Sabbath eve, the time for peaceful meditation. I imagine the flickering of candles in each Jewish home, swaying back and forth in their own light, and therefore I permit myself to greet you with the traditional . . . "[80] Whereupon Picon offered a version of the folk song "Gut shabbes, gut yor" (Good Sabbath, Good Year, or, idiomatically, "Nice to See You").

Although Picon conducted the program primarily in English and it technically violated the observance of the Sabbath, it still operated well within the cultural orbit of Yiddish radio. She used familiar Yiddish expressions, spoke with an insider's knowledge of Jewish life, and incorporated beloved selections from the traditions of Yiddish music into the program. To be sure, The Goldbergs, one of the most popular radio programs in the United States and a staple of NBC's lineup until 1947, portrayed Jewish life quite explicitly, too, and featured episodes about young Sammy's bar mitzvah and more than one celebration of a Passover seder. Yet Picon's program differed in both content and address. Whereas Gertrude Berg sought the broadest possible audience for her program, Picon spoke intimately to her Jewish audience and invited them into her program and herself into their homes. As Berg presented Jewish life for mass consumption, Picon performed alongside her audience and capitalized on the aesthetic of intimacy that characterized much of Yiddish radio, even though she spoke English. Culturally of Yiddish radio even if not properly Yiddish speaking, Picon's radio programs echoed her audience's desire, as well as a growing awareness among her producers and advertising agents that her audience had stopped expanding and that Yiddish radio producers needed to reach out in English to a new generation of Jewish listeners.

Sholom Rubenstein understood that this trend could be neither reversed nor stopped and recalled an exchange with WEVD's station manager,

Henry Greenfield, about developing English-language programming: "Henry Greenfield attacked me once, you know, when we made the switch over [to English], called me a traitor and so on. I said, 'Henry, what language do your children speak?' And he said, 'English.' And I said, 'The defense rests.'"[81] As Greenfield tried to hold on to his Yiddish audience, Rubenstein, a businessman, understood the direction the market had begun to take and refused to invest in something he believed could not deliver an audience. Rubenstein remained committed to Jewish programming but turned to English in the hope of attracting a larger audience. His first major undertaking was a program called *The American Jewish Caravan of Stars*, a variety show that often featured "conglomerates of English, Yiddish, and Hebrew."[82] The *Caravan* debuted in 1951 and broadcast from the MGM Theater Studios at 711 Fifth Avenue in front of a live audience of five hundred guests. The show featured a regular cast that included Jan Bart, the Barry Sisters, and the composer-accompanist Abe Ellstein, along with popular guest comedians. The show ran for ten years and, for Rubenstein, clearly indicated that the Jewish future would be in English.

In truth, Rubenstein came late to the promise of listeners who wanted Jewish programs in English. The *American Jewish Hour*, a variety show and the precursor to *Caravan*, debuted in 1938 on WHN with some of the same performers and essentially the same idea. The weekly show, hosted by an English-speaking Lewis Charles, offered an eclectic account of Jewish life in America during the late 1930s and 1940s that it presented in three regular segments: news dramatizations, elaborately staged productions about life in America, and jazzed-up versions of popular Yiddish songs. Every aspect of the program focused on Jewish life, from news stories about Jews in America and elsewhere to swing versions of popular Yiddish songs like "Zug es mir nokhamol" (Tell Me Again) or "Glick" (Luck) to cantatas about the pleasures of American life. Sometimes a bit obtuse, the program offered a combination of news and entertainment for an audience that still wanted Jewish content, even in English. The producers believed that by speaking English and identifying as Jewish, the program would attract a broader audience interested in Jewish programming but looking for entertainment that sounded Jewish, modern, and youthful, as opposed to the slow, scraping Yiddish sounds of the immigrant generation. According to Howard Dressner, one of the show's writers, the producer decided to call the program the *American Jewish Hour,* rather than the *American Yiddish Hour,* because he intended that very little Yiddish would actually be spoken on the air.[83] Speaking English and swinging Yiddish classics gave the program a modern-sounding makeover without losing its connection to the language that would have attracted its audience in the first place.

The writers and producers, in echoes of *Der tog* and the *Forward* earlier in the decade, explained what set their program apart from the rest of Yiddish radio's substandard fare. Because the *American Jewish Hour* did not have a dedicated newspaper outlet, producers left the announcers to do the explaining. A typical introduction to the program went, "They do it to 'Elimelech.' They do it to 'Reb Duvidl.' They even do it to 'Yidl mit'n Fiddle.' . . . Yiddish Swing takes old Yiddish folk songs and finds the groove for them in merry modern rhythm."[84] Juxtaposing "old Yiddish folk songs" and "merry modern rhythm" gave the show a Jewish feel set to American rhythms in a way that spoke to more contemporary tastes. A souvenir program described the program similarly: "YIDDISH melodies in SWING, a half-hour musical show presenting traditional Yiddish folk-melodies in modern dance arrangements."[85] When Chicago's WGES purchased transcriptions of the program for broadcast in November 1942, the *Chicago Daily Tribune* described its features as "Hebrew-Yiddish folk tunes dressed in a 20th century cloak."[86] Like Yiddish adaptations of English programs, this program promised a similar product but in reverse; instead of adapting English-language programs to a Yiddish context, the *American Jewish Hour* updated Yiddish music with American rhythms. This became the program's trademark, including traditional holiday songs like "Dayeinu" ("It Would Have Been Enough," from the Passover seder) and modern songs like "Varenikes" (a song about pierogi-like dumplings) and "Ikh benk aheym" (I'm Longing for Home," a Zionist song). The program also included the occasional Yiddish translation of popular English songs and once featured a Yiddish version of Hank Williams's "Jambalaya," which had the humor and audacity to rhyme the titular uber-unkosher sausage-and-seafood stew with the Yiddish *mekhaye,* meaning "pleasure."

In its effort to provide the most modern takes on Yiddish music, producer Maurice Rapel made certain to hire some of Yiddish-speaking New York's most popular and accomplished performers, including Sam Medoff as the program's musical director. Medoff came from an active musical family: Sam's brother, Dave, had long been involved in Yiddish theater productions, and the Medoff family regularly advertised their musical services to readers of the *Forward*. Medoff eventually broke into mainstream music and had some success writing popular music under the pseudonym Dick Manning.[87] Medoff's bandleader was a clarinet player named Dave Tarras, widely respected for both his work ethic and his musicianship and now revered as a master of klezmer-style clarinet.[88] Jan Bart, a popular Borscht Belt performer, supplied his mature, steady tenor, while the younger Barry Sisters supplied the program's version of tight girl-group harmonies made popular by other sister acts like the Lennon Sisters and the Andrews Sisters, whose 1937 recording of Sholom Secunda's "Bei mir bistu sheyn" catapulted that Yiddish number into the catalogue of American popular song.[89] Behind the fluke success of Secunda's song and the widespread popularity of swing jazz in America at the time, the *American Jewish Hour* heard an opportunity to capture a Jewish audience by capitalizing on their American tastes but retaining the audible boundaries of the Jewish community.

For its assertive American rhythms, the program still relied on its roots in the Yiddish-speaking community. Like Picon's program, which grafted itself onto Friday nights, the *American Jewish Hour* made its debut at one o'clock on Sundays, planted firmly in the wake of the *Forward Hour* and *Bay tate mames tish*. It advertised regularly in the Yiddish press and featured performers with popular followings within the Jewish community and little name recognition beyond it. The program's Yiddish musical numbers drew primarily from the same sources as Packer's amateurs, skimming only the most popular Yiddish songs from the vast resources of Yiddish theater and folk music. Thus, even though Medoff could make "your old Yiddish folk songs do many a rollin' ridin' and rhythm-a-tic," he used a sensibililty similar to that of Packer's amateurs when it came to repertoire.

Even in its digests of the week's news, the *American Jewish Hour* hewed

closely to the prevailing sentiments about what constituted Jewish entertainments. Serious stories rarely strayed from news about Jews and
focused on events in Nazi Germany or the progress of Jewish settlement in Palestine, alongside other events of Jewish interest. In addition
to these kinds of features, the program specialized in dramatizations
of human interest stories, like that of the tragic love affair between
Kitty Smigal and Alan Berlinerberg, a Jewish Palestinian bus driver,
or the story of Bela Futterman, who was revived in her apartment by
her doctor.[90] Sports, local politics, even entertainment news did not fit
the program's Jewish framework, despite the popularity of those subjects among younger Jews, as reflected in the pages of the Yiddish and
mainstream English press. By narrowing its address, the *American Jewish
Hour* provided a cultural frame in which Jewish concerns transcended
the Yiddish language, even as the program maintained a fairly circumscribed notion of what constituted these concerns.

Despite the Yiddish musical selections and the Jewish content of
its news stories, the *American Jewish Hour* performed Jewishness that
sounded as American as possible. From the uptempo versions of Yiddish
songs to Lewis Charles's sassy interactions with the Barry Sisters, the
program, like many other Yiddish programs, took inspiration from the
most popular programs of the day. As with Packer's program, the combination of a charming male host and a pair of witty, younger female
singers was a popular characteristic, but one element of the program
amplified these tendencies more than any of the others.

In 1940, the program began presenting elaborately staged original
English-language cantatas, all of which celebrated the pleasures of life in
America. At the time, poetic, rhyming productions like these had become
popular radio fare. The writer Norman Corwin, who began his career
on CBS in 1938, became the master of the genre, through programs such
as "The Plot to Overthrow Christmas" and "They Fly Through the Air
with the Greatest of Ease." By 1941, Corwin had established himself as
the writer for CBS's prestigious *Columbia Workshop,* and he also penned
radio's all-star tribute to the 150th anniversary of the Bill of Rights, titled
"We Hold These Truths." The *American Jewish Hour*'s English-language
cantatas were small-scale versions of Corwin's declamatory epics. Filtered

through the program's Yiddish cultural context, their Jewishness became audible only implicitly and, often, by omission.

Generally, the cantatas had no Jewish content at all. "Highways of Happiness" described the beauty of traveling America by car, and "Take off to Tacoma" celebrated the ease and glamour of air travel.[91] Occasionally, as in the presentation called "Suburban Serenade," the cantatas only obliquely referenced their audience's Jewishness, as it described the peaceful life in "Mekhaye Village," a fictional suburb that took its name from the Yiddish in order to both mock and mimic the popularity of such names for new housing developments.

Sometimes the program took an even more understated approach to vocalizing its Jewishness. For Thanksgiving 1940, the *American Jewish Hour* staged the "Ballad for Thanksgiving," which celebrated "our country, our America" by imagining the nation as a ship full of immigrants whose "course is set for the new world . . . toward justice, liberty, peace and the pursuit of happiness." However, when recounting the places from which Americans had emigrated, the program omitted "Jewish" sites like Poland and Russia in favor of Mandalay and "Timbuctoo."[92] An adaptation and a summation of themes explored in NBC's popular series *Americans All Immigrants All*, the "Ballad of Thanksgiving" concluded with the following hopeful exchange:

CAPTAIN: It is November 21st, 1940. We are still just at the beginning of our great adventure.

WOMAN: Our homes are peaceful . . . and our sons walk in the ways of peace.

CAPTAIN: Our ship of state, the United States of America, is strong and united!

MAN: There are 130,000,000 of us!

CAPTAIN: Our course is set in the new world . . . toward justice, liberty, peace, and the pursuit of happiness. For this we humbly give our thanks for the great blessings to this . . .

CAST: Our country . . . Our America!!

ORCHESTRA AND TRIO: For America is a land of hope and freedom . . . And so it was . . . And so it shall be!!!![93]

For American Jews in 1940, such unwavering hope likely seemed scarce. With Europe at war and the situation facing the Jews of Eastern and Central Europe growing more dire each day, the 1940s hardly seemed like a decade of "great adventure." But English-speaking Jews on the radio, ever conscious of what non-Jews might think, cast their lot cheerfully and hopefully with America, with scarcely an echo of their own immigrant pasts or their relationship to the Jews of Europe.

Nonetheless, the program evoked an acoustically Jewish effect insofar as it operated within the broader culture of Yiddish radio. Neither Picon nor the *American Jewish Hour,* which sometimes advertised itself as *Yiddish Melodies in Swing* and *Yiddish Swingtime,* hid their Jewish roots, even as they specialized in American-style, uptempo adaptations of popular Yiddish songs and the creation of new ones with names like "Boogie Woogie Freylekhs."[94] In carefully staging their Jewish performances with news about Palestine, references to Sabbath rituals, and trivia competitions, English-speaking Jewish broadcasters pitched an acoustic Jewishness that its primary audience would have clearly understood and to which its secondary, non-Jewish audience would not have objected. Broadcasting in English on the margin between Jewish and mainstream audiences meant moderating the tone of one's performances to maintain the acoustic community with which its audience identified but always with the understanding that someone else might be listening.

Although Jewish and non-Jewish audiences might have been listening to the same programs, how they listened was quite different. The advent of Jewish programs in English complicated the relationship between the two tongues. In English but in a Yiddish context, these programs boisterously broadcast American Jewish syntheses. For sponsors eager to capitalize on a Jewish audience, for listeners drawn in by the aesthetic of intimacy, for performers playing with language, and for musicians playing with rhythm, the expectations that Yiddish radio could provide a sound track to Americanization both reinforced and undermined how that process would sound. As advertisers and audiences imagined their own versions of a coherent Jewish community audience, broadcasters played with performances of Yiddish, of translation, and of culture.

THE BEGINNING OF AN END

On the verge of World War II, which stands as a turning point in the history of Yiddish and in narratives of its decline, Yiddish in America sounded both stronger and weaker than ever before.[95] Nineteen radio stations across the country carried Yiddish programming, and New York's radio stations offered nearly seventy-one hours of Yiddish each week.[96] Supported by the efforts of ABC and Joseph Jacobs, more and wealthier sponsors than ever invested in Yiddish radio broadcasting, helping to stabilize and expand its reach.

At the same time that the FCC recognized Brooklyn's need for broadcasting that suited its multiethnic and multilingual residents, it ushered in the end of broadcasting in the borough. Even though New York housed the largest Jewish population of any city in the United States and Brooklyn was called home by more Jews than any other borough, Brooklyn's four small stations stood on the brink of deletion. ABC and Jacob Jacobs paid these stations little attention, focusing instead on the larger contracts and audiences that they had found on WEVD. Moreover, the four Brooklyn-based stations remained wed to one another because they still shared time on a single frequency, raising the level of tension and competition among them.

In 1941, the FCC ruled that this situation compromised the overall quality of radio programming in Brooklyn. "Competition, under such circumstances," it held, "is necessarily severe and operates as a definite handicap to each station in rendering efficient service to the public."[97] As a result, the FCC recommended that the four independent stations pool their resources and become a single station to serve the entire borough. With Aaron Kronenberg as its president and WBBC's old slogan, "Brooklyn's Own Station," as its tagline, the new station made its debut under the call letters WBYN on 1 May 1941. Although WBYN was a new company and a new station, much of the existing programming continued, including the large number of Yiddish programs. But the new agreement could not replace the years of competition and tension that had built up between the stations and their managers. The four new partners continued to disagree with one another, and Brooklyn's first full-time radio station found itself for sale only two years later.

That the disappearance of Yiddish radio in Brooklyn coincided with America's entrance into World War II is only a coincidence. And the juxtaposition of the two events suggests that narratives of the decline of Yiddish in America can be traced to the fulcrum of the early 1940s. But to do so would be to diminish the ongoing allure of Yiddish, especially during the war, as well as the expansion of radio stations nationwide on the heels of Jewish migrations west and south, and the persistence of WEVD as a powerful voice of Jewish immigrant America not only during the war, but through the early 1980s. Yet, with the establishment of WBYN and the effective consolidation of New York's Yiddish radio at WEVD, 1941 does mark a turning point in the cultural history of Yiddish radio.

As American Jews began debating among themselves about the role that America would and should play with respect to the war raging in Europe, Yiddish radio became an important vehicle for broadcasting messages among Jewish immigrants that articulated their collective Jewish identity as they simultaneously expressed their allegiance to America. Still catering primarily to an audience of immigrants, and in spite of producers' hopes for English programs, Yiddish radio continued to powerfully echo the sounds of a Jewish community wrestling with its role both as residents and citizens of the United States and as members of a global Jewish community. These two dimensions of identification found both harmonious and dissonant expressions on the air, as audiences, performers, and sponsors hoped to replicate on the Yiddish airwaves the community they sought on the ground.

FIVE At Home on the Air, 1941–1949

As you know, it is the policy of this Commission and of the
Office of War Information to encourage broadcasting in foreign
language broadcasts, since they explain the purposes of the
war to foreign language groups in their own tongue.

Letter from Marcus Cohn to the California Assembly, explaining
the FCC's policy on "foreign language" broadcasts, ca. 1943

For seven years we haven't laughed, and not only for seven
years have we not laughed, but for the whole seven years we
have not even been tempted to laugh. And now, we want you
to come to us and remind us how to laugh.

Molly Picon, 1948

By the early 1940s, even the latest arrivals from Eastern Europe had been living in the United States for more than fifteen years. Radio ownership rates in the urban areas of the Northeast, central Midwest, and West topped 90 percent, and Yiddish radio programs could be heard on more stations and in more parts of the country than ever before. Yet a steady undertone of American anti-Semitism, from Henry Ford to the infamous "radio priest" Father Coughlin and pro-Nazi rallies, reminded American Jews that although they called the United States home, they were not entirely welcome in all of its quarters.[1] The firm and persistent boundaries that kept the majority of America's Jews on the margin were less limiting on the radio. Jews could not only listen to the same English-language programs that everyone else did, but they could also tune in to Yiddish programming to hear their own voices over the same medium as the mainstream. The Yiddish programs they heard reflected back to them the sounds of their acoustic community through the aesthetic of intimacy, performances of translation, and the sheer presence of programming that most of America could not understand. Yet, as immigrants and as Jews, they kept their ears tuned not only to their local communities but to those that remained in Europe as well.

As Europe exploded in conflict in 1938, American Jews turned their attention to the situation facing Jews in Germany and Eastern Europe. The Yiddish press had been covering Hitler's rise to power and his anti-Semitism for some years, so when the war started American Jews were already aware of the danger facing their friends and families abroad and began to consider what responses would be appropriate. However, keenly aware of their marginal position in American society and fearful of being labeled warmongers or war profiteers, American Jewish leaders hesitated to advocate for American intervention in Europe on behalf of the Jews. The historian Marc Dollinger explained the calculations of American Jewish political and communal leaders that measured their concern for European Jewry against the security of their position in the United States. According to Dollinger, the self-interest of the American Jewish community "did not always match the military needs of the Allied governments. . . . Jewish leaders had little choice but to channel their anti-Hitler campaign through the State Department; anything less opened Jews to charges that their ethnic interests outweighed the need for victory."[2] Fearing both the reaction of Americans and for the future of Jews in Europe, American Jewish leaders took a more tepid political stance in English than they did in Yiddish.

In Yiddish, writers and performers began addressing the war overtly, giving voice to the common concerns of American immigrant Jews and strengthening and expanding their acoustic community. Programs such as *Zayn vaybs yidine* and announcers such as Nukhem Stutchkoff and Zvee Scooler used their access to the airwaves to explore and express the situation in which American Jews found themselves, and they, alongside a number of other broadcasters, helped to frame the emerging relationship between Jews, the United States, and the war.

Under the circumstances, the contours of the Jewish community flexed to engage specifically the Jews' relationship to America as both their home and the best hope for intervening in Europe. As immigrants and as an ethnic group with a particular interest in the defeat of Hitler, American Jews aggressively and overtly laid claim to their American identities and to their place in American society but only in Yiddish. Opening up the relationship between Jewish communities and their American homes meant both strengthening the notion of a Jewish community globally and articulating that community on the air in the United States. Audiences, in turn, tuned in to Yiddish programs not to hear the latest news but to hear the war reported from a Jewish perspective and reinforce the sense of their acoustic community. And in the years following the war, as the dimensions of that community warped to fit broader social changes, audiences continued to tune in and change how they listened but not what they wanted to hear.

RADIO RESEARCH

Until the late 1930s, the FCC regarded non-English-language radio broadcasting as a nuisance but not a threat. The stations that carried such programming often kept poor records, aired shows that could not be adequately supervised, and had too many commercials. With television still in its experimental stages, radio seemed the domain of the increasingly powerful networks, with local stations at best a distraction from and at worst a hindrance to quality programming. Despite these attitudes, that certain stations specialized in non-English programming did not warrant special attention beyond the FRC's and the FCC's insistence that it help to Americanize their listeners. It represented a small segment of the industry that occasionally needed a little additional assistance to maintain its commitment to the "public interest" but not much more than that. By the late 1930s, however, with the increasing likelihood of the United States joining a war already under way in Europe, interest in the content and intent of non-English-language broadcasts in America began to grow. Civilian listeners, who until this time lodged few complaints about non-English-language programming, began filing objections with the FCC. A listener from Palo Alto,

California, wrote, "We do not understand Italian, but we can certainly hear 'Mussolini' being endlessly repeated in their news broadcasts. We think that the US is not the place for foreign language 'newscasting.'"[3] Another listener believed that immigrants pitifully misunderstood the notion of American freedom and should therefore be denied access to the airwaves: "Our conception of freedom was not intended to promote the use of any foreign tongue in place of the English language. Foreign language broadcasts will not encourage the foreign born to understand or appreciate the American tongue or the American way, and they do not serve the necessity, convenience, needs or purpose of the great majority of American People."[4] Listeners objected especially to the activities of German- and Italian-speaking broadcasters, but suspicion shadowed practically every non-English-speaking broadcaster and raised difficult questions about the compatibility of multilingual radio and American interests in wartime.

Prior to this, the FCC treated the issue with so little concern that it did not even know how many stations carried programs in languages other than English. So, with the specter of war looming, it initiated a covert investigation of multilingual stations. In fall 1938, E. K. Jett, chief engineer of the FCC, posted a memo ordering his staff to record and submit all the information they could gather, including station call letters, titles and types of programs, broadcast times, and names of management and announcers. Illustrating the often-tense relationship between the stations and the FCC, Jett instructed his staff to "obtain the information . . . in a *strictly confidential* manner and particularly without knowledge of any broadcast station licensee or his representative."[5]

Jett's covert initiative did not yield sufficiently detailed results, so the FCC launched a formal investigation of radio's multilingual stations in order to determine the scope of the issue at hand. Sensitive to accusations of censorship, the FCC surveyed every station in the country, the results of which were published in December 1940, as part of the Wartime Survey of Foreign Language Broadcasts. The survey found that "a total of 199 stations now schedule broadcasts in one or more foreign languages," which amounted to 1,721 programs, or 1,330 hours of programming, each week. On the low end of the scale, the survey found one station that broadcast a program in "Slovene" and another that carried a show in Mesquakie, the language of the Sac and Fox tribe in Iowa.[6] Meanwhile, Italian, Spanish, German, Polish, and "Jewish" programs accounted for nearly 75 percent of all non-English broadcasts. Only 43 stations carried 10 or more hours of non-English programming each week, and 108 of the stations identified in the survey operated on 250 watts or less. Nearly one quarter of all non-English programming aired in Italian, while Yiddish accounted for approximately 10 percent, or 137 broadcast hours, of the total output.[7] In the context of radio generally, at the end of 1940, 850 radio broadcast stations operated in the United States, 24 percent of which carried programming in languages other than English.

Having assembled the basic statistics on non-English-language broadcasting in the United States, the FCC still knew precious little about its content. It turned to the four-year-old Princeton Radio Project, a partnership of the Rockefeller Foundation and Princeton University, for assistance. Directed by the German émigré sociologist Paul Lazarsfeld, the Princeton Radio Project hosted leading scholars—the German Marxist cultural critic Theodor Adorno, the social psychologist Hadley Cantril, the future president of CBS, Frank Stanton—to study radio's social effects.[8] Lazarsfeld brought the Radio Project to Columbia University in New York, where, in 1941, he published *Radio Research*, one of the first academic studies of radio broadcasters and listeners.[9] The war in Europe indelibly marked the volume, and Lazarsfeld acknowledged its impact in the book's introduction. "Some time ago," he wrote, "the question was raised whether foreign language programs originating over local American stations served in any way to further activities harmful to the country in the present emergency."[10] The war left an even greater impression on the volume's lead article—an investigation of foreign-language broadcasting in the United States.

The article, by Rudolf Arnheim and Martha Bayme, examined the significance of non-English programs "at a time when the country is most interested in speeding up the assimilation of its national minorities who have recently immigrated."[11] Arnheim and Bayme set up fifty-nine "listening posts" across the United States that they staffed with researchers who logged the content of non-English programs for two weeks in January and Feburary 1941. Their research provided a more nuanced account of program content, genre, advertising strategy, and general attitude than anything published previously, and they offered general impressions of the ways in which non-English-language broadcasts helped or hindered "the assimilation of national minorities." In one instance, Arnheim and Bayme concluded that sponsors "unconsciously retard this process by utilizing the national feelings of these groups as a sales appeal for [their] products."[12] Elsewhere they observed that these programs helped listeners to cope with feelings of "helplessness," "disappointment," and "isolation from the American community."[13] For Arnheim and Bayme, these two tendencies highlighted "the social problem of foreign language groups as a whole" and illustrated the ways in which non-English-language radio hindered the integration of immigrants into American culture and life.

Specifically with respect to news, Arnheim and Bayme observed the tendency to mobilize "national feelings" as most likely to foment sedition or allegiance to the listeners' countries of origin. With the war on the horizon, they observed, "on the Polish, Yiddish, Spanish and probably on the Lithuanian programs, this country's pro-democratic and anti-Axis policy is shared sincerely and wholeheartedly, while on the German and many of the Italian programs there is a cautious maneuvering ranging from camouflaged favoring of the former country's interests to a carefully balanced attitude of neutrality."[14] Yiddish programs earned subtle praise for their articulation of American politics and views: "Their political interests correspond to the aims proclaimed by American radio stations. Their main enemy is fascism, their hope is Britain's victory and Hitler's defeat. As one commentator put it: 'The same blow will throw down Nazi-Germany and anti-Semitism.'"[15]

In their conclusion, Arnheim and Bayme reiterated the FCC's preference for programming that encouraged Americanization. They recommended that radio follow an aggressive course of cultural intervention, including integrating "the American view" into news programs, broadcasting English classes "in a light, humorous style," "linking up American ideals and principles with those of his mother country," and translating "current American songs" and speeches by the president and other "outstanding American Politicians."[16] In so doing, they failed to hear the ways in which Yiddish radio, for example, amplified ethnic connections while also serving as a medium for discussions of Jewish community life in America. Despite the depth and sensitivity of their research, Arnheim and Bayme seemed able to hear only Americanization or the strengthening of ethnic bonds over the air, when in reality Yiddish radio never broadcast either message with such clarity. Specifically with respect to the "present emergency," Yiddish radio programs certainly supported American intervention in the war, but they sounded a slightly different set of concerns than that of mainstream, English-speaking America. Although Arnheim and Bayme picked up on a critical difference between Yiddish and other languages on the American airwaves, they were unable to hear specifically Jewish undertones in Yiddish broadcasts. Where Arnheim and Bayme heard harmony between Jewish and American politics, Jewish audiences heard counterpoint.

THE WAR OVER LANGUAGE

With suspicion about non-English-language broadcasters on the rise, Arhneim and Bayme, along with the FCC, helped to catalyze American radio policy during the months prior to the U.S. entry into the war. The Nazis' effective use of radio propaganda raised additional concerns about the political power of radio, and the attack on Pearl Harbor pressed the Office of Censorship to issue a code of wartime broadcasting. However, the FCC recognized two important factors that ultimately shaped the nature of the code. First, bitter memories of the Creel Commission's censorship of the press during World War I remained strong, so the FCC, fearing a similar response, resisted adoption of a firm set of restrictions.[17] Second, the radio industry stood to lose millions of dollars should the war interrupt regularly scheduled programming. So, in cooperation with the Office of Censorship, the industry adopted a voluntary Code of Wartime Practices for American Broadcasters. J. H. Ryan, assistant director of censorship, explained, "The very anomaly here demanded that the actual working of censorship must be voluntary, a problem for each broadcaster to solve for himself. If free speech—call it free radio, if you will—was important enough to fight and die for then more than likely it was important enough to warrant the exercise of certain controls."[18] Behind this logic, the code proved voluntary in name only, as those who violated it faced stringent and unwanted scrutiny from the FCC and, moreover, risked accusations of unpatriotic behavior for failing to willingly support the war effort.

But the FCC did not entirely trust everyone equally, and it instituted a separate stipulation for broadcasters who spoke languages other than English. "It is requested," continued the code, "that full transcripts, either written or recorded, be kept of all foreign language programs; it is suggested that broadcasters take all necessary precautions to prevent deviation from script by foreign language announcers and performers."[19] Furthermore, the code asked these stations to "cooperate whole heartedly . . . with pro-democratic groups in the selection of program material."[20] These additional demands by the Office of Censorship increased pressure on these stations to actively incorporate civic messages in their programs and announcements.

In order to facilitate cooperation, President Roosevelt, well aware of the power of radio because of the success of his "fireside chats," sought a more aggressive radio policy and merged the Office of Facts and Figures into the Office of War Information (OWI) in June 1942.[21] The Office's three primary tasks were to manage the dissemination of information about the war, explain what citizens could do to help, and keep public morale high. The Radio Bureau of the OWI decided early on that direct appeals to its audience would not be as productive as subtler incorporation of war materials into popular programs, so the OWI turned again to radio producers to volunteer. It asked producers to subscribe to its "Network Allocation Plan," which called for "voluntarily" including "an average of three messages a week" supporting the war effort in their most popular programs. The request could be fulfilled through spot announcements, thematic adaptations of normal programs, or advertisements. To help broadcasters, the Radio Bureau supplied "fact sheets" and "background information" for writers and producers to use as references.[22]

Most broadcasters found the government's hands-off policy satisfactory and employed a relatively light touch, shading wartime broadcasts with a "khaki tint."[23] Scriptwriters fabricated opportunities for proclamations of faith in America or created opportunities for characters to sing the national anthem or "God Bless America." Amateur hours welcomed enlisted men to appear as contestants and tell their stories. *The Goldbergs* even broadcast live from New York's Pennsylvania Station when fictional son Sammy joined the army. The prolific soap opera writer Irna Phillips created *Lonely Women,* a program about women separated from their men by war, while other shows such as *Counterspy, The 22nd Letter,* and *Alias John Freedom* repackaged the familiar spy genre in wartime camouflage. Both *Dick Tracy* and *Jack Armstrong—All American Boy* adopted wartime story lines that found Tracy tracking ration-book counterfeiters and Armstrong pursuing fifth columnists in America and Nazis in Morocco.[24] Jack Benny began regularly reminding his African American valet, Rochester—and his audience—to conserve gas, oil, and rubber when they took their cars out for a drive. The popular comedy team of George Burns and Gracie Allen, whose humor often relied on Gracie's scatterbrained antics, offered the following typically instructive exchange when Eddie Cantor paid them a visit.

CANTOR: Gracie, haven't you heard that gasoline is being rationed?

GRACIE: Well of course, I know that gasoline is being rationed! My goodness, what do you take me for, a dunce? I've read all about it. You're only allowed one cup a day.

CANTOR: Gracie, that's coffee.

GRACIE: Eddie, don't be silly. A car won't run on coffee.[25]

Yet the Office of War Information did not rely solely on the cooperation of broadcasters and occasionally took active steps to cooperate with or even create new programs that addressed wartime themes. Popular serials such as *Our Gal Sunday* and *Stella Dallas* devoted full weeks of programming to explain the war to their audiences. The Department of Agriculture commissioned a program about food productions, and the OWI produced *Hasten the Day,* a serial about the fictional Tucker family whose frugality

exemplified wartime living for its audience.[26] The government also produced three programs specifically to be translated into German, Italian,
and Spanish for immigrant listeners: *Uncle Sam Speaks, The Voice of Freedom,*
and *You Can't Do Business with Hitler.*[27] These shows carried messages of
American patriotism in support of the war effort and found common
cause with German and Italian refugee organizations that also wished to
see their ethnic communities avoid suspicion during wartime.

Unfortunately, these same refugee and aid organizations also coop-
erated with the Foreign Language Division of the OWI, which led to
the removal of nine New York broadcasters from the air.[28] The OWI
suspected these broadcasters of airing pro-Axis sentiments and made
them into examples of what other stations could expect if they did not
abide by the code. The tactic worked. Fearing the same kind of negative
attention, Philadelphia's WTEL voluntarily replaced all their German-
speaking announcers and New York's WOV replaced five of its Italian
speakers. However, even such preemptive actions could not save New
York's WHOM and WBNX, Philadelphia's WPEN, Chicago's WGES, and a
handful of others from being placed on temporary licenses in a coercive
effort to influence their policies and practices during the war. The FBI
even hired two employees of WEVD as confidential informants to inform
on the radio station's relationship to the German American Congress for
Democracy, albeit without much success.[29]

Some English-speaking Jewish groups had already begun to use the
airwaves to promote their own versions of pro-American sentiment even
before the adoption of the Code of Broadcasting. Sensitive both to American anti-Semitism and the fact that most Americans knew precious little
about what was happening in Europe, the American Jewish Committee
(AJC), one of the most powerful American Jewish political organizations,
outlined the four main objectives of its radio department in 1939.

1. To present a knowledge of and appreciation for Democracy as
   against all totalitarianisms to radio listeners by stressing the
   Americanism theme.
2. To impress listeners with the fact that America is a land of many
   peoples, and to combat pernicious race superiority theories. In
   short, "Immigrants All—Americans All."

3. To educate Americans to the threat of Nazism.

4. To present the Jew in a dignified light and his place as an integral part of American life and history.[30]

Unlike Yiddish-speaking broadcasters, the AJC spoke directly to the American public and hoped, thereby, to influence public opinion about America's involvement in war. The difference, like that between Gertrude Berg and Molly Picon, lay in the intention of their address, which left an indelible imprint on their content. Berg and the AJC spoke about Jews to a primarily non-Jewish audience over the networks, whereas Picon and Yiddish-speaking broadcasters spoke to Jewish listeners in the context of Yiddish radio.

Consequently, the AJC focused the majority of its radio efforts on English-language stations, featured well-known performers, and buried most overt references to Jews. The radio department of the AJC did not arrange programs in Yiddish, but it worked with Italian-language broadcasters to include pro-American and anti-Fascist messages in their programs. Wherever possible, the AJC supplied scripts and program ideas to established broadcasters and even wrote and produced a series called *Dear Adolph*, which used the conceit of letters from "average Americans"—a farmer, a housewife, a private in the U.S. Signal Corps, and a "foreign-born American"—to explain the war to American audiences. One episode of *Dear Adolph* featured the Yiddish actor Rudolph Schildkraut but did not identify him as Jewish. Instead, the AJC introduced the program as a production of NBC and the Council for Democracy, and Schildkraut did not mention Jews at all during the fifteen-minute broadcast. Like the *American Jewish Hour*'s Thanksgiving Cantata in 1940, *Dear Adolph* held its tongue about Jews, even in its conclusion, which featured a chorus of heavily accented voices reading the pledge of allegiance as Schildkraut exhorted, "Those, Adolph, are Greeks, Italians, Croats, Slovenians. Americans. Those, Adolph, are Romanians, Bohemians, Russians, Latvians, Norwegians. Americans. Those Adolph, are Danes and Swedes, Irish, French Spaniards. Americans. Americans."[31] The program sang the praises of American multiculturalism but did not utter a word about Jews.

Four years later, when the Jewish Theological Seminary launched its English-language program, it took the AJC's intention a step further and aimed at diminishing any apparent tension between American values and Jewish ones. The program, called *The Eternal Light*, intended "to show Judaism as a moral force in important moments of history" and to "explain Judaism to the American public and . . . give Jews a better appreciation of their own heritage," though it clearly put more emphasis on the former than the latter.[32] Behind the creative force of Morton Wishengrod, who had written successfully for NBC's *University of the Air*, among other programs, the program tried to synthesize Jewish and American stories in an obvious attempt to mitigate anti-Semitic sentiment about America's involvement in the war. A 1944 episode, "Maccabees," provides an excellent example of the program's general rhetorical strategy: "There was a tyrant who desecrated the Temple and massacred the innocent. Just as the nations of the free world in our time, the Maccabees were compelled to take up arms in order to destroy these forces which would suppress freedom and justice. . . . Our own American Revolution is a testament to the Maccabean spirit. So is the courageous defense of the Warsaw Ghetto."[33] Unlike Yiddish programs, the conflicts on *The Eternal Light* joined Maccabees, Minutemen, American GIs, and fighters in the Warsaw Ghetto on the same side of a struggle for freedom. Whereas Yiddish programming amplified the specifically Jewish aspects of American life, *The Eternal Light* inverted the logic and turned up the volume on the American aspects of Jewish life, appealing to a primarily non-Jewish audience with the intention of diminishing American anti-Semitism and strengthening support for the war.

The AJC's and the Jewish Theological Seminary's respective wartime radio shows echoed the self-conscious strategies of other American Jewish political leaders. Downplaying their Jewish roots in favor of their American identifications enabled them to take a public stand while attempting to diminish or deflate anti-Semitic attacks. These programs spoke English with a non-Jewish audience in mind and presented a kind of agreeable American-Jewish synthesis that avoided the explicit Jewish significance of the war.

THE WAR IN YIDDISH

In Yiddish, things sounded quite different. Where Arnheim and Bayme heard continuity and support for the war effort, Yiddish-speaking listeners likely heard a more assertively Jewish tone. Yiddish speakers felt free to speak openly about their concerns, as language formed a buffer between the Jewish community and the broader radio audience. English-speaking Jewish broadcasters had to take a subtler approach, and not even Molly Picon mentioned the war in her English programs until after Pearl Harbor. Because they spoke exclusively to a Jewish audience, Yiddish-speaking broadcasters often took political and personal concerns for granted. This gave Yiddish-language broadcasting a very different tone during the war, in which the audience's communal attachments reinforced both their commitment to America and their concern for Jews living abroad (see figure 19).

Yiddish-speaking radio performers and newspapers had been speaking warily of Hitler since the early 1930s and had been charting quite closely his rise to power and the deteriorating conditions of Jews in Central and Eastern Europe.[34] Stutchkoff's first program, *Annie and Bennie*, debuted in 1932 and revolved around the lives of a Jewish woman and her German Jewish refugee husband. Bennie's identification as a "refugee" referred to his recent, unintended emigration from Germany and relied on a general Jewish awareness of events in Germany, even if the program did not acknowledge them directly. Later in the decade, WEVD turned the microphone over to German Jewish refugees in *Yidish-daytsh flikhtling program* (Jewish-German Refugee Program), a weekly show that featured recently displaced Jewish German refugees in dramatizations of their own stories.[35] Sponsored by Horowitz-Margareten, the show featured a cast in which "every artist was famous overseas and has had to tear up the roots of a lifetime."[36] Presented for a Jewish audience, the program reinforced connections among immigrants, both new and old.

This perspective fueled the ways in which Yiddish radio outlets carried and reported on the news. Unlike English-language radio, which the war helped to establish as a news source independent of the press, Yiddish radio continued to rely heavily on Yiddish newspapers for content. The war made personalities of people like H. V. Kaltenborn and Edward R.

Figure 19. Molly Picon and her husband, Jacob Kalich, conducting a Passover seder for servicemen during World War II, on WDAS, Philadelphia. Courtesy of the American Jewish Historical Society of Newton Center, Massachusetts, and New York.

Murrow, who broadcast daily dispatches from theaters of war to American audiences, but Yiddish radio could not afford remote broadcast technology and relied instead on journalists from *Der tog* and the *Forward* to wire their stories home for publication. Announcers, too, came largely from the Yiddish press. The journalist Hillel Rogoff read news from the *Forward* on WEVD, while WVFW hired Morris Kramer from *Der tog* to serve as its newscaster. In Chicago, the *Idisher kuryer* (Jewish Courier), the city's Yiddish daily newspaper, debuted its own *Jewish Hour* in February 1939, which included a combination of music and news. By 1941, some stations subscribed directly to the Jewish Telegraphic Agency for wire reports, which they only sometimes rewrote before reading on the air.[37]

Gathering their news from the same sources as their audience freed radio announcers from the responsibility of reporting "breaking news" with authority and objectivity. When Yiddish news programs first appeared during the mid-1930s, they offered weekly "news digests," a format that combined news and commentary. Far from the authoritative voices of Kaltenborn and Murrow, Kramer, Rogoff, Scooler, and their colleagues presented sometimes humorous, sometimes poignant commentary about what the news *meant*, not what the news *was*. Yiddish-speaking newscasters delivered the news in rhymes, jokes, exhortations, criticism, interpretation, and explication rather than the serious objective tones of NBC or CBS. For the Yiddish broadcasts, this difference fostered a kind of freedom to publicly express political opinions that English-speaking Jews hesitated to. For example, when Scooler delivered his 1940 Thanksgiving "Grammeister" performance, he did not limit his thanks to America.

> America I thank you [modeh ani]
> And I thank Great Britain
> And, my friends, I thank
> Of great importance
> Those who fly in the sanctification of God's name [al kiddush HaShem],
> The RAF.[38]

Instead of saying "thank you" in Yiddish—"Ikh dank aych"—Scooler reverted to liturgical Hebrew—"modeh ani "—giving his thanks the gravity of prayer. He even extended the honor of the "sanctification of God's name," usually reserved for Jewish martyrs, to British airmen fighting a war of specific concern to America's Jews. As America retained its policy of neutrality and American Jewish leaders hesitated to encourage American involvement in the war, American Jews increasingly supported intervention, and Scooler delivered the news and commentary that they wanted to hear.

Other genres echoed this peculiar fusing of an identification with America and a global Jewish sensibility. An episode of *Zayn vaybs yidine* spoke explicitly about both the dire situation facing German Jews and the confusing responses of American Jews. One episode from January 1940 began with Fishbein complaining about a new pair of shoes that he had just purchased from a German Jewish store owner. When he asked for a larger size, the store owner replied by shaking his head and sadly sighing, "Oh, they mean the concentration camps, that's truly a horror . . . yes, yes. Oppression, terrible oppression, the Nazis know about it, yes, yes." After Fishbein repeated, "smaller, smaller," the shoe salesman replied, "Yes. Both small and large. The Nazis don't care about the difference. Everyone will be persecuted. Eight dollars and 16 cents, please." Befuddled and concerned but unable to deny the old man a sale, Fishbein found a simplistic American Jewish moral in his ill-fitting shoes: "We American Jews are too pampered. The world is going through all sorts of sorrows. . . . In Finland hundreds of soldiers are freezing. . . . In Poland, in Germany thousands of Jews are starving and dying. . . . Sailors are drowning in the cold seas. . . . Jews have too little happiness and enjoyment in their lives. Therefore, when I wear my own shoes, I'll want to take them off. And when I do, I'll feel a great happiness and enjoyment."[39] Nothing could have sounded further from the message of the AJC or the Jewish Theological Seminary. Instead of emphasizing similarities between Jewish and American values, *Zayn vaybs yidine* connected the sentiments of American Jews to Jews in Eastern Europe. Moreover, the point of identification did not rely on political or pragmatic allegiances but on affect and structures of feeling that tied American Jews to their European families and friends.

Messages of concern appeared regularly on Yiddish radio and often placed American characters in sympathetic relation to their counterparts in Eastern Europe. These stories began appearing well in advance of the U.S. entry into the war and emphasized the sense of connection between Jews living in the United States and those living in Europe. A December 1939 episode of *Bay tate mames tish* told this story through the Liebmans, a poor Lower East Side family whose daughter, Gertie, had been turned down from several jobs because she was Jewish. A meeting with Jacob Solomon, a local business owner, revealed that he refused to hire her because of her Jewish-sounding name. She angrily accused him of doing business with the Nazis, claiming, "Then I have a partner for you: Joseph Goebbels of the Hitler, Goebbels and Company!" The final scene of the program featured Gertie's father in synagogue railing against businessmen like Solomon, concluding, "Not to give work to

Jewish daughters is equal to anti-Semitism."[40] Despite the significant difference between bigoted American Jewish businessmen and Nazism, the points of identification sounded loudly and further reinforced the sense of communal sentiment among Jews globally while speaking from a position firmly rooted in the United States.

Yiddish announcers took almost every opportunity to comment on the current situation. Holidays, long a popular source of entertainment on radio, presented a rich vein of material on which radio performers could draw for their news, performances, and commentaries. Scooler celebrated Hanukkah 1940 by proposing the adoption of a "new dreydl," the four-sided top used in a popular children's holiday game.[41] Traditionally, a different Hebrew letter appears on each of the four sides—*Nun, Gimel, Hey,* and *Shin*—each letter representing a word in the phrase, "A Great Miracle Happened There." But instead of miracles, Scooler found a more immediate application of the letters:

> The *Nun*—Nazi darkness
> *Gimel*—Goering, Goebbels,
> Blot out their names and their memories
> *Hey*—Hitler, dog *[hund]*
> *Shin*—There *[shom].*[42]

Yiddish gave broadcasters like Scooler the freedom to be politically overt, even when the circumstances did not seem immediately appropriate. Yiddish radio provided a venue in which Jewish immigrants could explicitly and immediately respond to current events in ways that amplified their Jewish concerns and their American context.

While almost every holiday provided an opportunity for Yiddish radio to hold forth on American Jewish similarities, Purim supplied the most obvious historical parallel and thus became one of the most popular holidays for radio performers during the war. Traditionally, the holiday commemorates the victory of the Jews of Persia over evil Haman's plot to have them massacred (as told in the Book of Esther), and throughout World War II, each year brought more emphatic comparisons of Haman and Hitler. In *Zayn vaybs yidine*'s commemoration of Purim in March 1940, Ben Fishbein, frustrated by his failure to arrange a "meeting" between Adolph Hitler and his brutish Irish relatives on the police force, drew the program to a close by singing a song about his plans for the holiday.

> We're sending Hitler, Mussolini, MacDonald and maybe even Stalin the same dark curse.
> They are due the same quick defeat as Haman,
> Then every Jewish child will sing and dance
> Then no Jew [person] will know from agony
> In honor of Hitler's defeat, we'll celebrate an extra-special, joyous Purim.
> So let us celebrate, dear sisters, and make good things to eat.
> From today until next year, I'll teach you how to make Hitler-tashen.[43]

Fishbein replaced Haman, the holiday's traditional antagonist, with Hitler and substituted the sweet traditional holiday cookie, *hamantashen*, with one renamed for the current foe. In Yiddish, both Fishbein and Scooler expressed overtly political sentiments that specifically highlighted the Jewish concern for Hitler's defeat.

Listening to Yiddish programming, Arnheim and Bayme heard sentiments that they understood as perfectly congruous with American politics. But, within the culture of Yiddish radio, the anti-Hitler messages contained deeper resonances and explicitly Jewish overtones that were immediately apparent to anyone who knew how to hear them. Yiddish radio programs provided an opportunity for the expression and broadcast of popular anti-Hitler messages that emphasized the particular Jewish concerns about events in Europe. For non-Jewish listeners, they may have sounded similar to the messages broadcast by the AJC, but within the community of Yiddish-speaking listeners, the programs and the messages they contained emphasized sentiment over politics and Jewish commonality over American patriotism.

SELLING WAR BONDS IN YIDDISH

When Yiddish programs joined the formal war effort, they mobilized a distinctly Jewish approach that echoed the sentiments of other programs. The war effort began on radio in July 1941, when the Treasury Department launched *Millions for Defense* and the *Treasury Hour* to ready the nation for war on the home front.[44] Following the Japanese attack on Pearl Harbor in December of that year, radio changed its approach from programs supporting "defense" to those dedicated to selling war bonds and raising money and morale for the war effort. As soon as popular radio comedians like Eddie Cantor, Bob Hope, and Jack Benny begun selling bonds, their Yiddish-speaking counterparts joined them. The U.S. Treasury sponsored *Yiddish Treasury Programs* on WBNX, WHOM, and WEVD, while other Yiddish programs—for example, *Dos iz milkhome* (This Is War), *Ikh bin a flikhtling* (I Am a Refugee), *United Jewish War Effort,* WEVD's refugee theater programs, and at least one Mother's Day charity program that included a plea for buying war bonds—took a slighly different approach. The *American Jewish Hour,* too, began incorporating public service announcements to support the sale of war bonds through patriotic cantatas with titles like "Johnnie's Got a Date with Miss Liberty."[45]

Although Yiddish war bonds programs typically followed the same basic format as English ones, they relied on a different set of identifications (see figure 20). Emphasizing the audience's Jewish connections, *Bonds durkh gelekhter* (Bonds through Laughter) featured the popular comedians Menashe Skulnik, Zvee Scooler, and Yehuda Bleich singing, telling jokes, performing skits, and selling bonds in a variety-show format. The show emphasized Jewish interest in the war. Performed and transcribed in front of a live audience, the program opened with Scooler presenting verses in Hebrew, Russian, English, French, and Yiddish to "help our imprisoned brothers" by purchasing bonds. The Hebrew and Yiddish verses went:

> To strengthen the hand of our President
> Our guard and our sentry,
> Bonds through laughter.

> Help, Jews and forge the slaughtering knife
> To butcher and slaughter our slaughterer.
> Bonds through laughter.[46]

Scooler added a musical exclamation point to each verse by instructing his musicians to follow each verse with the opening bars of the

Figure 20. Newspaper advertisement for a Yiddish war bonds rally featuring some of the biggest names in radio. *Jewish Daily Forward,* 12 September 1943, 10. Courtesy of the Forward Association.

national anthem that matched the language of the verse. The band played "Le Marsailles" after the French verse and the "Star Spangled Banner" after the verse in English. The band answered the Hebrew verse with "Hatikvah," the Jewish anthem that Israel eventually adopted as its own. In response to the opening phrase from the Yiddish verse, the band played "Hail to the Chief," to emphasize listeners' American identification.

Stutchkoff also brought his gift for Yiddish radio melodrama to the war effort, matching Scooler and Skulnik with his own series bluntly titled *Der gehenom* (Hell). An excellent student of English-language programs, Stutchkoff modeled his show on the dramatic *Treasury Star Parade*, which debuted in April 1942 and starred the cream of the Hollywood crop in moralistic and patriotic vignettes that dramatized the dangers of unpatriotic actions. In one episode, Edward G. Robinson played a man who did not follow the rules of gasoline rationing, until the gas that he pumped into his car turned to blood.[47] The master of the aesthetic of intimacy, Stutchkoff prefaced each episode in this series with a warning in Yiddish that played on the program's affective register. "All of you who have weak nerves, weak hearts, or fear looking death in the eye," he warned, "go away from your radios so you can't hear. But if you listen not only with your ears, but also with your heart and souls, I've written this for you."[48] Working within his familiar oeuvre and within the bounds of a Jewish community, Stutchkoff relied on the familiar family conflict narrative to address his audience's opinions and concerns about the war.

One episode, set in Bensonhurst at the end of 1942, featured a family who had gathered to say good-bye to Harry, an American-born Jewish boy who was to report for boot camp in the morning. The program opened to the sound of Harry's grandfather crying out for God's intercession after reading a Yiddish newspaper's account of German soldiers forcing a group of Jewish women and children onto trains. Fixated on the plight of German and Polish Jews, much to the aggravation of his wife and the rest of the family, Harry's grandfather explained the attitude of his generation in Yiddish: "Because he [Harry] is going away in the morning, he ought to know why and for what he's going. He's not only going as an American, but as a Jew, too." By contrast, English-speaking Harry proved quite matter-of-fact about being drafted: "War is no picnic. . . . It's either kill or be killed." Imagining the service as a kind of extension of school, Harry continued, "[I want to] be a flier. . . . I'm pretty good at mathematics. I think they'll take me."

Caught between the grandfather's agitation and Harry's attitude about his military service, Harry's father tried to explain the situation, as much to the audience as to his fictional son. In Yiddish, he explained:

> I'm not only talking about you, but about all Jewish American children who had the fortune to be born here. When you talk about Jews of Europe, you're talking about strangers whom you have never seen with your own eyes. And for people you've never seen with your own eyes, it causes no pain in your heart. But us? Me, your mother, your grandfather and grandmother, when we talk about Jews of Europe, we are talking about people with whom we have grown up. People we lived with, people we played with, and they are a piece of us. For us Warsaw is not just a name on the map. But for us, it is part of your life, a part of our soul. . . . Could you imagine, Oh Lord, what would have happened, God forbid, if we had never come to America, but stayed there? Like the poor millions of Jews who stayed? If we didn't live on Bay Parkway . . . but in a dark ghetto?[49]

To Stutchkoff, fighting for America meant fighting for the Jews of Europe, and his explanation, while targeting a younger audience, likely reached more of those who shared his views than those who shared Harry's. Graphic, melodramatic, and overwrought, *Der gehenom* did not tell audiences anything new. Instead, it used the familiar device of family conflict to echo and reinforce the audience's understanding of the conflict and the special relationship between American Jews and the war effort, to which Jews on the home front could contribute by purchasing war bonds. In fact, the story had little to do with Hitler or Fascism at all, but it explicitly connected the experience of Jewish immigrants to the too-real possibility of their alternative fate.

For American Jews, operating within a broad understanding of a Jewish community that was both local and global, buying bonds provided an opportunity to support their country, express their patriotism, aid their families and friends suffering in Eastern Europe, and also begin, in the words of one episode of the *Jewish Treasury Hour*, to "honor the lives of the victims." Announcer Chaim Tauber made this explicit when he urged his listeners, "Say kaddish [the Jewish prayer of mourning] for the 39 young lives that were cut short . . . [and] make certain Hitler will be defeated. . . . Secure the future of America [and the] future of the Jewish people."[50] Connecting the memory of Hitler's victims to the "future of America" reinforced the sentiment that the purchase of war bonds served a Jewish purpose and turned that act into an act of memorialization. Yiddish radio used the intimate relationship between Jews in America and Jews in Europe to turn audiences from listeners into actors and to differentiate their intentions, if not their actions, from those of other Americans. Yiddish radio programs that sold war bonds to remember victims of Nazi violence reinforced the connection between the "future of America and the future of the Jewish people," even as it sonically set its audience apart from the American mainstream.

Like Americanization programs that began in the late 1920s, Yiddish wartime and war bonds programs promoted participation in the mass mobilization even as they did not always sound like the versions of Americanization or patriotism favored by the FCC or the OWI. Instead, they hewed closely enough to the mainstream ideological message but embellished and undermined those messages by emphasizing Jewish concerns. What emerges is a cultural formation that exists on the porous sonic boundary between the Jewish community and the broader American nation of which they were part. Audiences tuned in to Yiddish wartime programs to hear Jewish perspectives on news, holidays, and the war effort. But the sounds of the war in Yiddish resonated strongly with American Jews whose own identifications—with American Jews, with America, and with Jews in Eastern Europe—proved both confusing and congruent.

THE DIMENSIONS OF HOME

In the wake of the war, stations continued to carry Yiddish programs and largely attempted to return to normal. However, many changes had already taken place, both culturally and politically, that would have an impact on the shape of American Jewish communities—and the future of radio as well. Moreover, as survivors of the Holocaust settled in the

United States and Jewish political efforts focused on establishing a Jewish state, the aural culture of Yiddish radio opened up to echo both the past and the present and account for the rapidly shifting parameters of the global Jewish community. Responses to postwar Jewish life found expression in a variety of ways as Jewish communities adapted to the destruction of European Jewish life, the emergent power of the American Jewish community, and the possibility of a Jewish state.

Immediately following the war, the resources and energies of Jewish communities focused on resettling refugees and reuniting families who had been affected by the war. The Jewish Labor Committee (JLC), founded by a number of Jewish labor unions in 1934 as an organized response to the threat of Fascism to Jews in Europe, participated in this effort, turning to the two biggest Yiddish-language media: the *Forward* and WEVD. In print and on the air, the JLC reached out to Jewish immigrant families on behalf of survivors, often just reading lists of names of refugees and urging anyone who might know of their families to call the Committee. The work of the JLC, then, offers a clear example of this acoustic community in which broadcast media played a key role in establishing and reestablishing social bonds through sound.[51]

The bonds of this acoustic community reverberated along other, longer axes as well. WEVD's broadcast of the United Nations vote to partition Palestine and create a Jewish state stands as an outstanding example of the complex ways in which sound mediated the sense of community among listeners. The evening following the vote, WEVD announcer Miriam Kressyn, recalling the aesthetic of intimacy and the trend that Yiddish newscasts offered more commentary than news, presented her program as if she had been present. Providing a Yiddish voice-over to a rebroadcast of the original WBC coverage, she spoke to her viewers as if they were listening to a live simulcast. "The hall is filling up with people," she reported. "Delegates are coming in. Radio commentators, press, guests. Friends and enemies, yes."[52] She then feigned turning the microphone over to Oswaldo Aranja, president of the U.N. General Assembly, and allowed the entire vote to be read as it had, earlier that day. When the votes were tallied, Kressyn feigned surprise: "My heart is beating so fast I can hardly read." And after the announcement of the vote, she exclaimed, "Mazel tov, mazel tov, mazel tov, the 1900-year-old dream has become reality. . . . 33 for us. 13 against." Kressyn then feigned "running into the delegate hall," where she continued as if she had been there earlier that day. She edited together remarks from a few Jewish leaders and continued her description of the event she had not attended. "People are dancing, kissing, crying, dancing . . . "

WEVD's presentation of the U.N. vote on the partition of Palestine reinforced and amplified the multiple affiliations of its audience. By the time listeners tuned in to Kressyn's staged rebroadcast, most already knew the outcome and may well have listened to the original broadcast on NBC. But WEVD, an important outlet of Jewish communal politics and culture, attracted listeners who tuned in to hear the news not as it happened but, more important, to hear it in a Yiddish-speaking context. Like Yiddish news programs during the war, this program's cultural message exceeded its explicit content. The choice of how to listen to this historic event—and with whom—informed what the audience heard, as well as the ways in which they made sense of the broadcast's content.

In the days following the U.N. vote, Yiddish radio carried messages of collectivity and community that echoed recent events. The Sunday after the vote, Scooler responded by thanking God for allowing him to live to see this day, wishing his listeners a "mazel tov," congratulating everybody living in the Diaspora on this accomplishment, and sharing his hopes for "an end to our Jewish exile."[53] In the years that followed, the Israeli presence on WEVD deepened through regular visits from performers like the folksinger Yaffa Yarkoni and Ben Basenko's weekly program featuring news from Israel. Yiddish charity programs also turned their attention to Israel. One of the first began in 1934, when Esther Leibowitz solicited donations for the Zion Dov Ber Torah Fund to support Yeshiva Meah Shearim, a seminary in Jerusalem. Every Friday, Leibowitz composed an original fifteen-minute sermon, which she delivered on WEVD for the next forty years. Most of her donations came in $1 and $5 increments, and she dutifully rewarded donors by reading their names on the air. In addition to Mrs. Leibowitz, a handful of rabbis used the radio to solicit for their own institutions in Israel, and WEVD offered the religious-sounding *Brokhes far yisroel* (Blessings for Israel).[54]

Meanwhile, the Sova Israel Scrip Stores, a small California chain that carried Israeli products, introduced the *Voice of Israel* to Los Angeles on KWKW. Ironically, the *Voice of Israel* was bilingual; it spoke English and Yiddish.

Although Yiddish-speaking radio broadcasters celebrated and supported the young state of Israel and featured Israeli music and Hebrew-speaking performers, radio did not abandon Yiddish for Hebrew but folded this old-new language into its already bilingual broadcasting strategies. Scooler and Shoshana Spector introduced the program *Lomir lernen hebraish* (Let's Learn Hebrew), which taught modern Hebrew in Yiddish. Molly Picon celebrated the young state in an episode of her radio program dedicated to Jaffa, the older, historically Arab port city to the south of Tel Aviv. In Yiddish, Picon sang:

A song about out our people, about Zion
In a workshop by a spindle when one goes home from work
He hears a song of love and devotion
For exactly these people with their forgotten luck
A song of Jewish freedom.[55]

For Picon, the establishment of the state of Israel restored the hope that had been lost during the Holocaust. It gave Jews an opportunity to look to the future and to enjoy a new song, which, although often performed in Hebrew, Picon offered to her audience in Yiddish.

The aesthetic of intimacy that characterized Yiddish radio programs during the 1930s began to give way after the war to a more generalized acoustic Jewishness that capitalized on the dramatic changes wrought by the Holocaust and the founding of the state of Israel. Yet, even as its textures flattened out, Yiddish radio continued to speak to the concerns and desires of its audience. In the postwar years, the questions facing American Jews no longer sounded like those that had defined the Jewish neighborhoods from earlier in the century but were instead salient to American Jews who had grown a bit more at home in America, had experienced the Holocaust from an American Jewish perspective, and had celebrated the establishment of the state of Israel at a distance. These changes melded with broader changes in American popular culture, leaving Yiddish radio sounding in harmony with contemporary styles but always echoing the experience of the generation that remained its most dedicated audience.

HEARING LOSS

The changes in Yiddish radio did not take place without some strife, and despite the flexibility with which Jewish immigrant audiences listened to the various dimensions of their communities, broadcasters sometimes faced more difficult challenges keeping up with a rapidly changing industry in the immediate postwar years. Yiddish-speaking radio broadcasters faced more material changes that challenged them to reimagine the scope and breadth of Yiddish radio. In some cases, they found success and an awaiting audience, but more often than not, they tried to either follow trends in the broader industry or simply resist change outright. The growth of the medium during and after the war expanded opportunities for broadcasting, but the audience for Yiddish programming was not growing in turn. The same audience that had matured alongside Yiddish programming since the 1920s continued to tune in, but it had reached its maximum size, and there was nowhere for Yiddish-speaking broadcasters to go but to reconfigure their audiences or themselves.

By business standards, radio boomed during the war and carried that momentum into the immediate postwar years. Aided by the FCC's unwillingness to risk the ire of the industry, the war boosted radio's profitability due to a combination of paper rationing, which hurt newspaper production, and the imposition of a 90 percent "excess profits tax" intended to discourage wartime profiteering. The tax did not extend to advertising, so advertisers essentially received 90 cents on every advertising dollar spent. As a result, radio stations not affiliated with radio networks more than doubled their income, from $90.6 million in 1940 to $198.3 million by 1945.[56] The confluence of cheap wartime advertising, the concentration of Rubenstein and Kielson at WEVD, and the doomed union of the four Brooklyn-based Yiddish-language stations left WEVD

as virtually the sole remaining carrier of Yiddish-language programming in New York. With the support of Rubenstein and Kielson's ABC,
WEVD expanded its weekly Yiddish broadcasts, and by January 1943
every single Yiddish program on the station claimed a sponsor.[57] As the
leading outlet for Yiddish radio in the United States, WEVD was now
more successful than ever before. Yet it faced a strange predicament in
an aging audience, with few prospects for drawing in new listeners. The
generational shift in language challenged Yiddish-speaking broadcasters to recalibrate their address to suit the different voices of a postwar
American Jewish community.

WEVD, as the most consistent and prolific venue for Yiddish radio,
offers an excellent example of the changing relationship between the
Jewish audience and its aural cultures. When the *Forward* celebrated its
fiftieth anniversary in 1947, it took a moment to reflect on the role radio
played in the lives of New York's immigrant communities. Paying close
attention to the station's linguistic diversity, WEVD's station manager,
Henry Greenfield, observed, "The majority of the cultural programs
in the evening is in English. . . . [But] when the children of different
peoples, like Italians, Greeks, Armenians, Lithuanians, want to hear a
heymish [familiar] word, a *heymish* song that will warm their hearts,
they know where they can hear it: 'WEVD.'"[58] For Greenfield, immigrant
groups listened to WEVD in order to hear something evocative of their
homelands. The obvious omission from this list of immigrant communities was WEVD's largest dedicated audience, which listened to hear
something evocative of their homeland, too, except that their homeland
had become New York.

WEVD did not carry messages for Jewish listeners homesick for the old
country but instead audibly reinscribed the Jewish community within
the United States, and specifically New York. Focusing on the *Forward
Hour*, Greenfield explained, "It is clear that in all of the languages except
English, the most outstanding of all that can be heard on WEVD is our
unique, beloved *mameloshn* [mother tongue], our Yiddish language that
begins each week with the Sunday 'Forward' Hour, which has already
become an established artistic institution that Jews anticipate." The program gave Jewish performers from "across the sea" their first exposure

to Jewish America, served as a stepping-stone for American Jewish performers to achieve even greater success, and provided a vehicle for the "sons and daughters of American Jews who dedicated themselves to Yiddish art" to appear beside established Jewish stars. All these roles, he concluded, made the *Forward Hour* fulfill "an important cultural function in the Jewish life of this great Jewish city."[59] Reflecting on the past and imagining the future of WEVD, Greenfield expressed not only the station's commitment to Yiddish but also the service it provided to newly arriving immigrants and aspiring artists. The station's "cultural function," Greenfield asserted, would extend well beyond its artistic contributions and would, in a delayed echo of Saul Birns's predictions some twenty-four years earlier, provide a community service for its audience at home.

Supported by a more robust roster of sponsors, with an increasingly large percentage from the English-speaking world, WEVD continued to expand its Yiddish-language programming. Nukhem Stutchkoff contributed a handful of short-lived family dramas, in addition to other programs featuring beloved stars like Jennie Moskowitz and Rubin Goldberg.[60] In 1943, the Yiddish writer and poet Kadya Modlowsky serialized her autobiographical novel, *Fun lublin biz nyu york* (From Lublin to New York), which received critical praise for its literary and dramatic quality. As WEVD grew its daytime offerings, it again looked to the English-language industry for direction, targeting a female audience with programs like *Di yidishe baleboste redt* (The Jewish Homemaker Speaks), which proved so popular that it spawned a musical spin-off, *Di yidishe baleboste zingt* (The Jewish Homemaker Sings). Sherman Foods introduced a program about nutrition called *Es gesunterheyt* (Eat Healthily); and *Di frayndlikhe rothgeberin* (The Friendly Adviser), *Froyen in di nayes* (Women in the News), and *Fun a froy tzu a froy* (From One Woman to Another) all promised talk and information on issues of interest to women. Their attempt to appeal to female listeners, however, did not have the same effect in Yiddish as it did in English. Yiddish broadcasting, even with the introduction of programs oriented toward women, still relied on a hodgepodge of programming throughout the day that included quasi-religious programs—*Stavskys great sforim stor fun der luft* (Stavsky's Great Religious Bookstore of the Air)—alongside musical shows—*Star ekspres*—and old favorites like *Der yidisher filosof.*

Though WEVD kept Yiddish healthy and on the air, others sought Jewish audiences elsewhere, although still within the larger orbit of radio's aural culture. WBYN, the station created from the rubble of Brooklyn's radio stations, bet on a younger generation of English-speaking Jews and announced its new direction in an English advertisement in *Der tog*: "Radio station WBYN in its daily presentation of Jewish programs offers an outstanding and vital service to Jewish listeners of greater New York. With complete understanding of all phases of American Jewish life in the fields of education, religion, and popular entertainment, WBYN will continue to serve its vast audience of Jewish listeners with the kind of material and programs best designed to fill their needs and desires."[61]

Reinforcing its intention to attract a Jewish audience and its claim on Jewish community, WBYN did not run advertisements in the English-language press. It began carrying about 90 minutes of Jewish programming in both English and Yiddish on weekdays and 75 minutes on evenings, in addition to three hours every Sunday and 90 minutes on Saturdays.[62] Hoping to be the pioneer of the future of Jewish broadcasting, WBYN instituted a lineup that consisted primarily of light musical entertainment aimed squarely at the tastes of a younger audience. The station hired Wolf Younin as its musical director and featured performances by Lee Grant's Swing-phonic Quintet. It also launched a game show, *Sakhar far vaysn* (Payment for Knowledge), that quizzed contestants about the Bible, Jewish history, American Jewish life, and world events. Sponsored by Kosher Desserts Incorporated, the producers of CoJel Kosher Gelatin, the program was conceived generationally by the station, "so that Jews can recite what they once learned and so the younger generation can also participate in the program."[63] Despite its detailed plan and reinvigorated new identity, the station could not attract an audience and abandoned Jewish programming almost entirely after only one year.

Der tog found itself facing a similar situation with respect to its audience, so in 1944, the newspaper began printing a column in English for its younger readers, explaining, "The Jewish home in America has become bi-cultural." The newspaper explained the timing of its decision in terms of intergenerational communication and the need for a more robust American Jewish life, adding, "The immigrant father and mother no longer live solely on the spiritual fare they brought from the other side." "Immigrant parents," the paper said, still speak Yiddish, even though "their mode of living is also very much American," and despite their "studied indifference to things Jewish," their children "want to know about their Jewish background and the major problems facing Jews today." Instead of successive generations straying farther and farther from Jewishness, Der tog saw that the next generation's comfort with English would benefit American Jews. The newspaper's editors understood this return to Jewish concerns as a coming-of-age of American Jews; no longer limited by the stigmas attached to immigrant life, the younger generation was "more rooted in American soil, more secure in his Americanism, and no longer apprehensive."[64] Optimistic but perhaps too focused on Jewish community, the newspaper underestimated the interest in American popular culture purveyed by magazines, newspapers, records, and radio.

The contraction in Yiddish broadcasting and the turn away from Yiddish as the language of American Jews coincided with broader changes then under way within the culture of radio generally. Of the 199 stations that carried programs in languages other than English at the outset of the war, only about 150 remained by 1943; and at the end of the war, only 130 survived. Radio covered 91 percent of the country and remained the single most powerful medium for news, entertainment, and communication, but people were not listening to radio in the same ways. The invention of the transistor made it possible to leave behind the heavy, burdensome crystal and tube radio sets that typified the home market in the 1930s and 1940s and made smaller, portable radios possible. Millions of these smaller sets, designed for bedrooms, kitchens, and cars, sold at much lower prices than the older cabinet models. Between 1945 and 1955, the number of automobiles equipped with radios jumped from 6 million to 29 million, as people began listening to radio in previously unknown ways, at the beach, in their bedrooms, and at the office. Commuters began tuning in on their way home from work, giving birth to the phenomenon known as "drive time" radio. Teenagers, a lucrative market just beginning to emerge in the postwar years, began tuning in to programs that carried "black" music into the mostly white suburbs and used the change in musical taste as evidence of the difference between themselves and their parents.[65]

Both Jewish and not, younger listeners had developed tastes more in common with their broader age cohort and favored stations with gregarious disc jockeys whose personalities became a kind of signature for the station and a familiar friend for listeners. DJs played music that suited youthful, postwar American tastes and drew heavily on the influences of "black appeal [radio] stations" that broadcast from America's urban centers.[66] Chicago DJ Jack Gibson, who played rhythm and blues records on WCFL, claimed that 90 percent of his fan mail came from white listeners.[67] Radio transgressed racial boundaries with ease, giving young white audiences access to black music, helping to feed the burgeoning relationship between American youth and popular music. Hearing these shifts in the economics of radio, New York stations that once carried Yiddish music began seeking out new markets, too. WMCA and WWRL both abandoned their multilingual formats in favor of rhythm-and-blues-based programming. WLIB is an even more interesting case. Harry and Morris Novick, the same Morris Novick who got his start at WEVD, bought the station in 1949, with the intention of carrying Yiddish programming. Harry explained, "We thought there would be a market among second- and third- generation Jews for Yiddish music with English patter and ads. But we couldn't sell the advertisers on it, so we started concentrating on the Negro market."[68]

The trend away from Yiddish radio reverberated nationally. Chicago's WCFL, the "Voice of Labor," stopped carrying Yiddish and all other foreign-language programs in 1938.[69] In Los Angeles, KWKW, KFVD, and KOWL carried a handful of Yiddish shows, most of which aired once a week, but rarely for longer than a year or two. Baltimore's daily Yiddish program closed down in 1955, but Rabbi Max Resnick continued as the host of the weekly *Yidishe shtunde* (Yiddish Hour), along with a couple of other English-language programs with Jewish content. Philadelphia's *Idishe velt*, the city's only native Yiddish newspaper, could not survive the pressures of the depression and folded in 1942, hobbling Philadelphia's lively Yiddish radio industry, which managed to continue broadcasting sporadically through the 1940s. New York's WBBR, owned by the Watchtower Bible and Tract Society since 1941, ceased carrying Yiddish programming long before the Watchtower sold the station in 1957 to focus on publishing. WBNX had already moved away from its earlier incarnation as "the station that speaks your language," toward a more eclectic English-language lineup before going up for sale in 1960 to become one of New York's first full-time Spanish-speaking stations. Fortune and Generoso Pope, owners of *Il Progresso,* one of New York's Italian-language dailies, bought WHOM in 1946 in order to turn it into the premier outlet for Italian radio programming in New York. The following year, in response to the city's changing demographics, WHOM introduced some Spanish-language programming, in addition to shows targeting African American listeners. Even Molly Picon, who had a long and successful relationship performing for WHN, returned to WEVD in the late 1940s, when WHN adopted an all-news format, leaving no time for Yiddish.

The acoustic community of Yiddish radio had changed dramatically since Yiddish radio debuted in 1926. It had aged and migrated and had not been replaced by a new, younger generation of listeners. The radio industry, too, had changed, as it moved away from elaborate in-house productions of soap operas or variety programs and toward a more streamlined sensibility that favored recorded music, disc jockeys, and simple newscasts.[70] Yiddish-speaking audiences still wanted to hear themselves on the air, but the desire of an audience alone could not keep programs alive. In an effort to hold on to whatever income could still be earned from Yiddish programs, WEVD's Chaim Tauber, David Opatoshu, and Michl Goldstein organized the Yiddish Radio Guild of America (YRGA) in 1947. Its charter explained, "The object of this association is to form a union of men and women who are employed in the selling, production, preparation and broadcasting of radio programs in the Yiddish language so that a collective bargaining unit may be available to them in order to safeguard, protect, defend, advance and promote their rights and better their working conditions."[71] The YRGA constitution set members' dues at $2 per month and agreed that twice-monthly meetings would be held every month except July and August, when many performers left the city for the hotels and resorts of the Catskills.

The YRGA tried to capitalize on Yiddish radio performances by creating a system for the broadcast of and payment for Yiddish. When the YRGA signed an exclusive contract with Rubenstein and Kielson's Advertiser's Broadcast Company three years later, it effectively created little more than a pricing scheme for Yiddish. The contract promised that announcers would receive three weeks' vacation and that they would not work more than six days per week, while it fixed broadcast fees at $1.50 for five-minute programs and $4.50 for programs lasting thirty minutes. News broadcasts demanded steeper fees, $3.75 for five minutes and $8.25 for fifteen.[72] For all intents and purposes, YRGA membership did not extend much beyond the Yiddish-speaking staff of WEVD. Scooler and Kressyn and her husband, Seymour Rexite, joined, but Picon did not. In truth, the union seemed to benefit ABC more than its members, as it effectively turned ABC into the sole agent for every Yiddish-speaking performer. And, despite the creation of the YRGA, there existed no mechanism for monitoring or even accounting for every Yiddish broadcast across the country. As a result, the YRGA spent a good deal of energy chasing down stray Yiddish broadcasts—a fifteen-minute program in Los Angeles, an outstanding bill from Philadelphia—and trying to hold the stations that carried them responsible for payment.[73]

The YRGA, however, was fighting a battle that it could not win. No matter how virtuous it imagined its work to be, it could keep pace neither with the open market nor with the stagnant demographics of the Yiddish radio audience. Attempting to regulate the business seemed a well-intentioned but futile plan to organize an industry that had grown up on its own terms, and in which it was not uncommon for performers like Seymour Rexite to shuttle from station to station, as his contracts required. Rather, the formation of the YRGA represented a late effort to ensure the ongoing financial stability of Yiddish-speaking radio broadcasters and an almost retrograde attempt to sustain an industry and culture as they had been previously. The loss that Yiddish-speaking broadcasters heard during the late 1940s could not be mistaken, but this strategy proved shortsighted and not nearly as persistent, flexible, or creative as either the language or the audience itself.

OLD ENDS AND NEW BEGINNINGS

The biggest change in radio took place on television, which began to attract the attention of all the major networks and their sponsors almost as soon as the first set was sold. Between 1947 and 1955, networks poured money and attention into television as they paid increasingly less attention to radio. As a result, during those years, network affiliation among radio stations dropped from 97 percent to 50 percent.[74] But as radio eased back into the hands of local broadcasters, it did not return to its prenetwork ways. Instead, the FCC opened up the FM band and relaxed its restrictions for station ownership in the wake of World War II, which increased the number of available radio licenses. At the end of the war, about 900 radio stations broadcast in the United States. By 1952, the number of stations grew to 2,400, and by 1960, it ballooned to nearly 3,500, as FM stations proliferated.

In accord with some of these changes and despite the changes in the linguistic makeup of the Jewish community in America, the number of stations carrying Yiddish shows more than doubled, from 21 in 1941 to 46 in 1958.[75] The growth did not reflect a growing interest in Yiddish programming as much as it did the establishment of Jewish communities in new cities. The large urban centers of Jewish life continued apace, but new communities and audiences sprang up and multiplied the number of stations broadcasting in Yiddish. Zalmen Zylbercweig, editor of the six-volume *Lexicon of the Yiddish Theater,* broadcast a Yiddish-language program from his backyard in Los Angeles.[76] Jacob Shachter, who began his career on New York's WBNX, launched Miami's first Yiddish radio program on WEDR in 1946, following three years of wrangling with local radio executives for permission to air an ethnic program. Shachter's program became the first non-English-language program in Miami, and he opened the door for programs in Italian, German, Greek, Russian, and Spanish. Schachter established himself on WEDR, where he broadcast a variety of programs, entertained popular guests like Moyshe Oyhser, Molly Picon, and others, and used his position to raise money for the Jewish National Fund. As the Jewish community of Miami continued to grow during the 1950s, so did the number of Yiddish programs and the number of sponsors who wanted to reach out to South Florida's Jewish residents, flooding in from cities like Chicago and New York.

Los Angeles, home to an older and more established Jewish community, also saw a slight revival of Yiddish music on its airwaves when the singer, bandleader, and parodist Mickey Katz brought his "antic-semitism" to the airwaves from 1951 to 1956, during which time he claimed to be "Southern California's only American Jewish disc jockey." He read announcements and commercials "in English-Yiddish comic vein" and played "recordings with a Yiddish-Israeli flavor," including those of Al Jolson, Jan Peerce, Yaffa Yarkoni, and his own.[77] In the same vein as Packer's performances of Yiddish, Katz relied on his audience's desire to hear it but not necessarily their ability to understand it. Although he focused on a Jewish audience, radio kept communal boundaries porous, and Katz recalled taking great pleasure in the program's wide appeal: "Thousands of people of all faiths loved the haimish (homey) Jewish music and the lively *frailachs*. I got grateful letters from Catholic senior citizens and from many non-Jewish individuals and groups."[78] The performance of Yiddish, now for a broader audience, continued to resonate on the air, and Katz, who had a great ear for Yiddish parody, happily supplied it to whoever wanted to hear it.

Well-known outside the Jewish world, Katz was a bit of an anomaly. Most Yiddish-speaking broadcasters reached a primarily Jewish audience and, in large part, the same audience they had entertained for the better part of thirty years. According to Ruth Glazer, it continued to supply a sound track for Jewish life. In 1955, Glazer, "an occasional commentator on Jewish manners, morals, and cooking" for *Commentary*, published her impressions of WEVD in which she noted her appreciation for how little the station had changed in terms of community, not necessarily taste. With regard to news reports, Glazer observed the station's preference for the interests of older listeners: "I have yet, even at the height of the season, to hear a single baseball score offered over the station. For the WEVD listener, the Yankees, the Dodgers, the Rose Bowl, the four-minute mile are all strange figments of the imagination of the younger generation." Glazer praised Zvee Scooler, who delivered his programs and extemporaneous announcements "with such simplicity that, listening, it was as if one were overhearing a scholar at his studies," and she shared her distaste for programs in which "all sense of proportion gets swept away."[79] With respect to the station's musical selections, Glazer held particular dislike for "Anglo-Jewish composers and arrangers," whose music she found too often overburdened, mawkish, and sentimental. She could not stand songs like the Zionist ballad "Ikh benk aheym," which she described as "almost more than mortal flesh can endure." She dubbed Seymour Rexite the "Yiddish Liberace" and dismissed his delivery as "that light, slightly nasal tenor voice that ladies of a certain age find irresistible. It quivers, it trembles, it vibrates. In point of fact, it bleats." Critical as she was, overall, she appreciated the station's commitment to classic Yiddish music: "In view of the vast quantity of sentimental trash, smutty and otherwise, that floods the current Yiddish stage and record market, WEVD maintains a remarkably high-toned and even high-minded atmosphere."[80] In her implicit criticism of changes in Yiddish culture, Glazer made her preference for the olden days quite audible and praised WEVD for continuing to provide the sound track of a past time without sounding nostalgic.

In a similar way, when it introduced new dramatic programs, WEVD appealed to the tastes and sentiments of its established audience, sustaining the sound of an aging community. The station's final three Yiddish dramas, *Mein mutter un ikh, Eltern un kinder* (Parents and Children), and *Tsuris bay laytn* (People's Troubles), Stutchkoff's final contribution, bore titles that evoked the intergenerational conflict that characterized so much of earlier Yiddish radio drama, and each captured the last strains of these same intimate conflicts but with an attitude that aged with its audience. Glazer wrote, "In these sketches the older generation speaks Yiddish, which in the context of the station gives their characters depth and richness, and the younger generation speaks English, a particularly flat, nasal and unappetizing brand of English, so that by contrast with the limpid speech of their elders, they seem like incompetent self-centered children. And, as it almost inevitably turns out, that is just what they are."[81] For Glazer and Stutchkoff, American-born Jewish children no longer bore the hope they had when Stutchkoff introduced *Bay tate mames tish,* some fifteen years earlier. By the 1950s, younger characters had become weak, self-centered, and spoiled. They no longer spoke endearing variations of Anglicized Yiddish but gave over, instead, to speaking English entirely. Gone were the aspirations echoed on programs like *Uptown-Downtown* and the vibrant playfulness of *Zayn vaybs yidine.* Poetically and bittersweetly, Stutchkoff's *Tsuris bay laytn* placed many of its aging protagonists in the Jewish Hospital for Chronic Diseases, a real-life hospital in Brooklyn that doubled as the program's sponsor.

Always more conservative than its radio announcers, the audience for Yiddish radio preferred to hear itself as it once was rather than as what it had become. Sholom Rubenstein recalled an episode in which he encouraged the comedian Menashe Skulnik to incorporate some new material into his act: "Menashe's material always got tremendous laughs but to me the jokes were old and shopworn. One day I suggested to Menashe that he provide some fresher scripts. Said Menashe: 'you want fresh, you'll get fresh.' He set to work with his writer and prepared some new skits which I thought were very funny and original. That week at the taping session we got a few chuckles, a giggle and maybe somebody smiled. Not one big laugh. Menashe didn't say a word but the next batch of scripts were back to the old, tried and true material."[82] Although his audience did not want to hear anything new, it did want to keep listening. During World War II and through the end of the 1940s, the audience of Yiddish radio continued to tune in to hear the sounds of themselves on the air.

Throughout the 1940s, the audiences of Yiddish radio listened for the sounds of Jewish voices that spoke to their experiences as immigrants, as Jews, and as Americans. The war stretched some of these allegiances and their sonic sensibilities while also reinforcing connections among and between Jews and their collective identifications. Yiddish newscasts carried more opinion than fact, while Yiddish dramas and war bonds programs reinforced the specifically Jewish concern for the war and the war effort. Meanwhile, audiences could hear identifications with Jews in America, in Europe, and, eventually, in the young state of Israel. In the postwar years, the broad social changes that reshaped Jewish communities across the United States also reshaped the radio dial. However, Yiddish broadcasting continued to ascribe to a set of aesthetic and affective criteria that its listeners sought all along. While never exactly progressive or avant-garde, Yiddish radio's ability to respond to the new postwar social context should not be surprising. Thus what is perhaps most poignant about this moment is that Yiddish radio kept speaking to the community that created it. Yiddish, while it did not properly disappear, had ceased to be the majority language of America's Jews. Yet it still reverberated with the multiple dimensions of Jewish communal life, for those who still chose to listen.

SIX Listening for Yiddish in Postwar America

> During the war years, the American Yiddish radio frequently
> succeeded in providing programs of interest for three generations
> of listeners. Since that time its audience has narrowed radically
> to the generation of grandparents. In that generation it still has a
> large and loyal following for whom it provides unique entertain-
> ment and topics of discussion in a manner unequalled by other
> media of mass communication. During the past few years, the
> Yiddish radio has held its own quite successfully.
>
> Joshua Fishman, commenting on the postwar life of Yiddish radio

> The *simkhe* continues.
>
> Slogan of WEVD disc jockey Art Raymond's program, ca. 1985

Perhaps most remarkably, the audience that chose to listen to Yiddish radio during the 1930s continued to listen as long as they could. Although Yiddish radio never regained the diversity or magnitude of the 1930s and 1940s, it kept broadcasting as long as listeners were there to hear it, and it managed a fairly robust and lengthy life in postwar America. Although the number of radio stations that carried Yiddish radio dropped from forty-one in 1956 to three in 1980, the number of broadcast hours remained remarkably consistent, owing to WEVD's ongoing commitment to the language.[1] And thanks to the presence of a sizable population of listeners who grew up, matured, and built homes, families, and communities to a sound track supplied by Yiddish radio.

The aging population of Jewish immigrants found in Yiddish radio a medium to sustain their connections both to one another and to Jewish culture, as they understood it. As the health of this generation began to wither in the 1970s and 1980s and the audience began to shrink significantly, Yiddish radio seemed poised to slip from the airwaves for good, but something remarkable occurred: Yiddish culture in the United States experienced a resurgence, driven in large part by the power of music and the ability of a new generation to participate in it specifically as listeners.[2]

EXPERIMENTS IN YIDDISH

After World War II, the audience for WEVD's Yiddish programming stood at approximately 1.75 million people.[3] With their support, the station maintained a healthy and diverse Yiddish program, which, like most radio at the time, had abandoned original dramas, comedies, and live music in favor of news, talk, and records. Sholom Rubenstein and Meyer Kielson continued to work behind the scenes at WEVD and, despite the station's health, felt the pressure of television and tried to bring Yiddish into the new medium. They teamed up with longtime client Maxwell House Coffee to book a series of television programs on New York's Channel 13. Broadcasting live and without much of a budget, Rubenstein directed and produced a program of dramatizations called *Great Jewish Stories,* another with Rabbi Avrom Soltes called *Sabbath Candles,* and another featuring radio performers Miriam Kressyn and Seymour Rexite called *Jewish Matinee Time.* The programs were conducted primarily in English, but all featured Jewish stories and Yiddish music. Rubenstein, a tireless worker and creative mind, produced nine shows, directed seven, and wrote five episodes each week until the owners of Channel 13 sold the station and put an end to Yiddish on television. The failure of Yiddish on television in the 1950s, however, came not for lack of an audience but for lack of a station.

The audience remained, and Yiddish retained its allure for listeners and continued to speak powerfully to its audience's desire to hear voices that sounded like their own. While the station satisfied the majority of its listeners, one member of the audience heard trouble in the variety of accents and inconsistencies in pronunciations among the station's staff. Much like earlier critics, B. Gutmans found that WEVD sounded like a hodgepodge in need of uniformity rather than a community. In 1958, this listener undertook a systematic study of the station, which he published in the journal *Yidishe shprakh* (Yiddish Language). To his dismay, Gutmans found at least nine different accents and found that some announcers even switched accents midreading. He observed that certain announcers favored English pronunciations of proper names, even if the names in question had Yiddish origins. Similarly, announcers generally referred to institutions by their English names or used English words, even when Yiddish ones existed.

Looking for resolution and uniformity, Gutmans sought advice from the British Broadcasting Corporation, the Canadian Broadcasting Corporation, and Israel's state broadcasting system, Kol Yisrael, each of which enforced formal guidelines for pronunciation. He concluded that Yiddish radio announcers and performers ought to bring listeners, "when it is possible, perfection of the spoken realm," so that radio could "play the role of which it is capable and that it must play in our cultural life."[4] According to Gutmans, WEVD had the potential to become the cultural voice of Yiddish-speaking America and serve the same role as the BBC in England or Kol Yisrael in Israel. Failing to broadcast "perfection of the spoken realm," Gutmans concluded that WEVD failed to fulfill its cultural and communal promise and that its inconsistencies weakened the community that listened to it.

Gutmans failed to notice that Yiddish radio programming had never standardized its speech and had from the very beginning included English in its broadcasts, as well as a variety of accents. Concerned as he may have been about elocution, this was never a major issue for Yiddish-speaking radio announcers. Rather, Gutmans's comments revealed a greater concern about the diminishing place of Yiddish in Jewish cultural life in the United States generally and anxiety over the future of the American Jewish community. Nevertheless, Yiddish radio continued to resonate with its listeners. Ruth Glazer still felt that WEVD provided the ideal sound track to her own preparations for the Sabbath. Her Friday afternoons included cleaning the house, polishing candlesticks, and skimming fat off the chicken soup. "When things reach a real crescendo with a real *balebosta*," she said, "we have a correspondingly heightened mood on WEVD."[5] Standardized Yiddish or not, WEVD still suited the tastes of its Jewish listeners.

To maintain that harmony with its audience, WEVD tried to sustain its sound from the early 1940s by continuing to provide original programming in Yiddish. The *Forward Hour* kept its variety format and gave performers like Seymour Rexite, Miriam Kressyn, and Zvee Scooler a regular venue for new translations or serializations of novels such as Osip Dimov's *The Family Muskat*, Isaac Bashevis Singer's *In My Father's Court*, or the *Tzenarena*, a Yiddish translation of Bible stories originally written for women. On the strength of these programs and others, and contrary to prevailing impressions of the health of Yiddish in the United States, by 1964, Jewish listening to WEVD had reached "its highest point since 1935," and two years later, the station reported its "best year ever."[6] As the only outlet for Yiddish programming in New York, it had no competition and a captive audience that helped it to thrive. Its forty-four hours of Yiddish programming each week spoke to the same audience it always had.

Although the audience remained largely the same, the culture of radio had moved away from the soap operas and variety shows of the 1930s toward more streamlined formats featuring mainly news or music. Even as the *Forward Hour* continued much as it always had, WEVD began to change with the times, moving toward more English-language programming while retaining the tone of its Jewish address. The station hired Joey Adams, the popular English-speaking comedian who developed his career in the Jewish resorts of the Catskills, to fill its weekday morning slot. Adams took his signature style into the studio, telling stories and conducting interviews in English with a smattering of Yiddish. The station's most successful disc jockey, Art Raymond, began his career on WEVD in the early 1960s and by the 1980s hosted almost daily shows ranging from one to four hours in length where he spoke English and played primarily Yiddish records. English-speaking Ruth Jacobs's *Jewish*

Home Show became a midday staple of the station around this time, carrying conversations about Jewish homemaking and cooking. Still focused on Jewish listeners, WEVD offered new versions of the aesthetic of intimacy by inviting listeners to learn Jewish homemaking from Jacobs, to participate in Raymond's daily *simkhe* (celebration), or to hear stories from the Sages of Israel Home for Aging Rabbis. On a far smaller scale than it had in the 1930s and 1940s, WEVD continued to broadcast Jewish messages for listeners who continued to tune in. WEVD, which had adopted the slogan "The Station That Speaks Your Language" from now-defunct WBNX, ironically captured its multilingual tension, as its Yiddish programs increasingly featured Israeli songs and Yiddish recordings presented by English-speaking hosts.[7] With at least three languages speaking to Jewish listeners, the station's slogan meant something different from what it seemed to, especially when read aloud on the air in a Yiddish accent: *WEVD—de steyshun det spiks your lengvedge.*

Behind the strength and commitment of WEVD, Yiddish remained the most popular non-English language on New York radio until 1962. That year, WHOM began to broadcast Spanish play-by-play of every New York Yankees baseball game to cater to the growing Spanish-speaking audience of Puerto Rican and Latin American immigrants settling in New York. This decision vaulted Spanish over Yiddish to become the "first major language, after English, on New York radio."[8] The change in rankings did not come about because WEVD or the other stations stopped carrying Yiddish but because WHOM added 154 three-hour Spanish broadcasts to an already substantial schedule, supplemented by more and more stations each year. Almost oblivious to these changes, WEVD sustained an output of nearly fifty hours per week of Yiddish programming until the late 1970s, when its audience began to succumb to the passage of time or retire to warmer cities farther south and west, including Honolulu, Hawaii, which boasted its own Yiddish radio program in 1964.[9]

In fact, the number of Yiddish speakers in North America had been growing since the end of World War II, as displaced Eastern European communities resettled in North American cities. Between 1940 and 1952, the United States absorbed some 137,450 Jewish immigrants, a number of whom settled in Brooklyn, where they tried to maintain continuity between their Orthodox lives in Europe and those in their new home. In New York, the number of Yiddish speakers actually increased between 1960 and 1970, due to the Orthodox community's high birthrate and fierce commitment to maintaining a tight-knit community. According to David Fishman's calculations, the number of native Yiddish speakers increased from 422,000 in 1960 to 985,703 in 1970.[10] By 1980, when Rabbi Pinchas Teitz's weekly Talmud seminar, *Daf hashavuah* (Talmud Page of the Week), joined WEVD's Saturday night lineup, the station could be assured of a significant number of ultra-Orthodox listeners tuning in from Brooklyn, even though Teitz's program aired between two programs sponsored by secular and socialist Yiddish organizations, the Bund and the Workman's Circle.

Owing to religious and ideological differences, as well as those in community organizing and structure, these new religiously observant communities did not generally participate in the Yiddish culture established by the previous generation of immigrants. Somewhat distrustful of media that came from outside their community, they preferred to remain relatively insular, largely avoiding most newspapers, theater, and music even when they were in Yiddish.[11] This influx of Yiddish speakers did not share the same Yiddish culture as those who had arrived half a century before, and as a result, circulation of Yiddish newspapers from the older immigrant generation continued to decline. By 1969, circulation of the *Forward* dropped to 80,000, and in 1971, *Der tog–Morgen Journal* closed its doors for good.

THE RISE OF YIDDISH

A few years later, the klezmer musician and scholar Henry Sapoznik had a life-changing encounter with bluegrass musician Tommy Jarrell, and in 1977, the Klezmorim recorded *East Side Wedding*, the first full-length LP of what would come to be known as the klezmer revival.[12] The ethnomusicologist Mark Slobin reviewed the record for the academic journal *Ethnomusicology* and keenly noted its departure from the overwrought melodrama of much Yiddish music: "This is a new way of presenting the 'Yiddish' tradition on disc, as far removed from Theodore Bikel as from *Fiddler on the Roof.*" More significantly, Slobin rightly observed, "The Klezmorim must be viewed as part of a newer folk layer themselves. . . . They represent the new breed of ethnic ensemble we have hardly begun to study."[13] A new generation of listeners began paying attention, and other musicians followed Sapoznik's path through bluegrass, folk, and rock and roll to this new-old Jewish music. One of the first new wave Yiddish programs grew directly out of this creative moment. In 1979, Jack Falk, an influential musician in the klezmer scene and a member of Di naye kapelye (the New Band) inaugurated Yiddish radio in the Pacific Northwest. On community radio station KBOO, Falk broadcast the *Portland Yiddish Hour* every Sunday. Across the country, in Tampa, Florida, the *Sunday Simcha* debuted the same year, broadcasting a mixture of "klezmer, Chassidic, Israeli, Yiddish, Ladino, Mizrachi" music to Jewish residents every Sunday afternoon. By 1982, sixteen stations nationwide carried Yiddish programming, ranging from 30 minutes to 19 hours, in the case of WEVD, each week.

Practically simultaneous with this development, *The Third Jewish Catalog*, published in 1980, dedicated nearly thirty pages to Yiddish, including a brief history of the language, resources for study, information about the Yiddish press, sources of Yiddish records, information for obtaining Yiddish films, and even where to hear Yiddish radio. The first two catalogs, published in 1973 and 1976 respectively, virtually neglected Yiddish. The original *Jewish Catalog* devoted three paragraphs to "Yiddish songs" and did not mention the *Forward*. By the *Third Jewish Catalog*, the revival of Yiddish had begun, and it noted the chatter of Yiddish radio: "For beginners the content of a [radio] program doesn't really make much difference; just the fact that it's there is sufficient."[14] For the Yiddish revival, listeners did not have to understand or learn the language, but in a kind of distant rearticulation of their parents' and grandparents' sonic practices, just listening seemed enough.

Participating in Yiddish culture did not depend on fluency but a sense of attachment to the language. Joshua Fishman expanded the definition of the term *heritage speaker* to include anyone with "a language of personal relevance other than English."[15] By shifting the burden from comprehension to "personal relevance," Fishman enabled the possibility that listening would remain a viable performance of identification, whether one understands what she hears or not. This formulation recapitulates earlier mobilizations of Yiddish, as Herbert Ganz observed in the performances of Mickey Katz. Katz, he claimed, "is comprehensible even to the younger Jews who do not understand Yiddish, and can achieve a comic effect largely because of the incongruity between American material and a more or less Yiddish language."[16] Katz, like klezmer, appeals in spite of and sometimes because of the linguistic gap, which occasionally speaks louder than words.

To be sure, listening to music—even when accompanied by lyrics— and understanding a news broadcast or a family drama are two different skills. And although the primary audience of Yiddish radio could do both, and much of the younger audience could only manage the former, listening remains an important cultural act. In the case of Yiddish and Yiddish radio, the ability and opportunity to listen continued to resonate on a cultural level. In fact, Fishman's definition of *heritage speaker* continued to refract on a communal level when the audience for radio began to diminish. When the Forward Association voted to sell WEVD's AM station in 1981, a coalition of Jewish groups organized to stop the sale based explicitly on the connection between the medium and the community it served. The groups filed a petition with the FCC to stop the sale, claiming, "The transfer of the WEVD-AM license is not an ordinary commercial transaction. It is the eradication of an institution in Jewish American life." The petition argued that the sale of the station would result in the cessation of Yiddish programming and the loss of programming on Jewish subjects for listeners in the New York area. While the latter argument was true, it would not have meant a loss for New York but a loss for the Jews of the city, and in this way, it strengthened the connection between the community and the radio. Although the combination of a shrinking audience and the declining interest of sponsors led the Forward Association to pursue the sale, by 1981, WEVD was no longer just a radio station; it had become a community "institution," worthy of protecting for that reason alone. Against these objections, the sale went through, though a handful of Jewish programs left the station because their hosts felt "uncomfortable" with the new owner, a company that had been involved in Christian broadcasting. Nevertheless, in 1984, WEVD still carried some eighty hours of Jewish programming each week in English, Yiddish, Hebrew, and Russian, and WEVD-FM still carried Yiddish programming as well.[17]

With questions of language, heritage, generational change, and commercial viability in the air, in 1990, the *Forward* decided to begin publishing a weekly edition in English. When Howard Ostroff explained this decision, he commented, "We need a new way of reaching the grandchildren of Jewish immigrants who probably don't speak Yiddish but are no less concerned with their heritage."[18] This was a frank commercial assessment. Yet Ostroff keenly if unintentionally framed the *Forward* less as a newspaper and more as a time machine. In an echo of Yiddish newscasting from the 1940s, what seemed important in increasing readership was not its ability to deliver the news but its power to invoke the heritage of its readers. These issues resurfaced again in the Forward Association's 2001 decision to sell WEVD to Disney for $78 million. Barnett Zumoff, president of the Forward Association, explained its decision to leave broadcasting and focus solely on its newspaper: "Our primary mission is to provide American Jews with newspapers that hold a mirror to our culture, our politics, our values and our history."[19] Zumoff articulated what Ostroff implied—that Yiddish media do not speak like mainstream American media and that their audiences do not attend to it in the same way either.

LEARNING TO LISTEN AGAIN

As the immigrant generation began to pass away in the 1970s, a younger generation, most of whom were raised in English-speaking homes, began to tune their attention to the sounds of the American Jewish generation that they scarcely knew. Anthropologists began to observe the passing of this generation.[20] Writers, playwrights, artists, and poets returned to the rich Yiddish literary tradition for inspiration and source material.[21] For musicians, returning to Jewish roots meant reclaiming a tradition of Jewish music in Eastern Europe and America, and they have created a substantial body of klezmer and klezmer-inspired music since the late 1970s. Seth Rogovoy's *The Essential Klezmer* includes an "essential klezmer library," of which seventeen of twenty entries have been recorded since the 1970s; the vast majority of his discography has also been recorded during the last quarter of the twentieth century.[22] But for this generation of children and grandchildren of immigrants, recapturing the precise inflections of the generation just passed is less important than paying homage while translating the modes, rhythms, and references into the idiom of a new generation that is again, ready to listen. From *The Simpsons'* character Krusty the Clown to the New York Jewish Music and Heritage Festival, both musically and culturally, sounding Jewish in America still generally means speaking with a Yiddish accent, and American Jews still choose to listen in order to figure out what it means.

The Yiddish scholar Jeffrey Shandler calls this a "postvernacular culture," meaning that Yiddish culture in America is enjoyed primarily by people for whom it is not the native tongue.[23] It may be the *mameloshn* still, but that is a more sentimental word, suggesting a greater emphasis on the power of one's attachment than the language in which one was raised. Shandler is concerned with the use and production of Yiddish in this "postvernacular" context, but within the history of Yiddish radio, the question of consumption and absorption is equally as important. After all, throughout the history of Yiddish radio, most of the people who participated in the culture did so as listeners.

Conclusion

[Diaspora] is found in the Greek translation of the Bible, and originates in the verb "to sow" and the preposition "over."

At the end of the war [World War I] . . . broadcasting, a word that until then had meant 'to scatter seeds,' acquired a new meaning.

The culture of Yiddish radio took root before the first Yiddish radio broadcasts and has outlived the generation that was radio's primary audience. This might be an effect of the power of listening as a cultural practice. It might speak to the ongoing resonance of Yiddish among American Jews. It might also emerge from radio's powerful place in interwar American cultural life, as the the culture of Yiddish radio flourished during the vibrant and complicated 1930s and 1940s, the Golden Age of radio. Although networks and advertising agencies came to dominate the culture and business of radio generally, a handful of small, independent stations sustained the attention of immigrant communities in America's major cities by speaking to them in their own languages. Never to the total exclusion of network or English-language radio, these communities formed and sustained themselves in conversation with the programs they heard and developed sophisticated relationships among performers, station owners, sponsors, listeners, and federal regulators. Out of these relationships, a distinct aural culture emerged in which Yiddish radio became both a venue and a vehicle for the expression of Jewish communal desires and identifications.

Beginning in the late 1920s, low-power, local stations across the country entertained audiences of Jewish immigrants in every imaginable genre, from vaudeville-style comedy to sermons and concerts of sacred music. As radio in general adjusted to the spread of television and the changing patterns of listening and consumption, the stations that carried Yiddish programming changed, too, and began favoring disc jockeys and recorded music over dramatic serials and live musicians. Yet throughout, Yiddish-speaking broadcasters, stations, and their audiences still engaged in subtle, sometimes barely audible conversations about the meaning of Jewish life in America. From the very beginning, Yiddish-language programming engaged the American tastes of its audience and sought to reach them where they lived by presenting sounds of American Jews at home, even when those homes reverberated with conflict.

These cultural accommodations became part of the acoustic palette of Yiddish radio. Yet, no matter how "Americanized" Yiddish radio sounded, audiences continued to listen in order to hear Yiddish because they heard in Yiddish, something both comforting and alienating. Yiddish sounded familiar, it was the language of the home and the street, and it was the language that they spoke and grew up speaking. Yet it also sounded alien, as immigrants tried to make their way in America, where the future would undoubtedly arrive speaking English. Sometimes overtly and sometimes implicitly, this tension found expression on the air in family dramas, in the intentions of aspiring amateur performers, in wartime newscasts, and in Yiddish programs that took their cues from English ones. The structures of feeling fostered by Yiddish radio drew on affective connections among Jewish listeners in spite of their marginal status within the industry. In terms of content, Yiddish programs gave voice to these conflicts that characterized the immigrant generation.

In terms of form, Yiddish radio operated in two worlds—that of radio generally and that of the Yiddish media specifically. In terms of Yiddish media, radio did not so much replace as extend the cultures of newspaper, recording, and theater. Yiddish newspapers in a number of cities owned radio stations and published advertisements and radio listings. Newspaper editors and writers appeared on the air, and theater contributed both material and personalities without which the airwaves would have been empty. Yiddish radio's relationship to mainstream radio is slightly more complicated, as the stations that hosted Yiddish programs operated according to the same rules and regulations as the networks, even though they catered to different audiences. More important, for listeners, Yiddish appeared side-by-side with programs in numerous other languages, and for audiences, English was only a turn of the dial away. To attract audiences away from generally higher-quality English programs, Yiddish programs had to offer something else.

The presence of Yiddish certainly served this end and succeeded in speaking loudly to Jewish immigrant audiences drawn to the presence of voices that sounded like theirs. Engaged in broadcasting in this way, the Jewish immigrant audience constituted a community of listeners who actively engaged themselves in discussions about what and how they ought to sound on the radio. Always within earshot of English programming, the acoustic community allowed audiences to hear an obvious difference (of language) while participating in a common culture (of medium). Yiddish radio performers reinforced this sensibility, enabling a few station owners to argue that they, too, served the interests of their community. Meanwhile, the listeners who tuned in provided perhaps the strongest expression of this communal sensibility because they could always listen elsewhere but chose not to. At the same time, radio also undermined the communal boundaries that it allowed its audience to imagine. Yiddish-speaking broadcasters engaged in careful mimicry of English-language programs, spoke English on the air, and broadcast bilingualism as a key element of the culture of Yiddish radio. They copied the successful formulas of English-language programs, sought the support of non-Jewish sponsors, and generally listened to English-language programming for inspiration. Moreover, and perhaps more important, their audience also listened to English programming with at least as much energy and excitement.

As audiences tuned in to Yiddish programs to hear the Jewish community, they also turned the dial to hear echoes of English and access mainstream American culture. Through radio, Jewish immigrant audiences attended to both worlds, and immigrants took advantage of nearly everything it offered. Listeners did not see the choice of broadcast language as exclusive, even as they remained keenly aware of a particular language's cultural overtones. The choice of whether to listen to Yiddish or to English meant choosing one acoustic community over another—but only in fifteen-minute increments. These choices, like the communities they represented, were never permanent. Instead, radio provided a way for audiences to imagine themselves as a community of listeners. Radio is a medium, and in this case, it became a crucial vehicle for listeners, performers, sponsors, and federal regulators to spin out their imaginings of the communities in which they participated and with which they identified. To be sure, each group claimed a different purchase on their community, and each community took on a different shape and scope. And Yiddish, as a mass medium for minority voices, served as the conduit for these imaginings. Different kinds of imaginings have very real effects; when the FCC mandated the unification of Brooklyn's radio stations, it resulted in very concrete effects on the soundscape of New York and the diversity of that city's Yiddish broadcasting but also on the sponsors who relied on the station and the people who owned and operated it. Or, in another example, when Philadelphia's Rabbi Levinthal objected to a nonkosher butcher advertising in Yiddish, that, too, had concrete effects on the butcher and the radio station but also on the rabbi's hopes for the purity of his Jewish community.

The material effects of this ethereal culture find expression in the interplay between audience and community. This was what confused the fictional Reb Yankev Lieb in the cartoon from 1926, but it also enabled WMIL to ask for a special suspension of its services, Zvee Scooler to encourage his audience to buy war bonds, and Sheindele di Khazente to maintain her veneer of piety. The imagined communities enabled by radio did not exist solely as fantasies but as actual manifestations of shared sensibilities. Yiddish radio allowed one particular imagining to take place; English-language radio promised another. And neither existed exclusive of the other.

Yet these effects share the essential fact that they revolve around notions of community constituted by participation in a shared aural culture. When Bertha Hart asked her audience to sing the "Star Spangled Banner" and they failed, that, too, gave voice to the culture of Yiddish radio as a venue for communal expression and the articulation of its limits. The culture of Yiddish radio developed out of those sometimes contradictory desires and created a context in which they could be heard as complementary. American radio did not confirm contemporary fears that it would disintegrate community bonds by turning people's attention elsewhere. Nor did it succeed in affirming the hope that it could unify a nation. It worked far more subtly in both ways; it distracted some listeners and created audiences of others. In the case of Yiddish radio, these twin dynamics allowed audiences to listen themselves from an audience into a community and from a community into an audience.

Notes

INTRODUCTION

Epigraphs: *Jewish Daily Forward*, 4 February 1933; Joseph Rakhlin, "Di nudne lidlekh un di oysgedroshene khokhmes af di radyo programen," *Jewish Daily Forward*, 10 August 1932, 3.

1. Audio recording, *The Jewish Hour*, 9 November 1936, YIVO Sound Archive. See also Yiddish Radio Project [realmedia], David Isay and Henry Sapoznik, www.yiddishradioproject.org; accessed 5 March 2005.

2. Gleason L. Archer, *History of Radio to 1926* (New York: Arno Press, 1951); Erik Barnouw, *A Tower of Babel: A History of Broadcasting in the United States to 1933* (New York: Oxford University Press, 1966).

3. Mark Goodman, "The Radio Act of 1927 as a Product of Progressivism," available at www.scripps.ohiou.edu/mediahistory/mhmjour2-2.htm. Accessed 19 January 2005. The article was published electronically in the Media History Monographs series.

4. Herbert Hoover, "Opening Address," in *Recommendations for the Regulation*

of Radio Adopted by the Third National Radio Conference (Washington, DC: U.S. Government Printing Office, 1924), 3.

5. Ibid., 2–3.

6. Ibid., 2.

7. Charles Henry Stamps, *The Concept of the Mass Audience in American Broadcasting: An Historical-Descriptive Study* (New York: Arno Press, 1979).

8. None of the transcripts from the four radio conferences or any of the popular English-language journalism of the time paid any attention to the audiences of immigrants who may have wanted to listen to programs in languages other than English.

9. Herbert Hoover, "Opening Address," in *Proceedings of the Fourth National Radio Conference and Recommendations for the Regulation of Radio 7*, November 9–11, 1925 (Washington, DC: Government Printing Office, 1926).

10. Much has been written about audiences and much work has been dedicated to "reception theory." I restrict my notes here to a few works that shaped my thinking about and approach to this area: Ien Eng, *Desperately Seeking the Audience* (New York: Routledge, 1991); John Fiske, *Power Plays, Power Works* (New York: Verso, 1993); Stuart Hall, "Encoding/Decoding," in *Culture, Media, Language: Working Papers in Cultural Studies*, ed. Centre for Contemporary Cultural Studies, 1972–79 (London: Hutchinson, 1980), 128–38; Janice Radway, *Reading the Romance* (New York: Verso, 1987).

11. Michelle Hilmes and Jason Loviglio, eds., *The Radio Reader: Essays in the Cultural History of Radio* (New York: Routledge, 2001).

12. David Siegel and Susan Siegel, *Radio and the Jews: The Untold Story of How Radio Influenced America's Image of Jews* (Yorktown Heights, NY: Book Hunter Press, 2007).

13. Michelle Hilmes does this in the introduction to *Radio Voices*. Although she qualifies her argument by observing that the major broadcasting interests do not comprise "one uncontested discourse," she concedes that they were "the one that dominates out of the many . . . voices that make up the whole of broadcast experience" and subsequently focuses her critique on the networks almost exclusively. Michelle Hilmes, *Radio Voices: American Broadcasting, 1922–1952* (Minneapolis: University of Minnesota Press, 1997), xvii.

14. Tona J. Hangen, *Redeeming the Dial: Radio, Religion and Popular Culture in America* (Chapel Hill: University of North Carolina Press, 2002). More generally, there are a few books that contribute to our understanding of radio in the United States. For an ethnographic analysis of one particular acoustic community, see Howard Dorgan, *The Airwaves of Zion: Radio and Religion in Appalachia* (Knoxville: University of Tennessee Press, 1993). Hal Erickson compiled a catalog of programs and people involved in religious broadcasting, but his work attends only to English programs and gives almost no attention to Jewish programs of

any sort. Hal Erickson, *Religious Radio and Television in the United States, 1921–1991: The Programs and Personalities* (Jefferson, NC: MacFarland, 1992).

15. Another interesting story in need of further exploration is the story of Israeli radio and the place of Yiddish and Arabic within it. But that, too, is a totally different context from the one at issue in this book. See Derek Jonathan Penslar, "Transmitting Jewish Culture: Radio in Israel," *Jewish Social Studies* 10, no. 1 (Fall 2003): 1–29.

16. Some of the best examples of this scholarship are James Baughman, *Republic of Mass Culture: Broadcasting in the U.S. since 1941* (Baltimore, MD: Johns Hopkins University Press, 1997); Douglas Czitrom, *Media and the American Mind: From Morse to Mcluhan* (Chapel Hill: University of North Carolina Press, 1982); Robert McChesney, *Telecommunications, Mass Media and Democracy: The Battle for Control of U.S. Broadcasting, 1928–1935* (New York: Oxford University Press, 1993).

17. Some examples of this school of scholarship are Bill Crawford and Gene Fowler, *Border Radio: Quacks, Yodelers, Pitchmen, Psychics, and Other Amazing Broadcasters of the American Airwaves* (Austin: University of Texas Press, 2002); Jeff Land, *Active Radio; Pacifica's Brash Experiment* (Minneapolis: University of Minnesota Press, 1999); Jesse Walker, *Rebels on the Air: An Alternative History of Radio in America* (New York: New York University Press, 2004).

18. Susan Smulyan, *Selling Radio: The Commercialization of American Broadcasting, 1920–1943* (Washington, DC: Smithsonian Institution Press, 1994).

19. Fred J. Macdonald, *Don't Touch That Dial! Radio Programming in American Life from 1920–1960* (Chicago: Nelson-Hall, 1979).

20. Ruth Glasser, *Music Is My Flag: Puerto Rican Musicians and Their Communities, 1917–1940* (Berkeley: University of California Press, 1997); Rudolph Vecoli, Cathleen Neils Conzen, David Gerber, Ewa Morawska, and George Pozzetta, "The Invention of Ethnicity: A Perspective from the U.S.A.," *Journal of American Ethnic History* 12 (1992): 3–41; Rudolph Vecoli, "Contadini in Chicago: A Critique of the Uprooted," *Journal of American History* 1, no. 3 (1964): 404–17.

21. Hasia R. Diner, *Hungering for America: Italian, Irish, and Jewish Foodways in the Age of Migration* (Cambridge, MA: Harvard University Press, 2001); Rebecca Kobrin, "Conflicting Diasporas, Shifting Centers: Migration and Identity in a Transnational Polish Jewish Community, 1878–1952," Ph.D. dissertation, University of Pennsylvania, 2002; Kerby Miller, *Emigrants and Exiles: Ireland and the Irish Exodus to the United States* (New York: Oxford University Press, 1988).

22. Jacob Rader Marcus and American Jewish Archives, *To Count a People: American Jewish Population Data, 1585–1984* (Lanham, MD: University Press of America, 1990).

23. Seth Rogovoy, *The Essential Klezmer* (Chapel Hill, NC: Algonquin Books, 2000); Henry Sapoznik and Pete Sokolow, *The Compleat Klezmer* (New York: Hal

Leonard, 1987); Mark Slobin, ed., *American Klezmer* (New York: Oxford University Press, 2003).

24. David Biale, ed., *The Cultures of the Jews* (New York: Schocken Books, 2002); Emanuel Goldsmith, *Modern Yiddish Culture: The Story of the Yiddish Language Movement* (New York: Fordham University Press, 1997); Naomi Seidman, *A Marriage Made in Heaven: The Sexual Politics of Hebrew and Yiddish* (Berkeley: University of California Press, 1997); David Shneer, *Yiddish and the Creation of Soviet Jewish Culture: 1918–1930* (New York: Cambridge University Press, 2004). For the most comprehensive account of the history of the Yiddish language, see Max Weinreich, *History of the Yiddish Language* (Chicago: University of Chicago Press, 1980).

25. Sholem Aleichem, *In amerika: motl peysi dem hazns un andere mayses* (New York: Varheyt, 1918; reprint Amherst, MA: National Yiddish Book Center, 1999).

26. Sholom Aleichem, *Motl, the Cantor's Son*, trans. Hillel Halkin (New Haven, CT: Yale University Press, 2002), 266. All of the transliterations and translations that appear in connection with this text are Halkin's.

27. Aleichem, *In amerika*, 198.

28. Deborah Dash Moore, *At Home in America: New York's Second Generation Jews* (New York, NY: Columbia University Press, 1991), 11.

29. Hannah Kliger, *Jewish Hometown Associations and Family Circles in New York* (Bloomington: University of Indiana Press, 1992); Isaac Rontch, ed., *Di idishe landsmanschaften fun nyu york* (New York: Yiddish Writers' Union, 1938); Daniel Soyer, *Jewish Immigrant Associations and American Identity in New York, 1890–1939* (Cambridge, MA: Harvard University Press, 1997); Michael Weisser, *A Brotherhood of Memory: Jewish Landsmanshaftn in the New World* (New York: Basic Books, 1985).

30. Jeffrey Shandler, *Adventures in Yiddishland: Postvernacular Language and Culture* (Berkeley: University of California Press, 2005), 74. Shandler drew his statistics from Zalmen Yefroykin, "Yiddish Education in the United States" (in Yiddish), in *Algemeyne entsiklopedye* (General Encyclopedia), vol. *yidn: hey* (Jews: 5) (New York: Dubnov-fond, 1957), 209.

31. Barry Truax, *Acoustic Communication* (Norwood, NJ: Ablex, 1984), 58. Original emphasis.

32. *Jewish Daily Forward*, 30 December 1962; quoted in David Silverman, "The Jewish Press: A Quadrilingual Phenomenon," in *The Religious Press in America*, ed. Martin Marty (New York: Holt, Reinhart, and Winston, 1962), 132. See also S. Margoshes, "The Jewish Press in New York City," in *The Jewish Communal Register of New York City: 1917–1918* (New York: Kehillah [Jewish Community] of New York City, 1918).

33. Andrew Heinze, *Adapting to Abundance* (New York: Columbia University Press, 1991), 119.

34. Nahma Sandrow, *Vagabond Stars: A World History of Yiddish Theater* (Syracuse, NY: University of Syracuse Press, 1977); Mark Slobin, *Tenement Songs: The Popular Music of the Jewish Immigrants* (Urbana: University of Illinois Press, 1982).

35. Paul Gilroy, *The Black Atlantic: Modernity and Double Consciousness* (Cambridge, MA: Harvard University Press, 1993).

36. Slobin, *American Klezmer,* 11.

37. David Lifson, *The Yiddish Theater in America* (New York: T. Yoseloff and Sons, 1965).

38. Mordecai Soltes, *The Yiddish Press, an Americanizing Agency* (New York: Teachers College Press, 1950).

39. This is discussed in greater detail in chapter 2.

40. Lawrence W. Levine and Cornelia R. Levine, *The People and the President: America's Conversation with FDR* (Boston, MA: Beacon Press, 2002); Jason Loviglio, *Radio's Intimate Public: Network Broadcasting and Mass-Mediated Democracy* (Minneapolis: University of Minnesota Press, 2005).

41. There are countless books chronicling and cataloging this period of radio history. The two most helpful are John Dunning, *On the Air: The Encyclopedia of Old-Time Radio* (New York: Oxford University Press, 1998); and John Dunning, *Tune in Yesterday: The Ultimate Encyclopedia of Old-Time Radio, 1925–1976* (Englewood Cliffs, NJ: Prentice-Hall, 1976).

42. Christopher Sterling and John Kittross, *Stay Tuned: A Concise History of Broadcasting in America* (Belmont, CA: Wadsworth, 1990).

43. Claude S. Fischer, *America Calling: A Social History of the Telephone to 1940* (Berkeley: University of California Press, 1992), 9.

44. Clifford Geertz, *The Interpretation of Cultures* (New York: Basic Books, 1973), 20.

45. Dick Hebdige, *Subculture, the Meaning of Style* (New York: Routledge, 1989).

46. Raymond Williams, *Marxism and Literature* (New York: Oxford University Press, 1978), 132.

47. Benedict R. Anderson, *Imagined Communities: Reflections on the Origin and Spread of Nationalism,* rev. and extended ed. (London: Verso, 1991).

48. Moore, *At Home in America;* see also Gerald H. Gamm, *Urban Exodus: Why the Jews Left Boston and the Catholics Stayed* (Cambridge, MA: Harvard University Press, 1999).

49. The best account of Jewish communal activity during the 1930s is Beth S. Wenger, *New York Jews and the Great Depression: Uncertain Promise* (New Haven, CT: Yale University Press, 1996). For an account of Jewish activity in the Socialist movement earlier in the century, see Tony Michels, *A Fire in Their Hearts: Yiddish Socialists in New York* (Cambridge, MA: Harvard University Press, 2005).

50. For two interesting and divergent accounts of audience formation, see Richard Butsch, *The Making of American Audiences: From Stage to Television, 1750–1990*, Cambridge Studies in the History of Mass Communications (Cambridge: Cambridge University Press, 2000); and Stamps, *Concept of the Mass Audience in American Broadcasting*. Butsch builds an argument about the interaction of audiences and mass media. Stamps explores and critiques the notion of "audience" as used by the radio industry. More on this in chapter 2.

1. FROM THE MAINSTREAM TO THE MARGIN

Epigraphs:*Jewish Daily Forward*, 3 August 1924, 3; Carl Dreher, "As a Broadcaster Sees It," *Radio Broadcast* 6 (March 1925): 870.

1. Erik Barnouw, *A Tower of Babel: A History of Broadcasting in the United States to 1933* (New York: Oxford University Press, 1966).

2. Susan Douglas, *The Invention of American Broadcasting, 1899–1922* (Baltimore, MD: Johns Hopkins University Press, 1987).

3. Charles Coolidge Parlin, *The Merchandising of Radio* (Philadelphia: Curtis Publishing Company, 1925), 4, 6.

4. See Ben Singer, "Nickelodeon Boom in Manhattan," In *Entertaining America: Jews, Movies, and Broadcasting*, ed. J. Hoberman and Jeffrey Shandler (New York and Princeton: Jewish Museum, under the auspices of the Jewish Theological Seminary of America, and Princeton University Press, 2003).

5. John Kasson, *Amusing the Million: Coney Island at the Turn of the Century* (New York: Hill and Wang, 1978); Kathy Peiss, *Cheap Amusements: Working Women and Leisure in Turn-of-the-Century New York* (Philadelphia: Temple University Press, 1986).

6. Mordecai Soltes, *The Yiddish Press, an Americanizing Agency* (New York: Teachers College Press, 1950), 24, table 4. He reported that another sample yielded similar results, with 55 percent reading English papers in addition to Yiddish ones.

7. *New York Times*, 30 August 1923, 6:2.

8. *Jewish Daily Forward*, 13 September, 1923, 5.

9. Ibid., 6 October 1923, 14.

10. Ibid., 3 April 1926.

11. Douglas, *Invention of American Broadcasting*, 36.

12. *Jewish Daily Forward*, 3 April 1926.

13. Stephen C. Vladeck, "Interview with Stephen C. Vladeck," 1974, ed. Alice Herb, American Jewish Committee, Oral History Library.

14. Baruch Charney Vladeck to David Sarnoff, President of RCA, 22 August

1923, Baruch Charney Vladeck Papers, reel #9, Tamiment Library, New York University.

15. *Jewish Daily Forward,* 3 August 1924, 3.

16. Ibid., 5 September 1923, 2.

17. *Der tog,* 5 March 1924.

18. Rubin Goldberg and M. Brooks, *Shloime afn radio* (Columbia Records, Master no. E9103, June 1923).

19. *Der tog,* 22 May 1926.

20. Ibid., 20 November 1924.

21. Ibid.

22. J. Hoberman, *Bridge of Light: Yiddish Cinema between Two Worlds* (Philadelphia: Temple University Press, 1995). Hoberman noted that the 1927 film was adapted in 1934, given dialogue and a sound track, and rereleased as a new Yiddish film, *Oy iz dus a shviger* (Oh! What a Mother-in-Law).

23. Rubin Goldberg, *Moyshe koyft a radio* (arr. Alexander Olshanetsky) (Brunswick 67132, Master no. E28720, 10 November 1928).

24. Published by Solomon Rosowsky, 1914.

25. Picon appeared in character as Sadie the Saleslady on *Entin's Radio Program. Jewish Daily Forward,* 9 October 1929.

26. Picon kept the reviews of the performance, which were lukewarm, but each one made special mention of her return to the Yiddish stage. Scrapbook, 1928–1932, Molly Picon Collection, American Jewish Historical Society, New York.

27. *Jewish Daily Forward,* 27 January 1926.

28. The program aired at 11:20 P.M. on Tuesday, 9 February 1926. The listing appeared in the *New York Times,* 6 February 1926.

29. *Chicago Tribune,* 1 July 1927, 18.

30. *Kalifornyer idishe shtime* (California Jewish Voice), 9 October 1931.

31. Ibid. On 17 January 1936, the program celebrated its hundredth episode, but by 1941, Los Angeles's Jewish newspapers carried no information about Yiddish radio programming.

32. *Chicago Daily Tribune,* 3 August 1927, 18.

33. Nathan Godfried, *WCFL:Chicago's Voice of Labor, 1926–78* (Champaign: University of Illinois Press, 1997).

34. *Idishe velt,* 16 January 1928.

35. Ibid.

36. Seeking a broader audience, *Der tog* even ran a series of bilingual Yiddish-English advertisements in the *New York Times,* 5 October 1928. The ever-competitive *Forward* listed it in its pages only as a "Yiddish program."

37. At the corner of Christie and Delancy Streets, a hub of pedestrian and motor traffic on the Lower East Side.

38. *New York Times,* 18 May 1926, 2:5.

39. Ibid., 11 May 1926, 24.

40. *Jewish Daily Forward,* 21 May 1926.

41. Ibid., 23 May 1926.

42. Ibid., 3 June 1926.

43. Ibid., 20 June 1926.

44. Ibid., 18 May 1926.

45. Henry Sapoznik, liner notes to *Jakie Jazz 'em Up: Old Time Klezmer Music, 1912–1926* (Global Village Music, 1993). See Also Henry Sapoznik and Pete Sokolow, *The Compleat Klezmer* (New York: Tara Publications, 1986). The *1940 Radio Annual* included an advertisement for a Josef Cherniavsky, then the musical director of WLW-WSAI in Cincinnati, Ohio. Cherniavsky had created and conducted programs such as *Musical Steeplechase, Musical Camera,* and *My Lucky Break.* This was a far cry from the Lower East Side. Jack Alicoate, ed., *1940 Radio Annual* (New York: Radio Daily, 1940), 744.

46. *Wall Street Journal,* 7 January 1931. By 1930, approximately 15 percent of New York's Jews remained on the Lower East Side.

47. *Jewish Daily Forward,* 12 October 1927.

48. Ibid., 25 April 1926; 5 June 1926; 2 April 1928.

49. Ibid., 5 June 1926.

50. Ibid., 4 July 1926.

2. AMERICANIZATION, AUDIENCE, COMMUNITY, CONSUMERS

Epigraphs: Commerce Secretary Herbert Hoover, envisioning the radio audience at the fourth national radio conference, quoted in *Proceedings of the Fourth National Radio Conference and Recommendations for the Regulation of Radio* 7, 9–11 November 1925 (Washington, DC: U.S. Government Printing Office, 1926); Roy S. Durstine, "The Future of Radio Advertising in the United States," *Annals of the American Academy of Political and Social Science, Radio: The Fifth Estate* 177 (January 1935): 150.

1. The efforts to curtail European immigration are well documented. One of the most extensive efforts to connect racial pseudoscience and immigration policy is Edwin Black, *War against the Weak: Eugenics and America's Campaign to Create a Master Race* (New York: Four Walls, Eight Windows, 2003); John Higham, *Strangers in the Land: Patterns of American Nativism, 1860–1925* (New Brunswick, NJ: Rutgers University Press, 1955); Walter Nugent, *Crossings: The Great Transatlantic Migrations, 1870–1914* (Bloomington: University of Indiana Press, 1992).

2. President Calvin Coolidge, "State of the Union Address," 6 December 1923. www.presidency.ucsb.edu/ws/index.php?pid=29564. Accessed 10 July 2008.

3. Calvin Coolidge, "Whose Country Is This?" *Good Housekeeping* 72 (February 1921): 14. There is substantial literature on the racialism of the anti-immigration movement, most significantly, Higham, *Strangers in the Land.*

4. For discussion of this topic, see Ruth Crocker, *Social Work and Social Order:The Settlement Movement in Two Industrial Cities, 1889–1930* (Urbana: University of Illinois Press, 1992); Donna Gabaccia, *From the Other Side: Women, Gender, and Immigrant Life in the U.S., 1820–1990* (Bloomington: Indiana University Press, 1994); Rivka Shpak Lissak, *Pluralism and Progressives: Hull House and the New Immigrants, 1890–1919* (Chicago: University of Chicago Press, 1989); Joel Perlmann, *Ethnic Differences: Schooling and Social Structure among the Irish, Italian, Jews, and Blacks in an American City* (Cambridge: Cambridge University Press, 1988).

5. Susan Douglas, *The Invention of American Broadcasting, 1899–1922* (Baltimore, MD: Johns Hopkins University Press, 1987), 303–14.

6. J.M. McKibbin, "The New Way to Make Americans," *Radio Broadcast* 2, no. 3 (January 1923): 238–39.

7. Ibid., 239.

8. Quoted in Susan Douglas, *Listening In: Radio and the American Imagination* (Minneapolis: University of Minnesota Press, 2004), 76.

9. The Zenith Corporation, which owned WJAZ, effectively forced the issue by unilaterally changing both its frequency and its broadcast hours and interrupting a broadcast by a Canadian station. The U.S. Commerce Department, under whose auspices radio fell, responded by filing a suit against WJAZ in Illinois Federal District Court for violating the agreement. The text of the ruling is available on-line: www.fcc.gov/mb/audio/decdoc/misc/US_v_Zenith_Radio_Corporation.html. Accessed 5 May 2006.

10. Quoted in Erwin G. Krasnow, *The Public Interest Standard: The Elusive Search for the Holy Grail*, Briefing Paper Prepared for the Avisory Committee on Public Interest Obligations of Digital Television Broadcasters (1997). Available at www.ntia.doc.gov/pubintadvcom/octmtg/Krasnow.htm. Accessed 18 April 2001.

11. *Congressional Record*, 69th Cong., lst sess., 1926, vol. 67, pt. 5: 5479.

12. Richard Butsch, *The Making of American Audiences: From Stage to Television, 1750–1990*, Cambridge Studies in the History of Mass Communications (Cambridge: Cambridge University Press, 2000), 1–15.

13. *Congressional Record*, 70th Cong., 1st sess., 1928, vol. 69, pt. 4: 3987.

14. The precise reasons for the great disparity between ownership rates of African Americans as compared to native-born whites or even white ethnic immigrants remain the source of critical scholarly inquiry. To date, the most

insightful argument has been offered by Derek Valliant, who takes into account both cultural and economic differences. Derek Vaillant, "Sounds of Whiteness: Local Radio, Racial Formation, and Public Culture in Chicago, 1921–1935," *American Quarterly* 54, no. 1 (2002): 35–66.

15. *Congressional Record,* 70th Cong., 1st sess., 1928, vol. 69, pt. 4: 3876.

16. *New York Times,* 29 May 1928, 18.

17. Ibid., 9 July 1928, 26.

18. Ibid., 18 July 1928, 24.

19. Ibid., 28 July 1928, 15.

20. Ibid., 29 May 1928, 18.

21. Federal Radio Commission, General Order 40, U.S. Department of Commerce, *Radio Service Bulletin,* 31 August 1928.

22. *New York Herald Tribune,* 11 September 1928; reprinted in Bill Jaker, Frank Sulek, and Peter Kanze, *The Airwaves of New York: Illustrated Histories of 156 AM Stations in the Metropolitan Area, 1921–1996* (Jefferson, NC: McFarland and Co., 1998), 10; *New York Times,* 11 November 1928.

23. Douglas B. Craig, *Fireside Politics: Radio and Political Culture in the United States, 1920–1940* (Baltimore, MD: Johns Hopkins University Press, 2000).

24. FCC Order, 1 October 1935, WEVD Station File, Deleted Station Files, FCC Archives, Record Group 173, NARA, College Park, MD.

25. Neil Cowan and Ruth Schwartz Cowan, *Our Parents Lives: The Americanization of Eastern European Jews* (New York: Basic Books, 1989), xix.

26. *New York Times,* 18 December 1927, II:2.

27. Letter from Arthur Faske, Owner Radio Broadcast Station WMIL, to Federal Radio Commission, 30 September 1932, WBKN Station File; Federal Communications Commission Broadcast License Series, Federal Radio Commission Closed Segment of Active Stations 1927 through 7–11–34, FCC Archives, Record Group 173, NARA, Sutland, MD.

28. Commissioner's Report, 6 January 1933, In Re: Applications of WWRL Docket 1742 and 1735, WMBQ, Docket 1743 and 1733, WMIL Docket 1727, WBKN Station File; Federal Communications Commission Broadcast License Series,; Federal Radio Commission Closed Segment of Active Stations 1927 through 7–11–34, FCC Archives, Record Group 173, NARA, Sutland, MD.

29. Quoted in the *New York Times,* 2 March 1934, 16. In fact, Walker was really trying to bring the Brooklyn stations into line with the Davis Amendment. In his report, he concluded, "The denial of the [renewal] applications here involved would result in decreasing the present over-quota status of the state of New York." Examiner's Report 539, 23 February 1934, WBBC Station File, Deleted Station Files, FCC Archives, Record Group 173, NARA, College Park, MD.

30. G. August Gerber, 27 March 1934, excerpted in Examiner's Report 539.

31. Susan Smulyan, *Selling Radio: The Commercialization of American Broadcasting, 1920–1943* (Washington, DC: Smithsonian Institution Press, 1994).

32. FCC Order, 1 October 1935.

33. Ibid.

34. Spencer Miller Jr., "Radio and Religion," *Annals of the American Academy of Political and Social Science*, no. 177 (1935): 123–28.

35. Letter from Rabbi Levinthal to station WRAX, 7 January 1931, Levinthal Papers, Philadelphia Jewish Archives; Roger Tabak, "Orthodox Judaism in Transition," in *Jewish Life in Philadelphia: 1830–1940*, ed. Murray Friedman (Philadelphia: Ishi Publications, 1983), 48–64.

36. Gertrude Berg, *Molly and Me* (New York: McGraw Hill, 1961). Transliteration in the original.

37. *Jewish Daily Forward*, 19 May 1928.

38. Ibid., 4 February 1928; 10 March 1928.

39. Ibid., 1 September 1929.

40. Letter from Peter Testan of WBBC to James Baldwin, secretary of the FRC, 1 June 1931, WBBC Station File 61–3, Deleted Station Files, Record Group 173, Federal Radio Commission Collection, NARA, College Park, MD.

41. Ibid.

42. Copy of letter from FRC Secretary James Baldwin to Mr. A. Schiller, 31 August 1931, WBBC Station File 61–3, Deleted Station Files, Record Group 173, FRC Archives, NARA, College Park, MD.

43. FCC Examiner's Report I-40, 12 April 1935, WEVD Station File 89–6, FCC Station Files, Record Group 173, NARA, College Park, MD

44. FCC Order, 1 October 1935.

45. FCC Examiner's Report I-40, 12 April 1935.

46. Letter from Peter Testan to President Franklin Delano Roosevelt, 19 March 1934, WBBC Station File, Deleted Station Files, FCC Archives, Record Group 173, NARA, College Park, MD.

47. Western Union Telegram from Brooklyn Broadcasting Corporation to FRC, 20 April 1934, WBBC Station File, Deleted Station Files, FCC Archives, Record Group 173, NARA, College Park, MD.

48. Letter from Peter Testan to Secretary Sykes, 29 November 1934, WBBC Station File, Deleted Station Files, FCC Archives, Record Group 173, NARA, College Park, MD.

49. FCC Order, 1 October 1935.

50. FCC Examiner Report I-40, 12 April 1935.

51. Ibid.

52. Ira Rozenwaike, *Population History of New York City* (Syracuse, NY: Syracuse University Press, 1972), 133, table 64, "Population of the Boroughs of New York City by Race and Nativity, 1900–1970." See also Commissioner's Report; In

Re: Brooklyn Broadcasting Corporation, Station WBBC (Docket #1882), WEVD Station File, Deleted Station Files, FCC Archives, Record Group 173, NARA, College Park, MD.

53. Commissioner's Report, In Re: Brooklyn Broadcasting Corporation, Station WBBC (Docket #1882), WEVD Station File, Deleted Station Files, FCC Archives, Record Group 173, NARA, College Park, MD, 16.

54. Commissioner's Report, In Re: Brooklyn Broadcasting Corporation, Station WBBC (Docket #1882).

55. Commissioner's Report, In Re: The Voice of Brooklyn, Inc., Station WLTH (Docket #1967), WBBC Station File, Deleted Station Files, FCC Archives, Record Group 173, NARA, College Park, MD.

56. Ibid., 16.

3. LISTENING TO THEMSELVES

Epigraphs: Jack Alicoate, ed., *Radio Annual* (New York: Radio Daily, 1939), 919; *Teater un radio velt* 1, no. 1 (April 1935): 1.

1. U.S. Bureau of the Census, *Fifteenth Census of the United States: 1930: Population* (Washington, DC: U.S. Government Printing Office, 1933), 52–53.

2. Ibid., 70.

3. Harry Barron, "Leisure-Time Interests, Preferences, and Activities of Children on the Lower East Side of New York City" (Graduate School for Jewish Social Work, 1935), 175.

4. Ibid., 402.

5. Michelle Hilmes, *Radio Voices: American Broadcasting, 1922–1952* (Minneapolis: University of Minnesota Press, 1997), 86.

6. *Teater un radio velt* 1, no. 2 (October 1935): 4.

7. Sholom Rubenstein, "Speech Delivered at the New School University," 19 January 1993, National Jewish Archive of Broadcasting, New York.

8. *Jewish Daily Forward*, 10 October 1928.

9. The book appeared first in Yiddish under the title *Arum der velt mit yidishen teater* (Around the World with Yiddish Theater). In English, the book was published as *Der Payatz*. See note 10 below.

10. Herman Yablokoff, *Der Payatz: Around the World with Yiddish Theater*, trans. Belle Mysell (Silver Spring, MD: Bartleby Press, 1995), 309–10.

11. *Idishe velt*, 16 January 1928.

12. *Der tog*, 1 October 1928.

13. *Jewish Daily Forward*, 22 September 1932.

14. Ibid., 17 September 1932. *Patriotn* is a term for the devoted and sometimes thuggish groups of fans of Yiddish theater stars.

15. Interview with Baruch Lumet, by Anita M. Wincelberg, 12 December 1976 and 28 April 1977, William E. Wiener Oral History Library of the American Jewish Committee, Dorot Jewish Division of the New York Public Library.

16. Zalman Zilbercweig, ed., *Leksikon fun yidishen teater* (New York: Farlag Elisheva, 1931–69).

17. Interview with Baruch Lumet.

18. A serial called *Bay a glezl tey* (By a Glass of Tea) aired briefly in spring 1929 on WMCA.

19. Sidney Lumet went on to become a successful Hollywood director.

20. Interview with Baruch Lumet, 171.

21. Interview with Baruch Lumet, 173.

22. Molly Picon, *Molly! An Autobiography* (New York: Simon and Schuster, 1980), 75.

23. Ibid., 81.

24. Nathan Zolotareff, "Art Paramount Aim of Three Yiddish Stars," newsclipping, 1 April, 1938, no source, Sholom Secunda Collection, Box 4, YIVO Archives, New York.

25. Interview with Baruch Lumet, 173.

26. Interview with Freydele Oysher, audiorecording, YIVO Sound Archive, New York.

27. *Jewish Examiner,* 22 June 1934.

28. Raymond Williams, *Marxism and Literature* (New York: Oxford University Press, 1978, 132.

29. *New York Times,* 5 August 1927, 14.

30. "IN RE: Application of Debs Memorial Radio Fund, Inc.," Docket #969, 3 November 1931, Federal Communications Commission Broadcast License Series, Federal Radio Commission Closed Segment of Active Stations 1927 through 7–11–34, WEVD Station File, FCC Archives, NARA, Sutland, MD.

31. *New York Times,* 27 September 1931, 1:4.

32. WEVD Broadcast License Renewal Application, 30 December 1930, Federal Communications Commission Broadcast License Series, Federal Radio Commission Closed Segment of Active Stations 1927 through 7–11–34, WEVD Station File; FCC Archives, NARA, Sutland, MD.

33. WEVD Broadcast License Renewal Application, 27 September 1929 and 11 October 1930, Federal Communications Commission Broadcast License Series, Federal Radio Commission Closed Segment of Active Stations 1927 through 7–11–34, WEVD Station File, FCC Archives; NARA, Sutland, MD.

34. "Radio in Education," pamphlet issued at the dedication of the new WEVD Studios, 11 November 1938, WEVD File, Tamiment Archives, New York University.

35. Morris Novik, "Interview with Morris Novik [Novick]," ed. Seymour

Segal and Marcus Cohen, American Jewish Committee, Oral History Library, 1980. For more on Novick's involvement in WEVD and the Socialist Party, see Nathan Godfried, "Struggling over Politics and Culture: Organized Labor and Radio Station WEVD during the 1930s," *Labor History* 42, no. 4 (2001): 347–69.

36. FCC Order, 1 October 1935, WEVD Station File, Deleted Station Files, FCC Archives, Record Group 173, NARA, College Park, MD.

37. When asked to list its best programs in the *Radio Annual* in 1938, WEVD did not select any Yiddish programs.

38. Christopher Sterling and John Kittross, *Stay Tuned: A Concise History of Broadcasting in America* (Belmont, CA: Wadsworth, 1990).

39. *Der tog*, 1 May 1932.

40. Ibid., 4 September 1933.

41. Ibid., 16 April 1934.

42. *Jewish Daily Forward*, 15 September 1932.

43. David Isay and Henry Sapozkik, Yiddish Radio Project [realmedia], David Isay and Henry Sapoznik, www.yiddishradioproject.org. Accessed 5 March 2005.

44. Mendel Osherovitch Collection, Files 43–62, YIVO Archives, New York.

45. Max Oxenhandler, "The Jewish Youth of the East Side," *Jewish Forum* 6, no. 1 (January 1923): 61. Quoted in Jeffrey S. Gurock, *From Fluidity to Rigidity: The Religious Worlds of Conservative and Orthodox Jews in Twentieth-Century America*, pamphlet (Ann Arbor: Jean & Samuel Frankel Center for Judaic Studies, University of Michigan, 1998).

46. *Jewish Daily Forward*, 30 March 1931.

47. *Chicago Jewish Chronicle*, 6 May 1932.

48. Kadya Molodowsky, "Bronzvil [Brownsville]," in *Der melekh dovid aleyn iz geblibn* (King David Alone Remains), trans. Kathryn Hellerstein (New York: Papirene Brik, 1946), IV.1–12, 17–20. Cited in Kathryn Hellerstein, "Finding Her Yiddish Voice: Kadya Molodowsky in America," *Sources* 12 (2002): 48–68.

49. *Jewish Daily Forward*, 2 November 1938.

50. *Der tog*, 22 December 1936. Also, the cover of one of the booklets was reprinted in J. Hoberman and Jeffrey Shandler, eds., *Entertaining America: Jews, Movies and Broadcasting* (Princeton, NJ: Princeton University Press, 2003).

51. Jason Loviglio, *Radio's Intimate Public: Network Broadcasting and Mass-Mediated Democracy* (Minneapolis: University of Minnesota Press, 2005), xxiv–xxv. Elena Razlogova begins her dissertation on listeners' letters with a slightly different account of radio's intimacy. Elena Razlogova, "The Voice of the Listener: Americans and the Radio Industry, 1920–1950," Ph.D. dissertation, George Mason University, 2003.

52. Deborah Dash Moore, *At Home in America: Second Generation New York Jews* (New York: Columbia University Press, 1991).

53. *Jewish Daily Forward*, 8 March 1937, 8.

54. "The Jewish Philosopher's League Charter," *Jewish Philosopher* 1 (November 1937): 1.

55. All the recordings of Der yiddisher filosof that are cited here are available, with translations, through the Web site of the Yiddish Radio Project: www .yiddishradioproject.org. Accessed 5 March 2005.

56. Yiddish Radio Project, at www.yiddishradioproject.org.

57. Zachary Baker, ed., *The Lawrence Marwick Collection of Copyrighted Yiddish Plays at the Library of Congress* (Washington, DC: Library of Congress, 1998), 1170.

58. Ibid., 1162.

59. *Der tog*, 14 December 1936.

60. *Mein mutter un ikh*, radio script, Episode 1, 5 January 1942, WEVD Collection, Box 18, YIVO Archives, New York.

61. Ibid.

62. Ibid., Episode 18.

63. Marc Schweid, *Jews in American History*, radio script, Marc Schweid Archive, Box 2, YIVO Institute, New York.

64. Ibid., Episode 4.

65. *Jewish Daily Forward*, 22 September 1932; 9 November 1932; 4 February 1933.

66. Letter from Rae Innerfeld to Zvee Scooler, 18 October 1942, File 43, Zvee Scooler Papers, YIVO Archives.

67. Letter from Ben Gutwilling to Victor Packer, 12 March 1935, Box 10, Victor Packer Papers, unprocessed, YIVO Archives.

68. For example, Rabbi Joseph Leibowitz, who served the East Flatbush Jewish Community Center, used WLTH to broadcast his Friday afternoon sermons, whose titles included "Laughter, Derision and Ridicule," "Gossip," "The Truth and the Lie," "A Contemporary Treatise on Kosher Meat," and other contemporary interpretations of the weekly Torah portion. Rabbi Jacob Leibowitz, *Radyo redes* (Radio Addresses) (Brooklyn, NY: Printed by author, 1940).

69. Mark Slobin, *Golden Voices: The Story of the American Cantorate* (Bloomington: University of Illinois Press, 2002). For accounts of the recording careers of specific cantors, see Zevulun Kwartin, *Mayn leben* (My Life) (Amherst, MA: National Yiddish Book Center, 2000; orig. pub. Philadelphia: Gezelshaftlikhen komitet, 1952); Rabbi Samuel Rosenblatt, *Yossele Rosenblatt: The Story of His Life as Told by His Son* (New York: Farrar, Straus and Young, 1954).

70. Interview with Freydele Oysher, audiorecording, YIVO Archives, New York.

71. "Biographical Sketch," 25 January 1944, handbill, Jean Gornish Collection, National Museum of American Jewish History, Philadelphia.

72. Ibid.

73. "Rabbi Rubin's Court of the Air," *Yiddish Radio Project* (CD, Highbridge Audio, 2002).

74. *American bord sholom v'tzedek,* audiorecording, YIVO Sound Archive, New York, NY.

75. WBBC unveiled the *Yiddish Goodwill Court* in 1936, and WLTH kicked off its fall 1937 season with the *Court of Arbitration Program.* WARD introduced *In the Court of Justice* the following January, and in April WVFW followed with its own court program.

76. This calculation is based on radio listings printed in *Der tog,* the *Forward,* and *Teater un radio velt* for April 1935.

4. AN ACOUSTIC COMMUNITY

Epigraphs: Mildred Schartz, application with transcribed notes, 30 April 1935, Victor Packer Collection, Box 3, YIVO Archives, New York; radio script, *American Jewish Hour,* Sunday, 18 November 1940, Howard Dressner Papers, used with permission of Howard Dressner.

1. *Jewish Daily Forward,* 9 January 1937.

2. Lyrics by Jacob Jacobs, music by Alexander Oleshanetsky.

3. Federal Writers' Project, *Yidishe families un familye krayzn fun nyu york* (New York: Yiddish Writers' Union, 1939).

4. Ibid.

5. Hannah Kliger, *Jewish Hometown Associations and Family Circles in New York* (Bloomington: Indiana University Press, 1992), 95, 99.

6. According to calculations based on daily radio listings in *Der tog* and the *Forward.*

7. Jack Alicoate, ed., *Radio Annual* (New York: Radio Daily, 1938).

8. Flyers, posters, and handbills document the activities of stations CNCW and CMBG in Havana during the late 1930s and early 1940s. These can be found in the Leyzer Ron Collection, Record Group 327, Box 17, YIVO Archives, New York. The YIVO Archives also hold microfilm runs of *Havana lebn.*

9. "Foreign Language Market," statistics supplied by the Foreign Language Department of Forjoe and Company, Jack Alicoate, ed., *Radio Annual* (New York: Radio Daily, 1940), 203.

10. Alicoate, *Radio Annual* (1940).

11. Ibid.

12. *WLTH Radio Theater News* 1, no. 1 (21 April 1935), pamphlet, Victor Packer Papers, Box 10, YIVO Archives.

13. "WEDC Radio Station," pamphlet, WEDC Collection, Chicago Historical Society, Chicago, IL.

14. Jack Alicoate, ed., *Radio Annual* (New York: Radio Daily, 1941).

15. Ibid.

16. Christopher Sterling and John Kittross, *Stay Tuned: A Concise History of Broadcasting in America* (Belmont, CA: Wadsworth, 1990).

17. Sholom Rubenstein, transcript of lecture delivered at the New School for Social Research, 19 January 1993, National Archive of Jewish Broadcasting, the Jewish Museum, New York. See also "Radio Reminiscences," YIVO Sound Archives, New York, n.d. (audiorecording of an interview with radio performers Seymour Rexite, Miriam Kressyn, and Sholom Rubenstein).

18. Sholom Rubenstein, transcript of lecture.

19. Alicoate, *Radio Annual* (1938), 476.

20. Author's calculation based on available information.

21. Andrew Heinze, *Adapting to Abundance* (New York: Columbia University Press, 1991).

22. "Molly Picon's Theater of the Air," radio script, Molly Picon Collection, Box 46, File 876, American Jewish Historical Society, New York.

23. "Radio Reminiscences."

24. *Bay tate mames tish* ('Round the Family Table), Episode 1, audiorecording, New York Public Library for the Performing Arts, New York.

25. Ibid., Episode 6.

26. "Tam Tam Commercials," audiorecording, n.d., YIVO Sound Archives.

27. Ibid.

28. Ibid.

29. Sterling and Kitross, *Stay Tuned*, 164.

30. Moses Asch, interview with Izzy Young, 13 June 1970. Transcript in possession of the author.

31. Hyla Kiczales, "Development of the Italian Radio Market in the East," in *Radio Annual* (1938), ed. Jack Alicoate, 524.

32. Alicoate, *Radio Annual* (1941).

33. Ibid.

34. *Philadelphia idisher kuryer,* 18 March 1936; 24 May 1936.

35. *Chicago Tribune,* 15 November 1942, W5.

36. Peter D. Goldsmith, *Making People's Music: Moe Asch and Folkways Records* (Washington, DC: Smithsonian Institution Press, 1998).

37. Letter from Harry Dubrow to Zvee Scooler, 4 September 1947, File 613, Zvee Scooler Papers, YIVO Archives.

38. *Bay tate mames tish,* audiorecording, YIVO Sound Archives. Also available with translation at Yiddish Radio Project, www.yiddishradioproject.org. Accessed 5 March 2005.

39. *Bay tate mames tish*, Episodes 15–17, audiorecording, New York Public Library for the Performing Arts.

40. *Bay tate mames tish*, Episode 18, audiorecording, New York Public Library for the Performing Arts.

41. Beth S. Wenger, *New York Jews and the Great Depression: Uncertain Promise* (New Haven, CT: Yale University Press, 1996).

42. Rudolph Arnheim and Martha Collins Bayme, "Foreign Language Broadcasts on Local American Stations," in *Radio Research*, ed. Paul Lazarsfeld and Frank Stanton (New York: Duell, Sloan and Pearce, 1941), 1–41.

43. *Zayn vaybs yidine* (His Wife's Wife), Episode 9, radio script, Tuesday, 2 January 1940, Congress for Jewish Culture, New York.

44. "Kibitzers Incorporated," 20 September 1936, radio script, Zvee Scooler Papers, Box 6, Folder 69, YIVO Archives.

45. "Kibitzers Incorporated," 10 October 1937, radio script, Zvee Scooler Papers, Box 6, Folder 71, YIVO Archives.

46. "Kibbitzers Incorporated," 7 June 1936, radio script, Zvee Scooler Papers, Box 6, File 69, YIVO Archives.

47. Selma Cantor Berrol, *Immigrants at School, New York City, 1898–1914* (New York: Arno Press, 1978). See also Ronald M. Bayor, *Neighbors in Conflict: The Irish, Germans, Jews, and Italians of New York City, 1929–1941*, 2d ed. (Urbana: University of Illinois Press, 1988); Joel Perlmann, *Ethnic Differences: Schooling and Social Structure among the Irish, Italian, Jews, and Blacks in an American City* (Cambridge: Cambridge University Press, 1988).

48. Wenger, *New York Jews and the Great Depression*, 56.

49. "Kibbitzers Incorporated," Sunday, 4 September 1938, radio script, Zvee Scooler Papers, Box 7, File 75, YIVO Archives.

50. There is a wonderful transcription of 1,400 kc from 1940 that captures just how eclectic these stations really were. "Abstract of Transcriptions Made of Programs Broadcast by Stations WLTH, WARD, WVFW and WBBC," 20 June 1940, WBBC Station File, Deleted Station Files, FCC Archives, Record Group 173, NARA, College Park, MD.

51. Letter from Louis Zaslow to Victor Packer, 14 April 1940, Victor Packer Papers, Box 10, YIVO Archives, New York.

52. Letter from R. W. Eschwege to Victor Packer, 6 June 1940, Victor Packer Papers, Box 10, YIVO Archives.

53. Letter from Louis Greenberg to Victor Packer, 17 April 1935, Victor Packer Papers, Box 10, YIVO Archives.

54. Letter to Zvee Scooler, unsigned, 3 August 1942, Zvee Scooler Papers, Box 3, File 41, YIVO Archives.

55. Postcard from Rose Kaross to Zvee Scooler, n.d., Box 3, File 41, Zvee Scooler Papers, YIVO Archives.

56. Postcard to Zvee Scooler, unsigned, 6 October 1940, Box 3, File 49, Zvee Scooler Papers, YIVO Archives.

57. Postcard from Rae Innerfeld to Zvee Scooler, 18 October 1942, Box 3, File 43, Zvee Scooler Papers, YIVO Archives.

58. Letter from Sally Gotthelfman to Zvee Scooler, 18 October 1942, Box 3, File 43, Zvee Scooler Papers, YIVO Archives.

59. Letter from Max Flagler to Zvee Scooler, 18 May 1941, Box 3, File 42, Zvee Scooler Papers, YIVO Archives.

60. Lizabeth Cohen, *Making a New Deal: Industrial Workers in Chicago, 1919–1939* (Cambridge: Cambridge University Press, 1990).

61. Packer and a handful of other Yiddish-speaking radio performers, including Freydele Oysher, Sholom Secunda, Nukhem Stutchkoff, and Al Entin, inaugurated their own amateur hours for Jewish immigrant audiences.

62. Questionnaires, Victor Packer Papers, Box 3, YIVO Archives.

63. Questionnaire, Fyvush Finkel, 24 September 1936, Victor Packer Papers, Box 3, YIVO Archives. When asked what he wanted to be, the young Finkel replied, "Jewish singer." The song was written by Alexander Oleshanetzky.

64. Packer's papers contain hundreds of these questionnaires, many of which have been written over in Packer's telltale scrawl, as he transcribed the interview that accompanied each audition. Box 3, Victor Packer Papers, YIVO Archives.

65. Packer hosted two such programs, the *Sterling Salt Program* and *Shtimen fun der gas* (Voices in the Street), sponsored by Foremost Milk. Selections of both programs are available at the YIVO Sound Archives.

66. *Shtimen fun der gas,* 6 February 1940, YIVO Sound Archives.

67. Kathryn Hellerstein, Introduction to Moshe-Leib Halpern, *In New York,* ed. and trans. Kathryn Hellerstein (Philadelphia: Jewish Publication Society, 1982).

68. Radio scripts, Victor Packer Papers, Box 5, YIVO Archive. Some recordings of Packer reciting his poetry are also available on-line at the Yiddish Radio Project, www.yiddishradioproject.org.

69. Arnheim and Bayme, in "Foreign Language Broadcasts over Local American Stations," note that advertisers began advertising their ability to speak Yiddish as a way of appealing to Jewish audiences.

70. *Jewish Daily Forward,* 10 September 1929.

71. A. Muzikant, *Dos naye opera bukh* (The New Opera Book) (New York: M. Yankovitsh, 1923).

72. Though sales of opera recordings to Jewish immigrants are nearly impossible to trace, some circumstantial evidence testifies to its popularity. Advertisements in the Yiddish press for phonographs often included listings of the latest operatic releases, including Yiddish ones. Cantors often earned comparisons to opera singers, for example, "the Jewish Caruso," in the case of Joseph Schmidt.

73. *Jewish Daily Forward*, 31 December 1933.

74. *Bay tate mames tish*, Episode 5, audiorecording, New York Public Library for the Performing Arts.

75. Joshua Fishman, "Three Centuries of Heritage Language Education in the United States," in *Heritage Languages in America: Preserving a National Resource*, ed. S McGinnis, J. K. Peyton, and D. A. Ranard (McHenry, IL, and Washington, DC: Delta Systems and Center for Applied Linguistics, 2001): 81–97.

76. The Twins appeared on radio at least once in 1936, on WLTH. See *Der tog*, 15 June 1936. But they do not appear regularly until the end of the decade.

77. *Hammer's Beverage Program*, 21 November 1940, audiorecording, YIVO Sound Archives.

78. *Hammer's Beverage Program*, 28 November 1940, audiorecording, YIVO Sound Archives.

79. Both Scooler's and Packer's papers contain scripts like this one, as does Molly Picon's collection. Single lines or specific idioms in transliteration—both English and Yiddish—were very common and appeared in the majority of radio scripts.

80. "Maxwell House Coffee Program," n.d., radio script, Molly Picon Collection, Box 44, File 798, American Jewish Historical Society, New York.

81. "Radio Reminiscences."

82. William and Sarah Schack, "And Now—Yinglish on Broadway," *Commentary* 12, no. 6 (1951): 586–89.

83. Howard Dressner, pers. com., Sunday, 22 July 2001.

84. *American Jewish Hour*, Sunday, 24 November 1940, Catalogue no. 8.07; YIVO Sound Archives, New York. Also available on the Yiddish Radio Project Web site, www.yiddishradioproject.org.

85. "Yiddish Melodies in Swing," n.d., program script, Howard Dressner Collection. Original emphasis.

86. *Chicago Daily Tribune*, 15 November 1942, W5.

87. The Medoff Family advertised their services fairly regularly in the Yiddish press and appeared to be quite successful. Sam Medoff also had a successful songwriting career as Dick Manning. His most famous compositions include "Hot Diggity" (1956), which he wrote with Al Hoffman, and "Papa Loves Mambo" (1954), which he wrote with Bix Reichner.

88. *Dave Tarras: Yiddish-American Music, 1925–1956* (Yazoo Records, 1992). Some of his more famous selections have been included in Henry Sapoznik and Pete Sokolow, *The Compleat Klezmer* (New York: Hal Leonard Publishing Co., 1987).

89. Victoria Secunda, *Bei Mir Bist Du Schön: The Life of Sholom Secunda* (Weston, CT, and New York: Magic Circle Press, distributed by Walker, 1982). Also, the Yiddish Radio Project Web site includes a wonderful synopsis of the

story, with examples of different versions of the song: www.yiddishradioproject. org/exhibits/ymis/ymis.php3?pg = 2.

90. *American Jewish Hour*, 1 January 1940 and 3 March 1940, audiorecordings, YIVO Sound Archives.

91. *American Jewish Hour*, 28 July 1940 and 24 November 1940, audiorecording, YIVO Sound Archives.

92. *American Jewish Hour*, program 47, 17 November 1940, radio script, Howard Dressner Collection.

93. Ibid.

94. *American Jewish Hour*, n.d., audiorecording, YIVO Sound Archives.

95. Joshua Fishman, *Yiddish in America* (Bloomington: Indiana University Center in Anthropology, Folklore, and Linguistics, 1965); Benjamin Harshav, *The Meaning of Yiddish* (Berkeley: University of California Press, 1990); Jeffrey Shandler, *Adventures in Yiddishland: Postvernacular Language and Culture* (Berkeley: University of California Press, 2006); Miriam Weinstein, *Yiddish: A Nation of Words* (South Royalton, VT: Steerforth Press, 2001); Janet Hadda, "Yiddish in Contemporary American Culture," in *Yiddish in the Contemporary World: Papers of the First Mendel Friedman International Conference on Yiddish*, ed. Gennady Estraikh and Mikhail Krutikov (Oxford: Legenda Press, 1999), 94–105.

96. Jack Alicoate, ed., *Radio Annual* (New York: Radio Daily, 1939). The figure for weekly New York broadcasting is a result of the author's calculation based on listings in the *Forward* and *Der tog*.

97. Commissioner's Report; In Re: Brooklyn Broadcasting Corporation, Station WBBC (Docket # 1882), p. 16, WBBC Station File, Deleted Station Files, FCC Archives, Record Group 173, NARA, College Park, MD.

5. AT HOME ON THE AIR

Epigraphs: Letter, Marcus Cohn, chief of the War Problems Division of the FCC, to the California Assembly (no. 195), FCC Office of the Executive Director General Correspondence, 1927–1946, File 67–4, FCC Archives, Record Group 173, NARA, College Park, MD; radio script, "Immigranten," 1948, Molly Picon Collection, Box 33, File 566, American Jewish Historical Society, New York.

1. Marc Dollinger, *Quest for Inclusion: Jews and Liberalism and Modern America* (Princeton, NJ: Princeton University Press, 2000).

2. Ibid., 80.

3. Letter from Mrs. V. Robbins to FCC, n.d., FCC Office of the Executive Director General Correspondence 1927–1946, File 67–4, FCC Archives, Record Group 173, NARA, College Park, MD.

4. Letter from Henry Harriman Grimm to FCC, 10 April 1939, FCC Office of

the Executive Director General Correspondence 1927–1946, File 67–4, FCC Archives, Record Group 173, NARA, College Park, MD.

5. Memo, E.K. Jett, 24 September 1938, FCC Office of the Executive Director General Correspondence 1927–1946, File 67–4, FCC Archives, Record Group 173, NARA, College Park, MD. Original emphasis.

6. It is worth noting here that these Native American languages were included in the accounting of "foreign languages," despite the fact that they were not, by strict definition, "foreign." Clearly, the designation "foreign language" emerged as a blanket term to describe all non-English-language broadcasting.

7. "Wartime Survey of Foreign Language Broadcasts," 13 February 1942, FCC Office of the Executive Director General Correspondence 1927–1946, File 67–4, FCC Archives, Record Group 173, NARA, College Park, MD.

8. For more on the history of the Princeton Radio Project, see Douglas Czitrom, *Media and the American Mind: From Morse to McLuhan* (Chapel Hill: University of North Carolina Press, 1982); Todd Gitlin, "Media Sociology: The Dominant Paradigm," *Theory and Society* 6, no. 2 (1978): 205–53; David E. Morrison, "The Transferrence of Experience and the Impact of Ideas: Paul Lazarsfeld and Mass Communications Research," *Communication* 10 (1988): 185–210.

9. Paul Lazarsfeld and Frank Stanton, eds., *Radio Research* (New York: Duell, Sloan and Pearce, 1941).

10. Ibid., viii.

11. Rudolph Arnheim and Martha Collins Bayme, "Foreign Language Broadcasts on Local American Stations," in Lazarsfeld and Stanton, eds., *Radio Research*, 4.

12. Ibid..

13. Ibid., 59.

14. Ibid., 24–25.

15. Ibid., 56.

16. Ibid., 63.

17. During World War I, the Creel Commission, also known as the Committee on Public Information, was organized by President Woodrow Wilson to rally public support for the war effort through the use of mass-mediated propaganda. In addition to pamphlets and the like, the commission worked closely with a handful of Hollywood filmmakers to produce pro-war popular films. It drew criticism, however, for tapping phone lines and spreading unfounded suspicions about the presence of German spies.

18. J.H. Ryan, "Radio Censorship 'Code,'" in *Radio Annual*, ed. Jack Alicoate (New York: Radio Daily, 1942), 67.

19. "The Code—Effective Jan. 16, 1942," in Alicoate, ed., *Radio Annual* (1942), 73. See also T.J. Slowie, Secretary of the Federal Communications Commission to

Senator Langer, 11 January 1943, FCC Office of the Executive Director General Correspondence 1927–1946, File 67–4, FCC Archives, Record Group 173, NARA, College Park, MD.

20. *New York Times*, 28 June 1942.

21. Gerd Horten, "Unity on the Air? Fifth Columnists and Foreign Language Broadcasting in the United States during World War II," *Ethnic Forum* 13, no. 1 (1993): 13–25.

22. Michelle Hilmes, *Radio Voices: American Broadcasting, 1922–1952* (Minneapolis: University of Minnesota Press, 1997), 243.

23. George A. Willey, "The Soap Operas and the War," *Journal of Broadcasting* 7, no. 4 (1963): 348.

24. Jim Harmon, *Radio Mystery and Adventure and Its Appearances in Film, Television and Other Media* (Jefferson, NC: MacFarland, 1992), 32.

25. Arthur Frank Wertheim, *Radio Comedy* (New York: Oxford University Press, 1979), 280.

26. Fred J. Macdonald, *Don't Touch That Dial! Radio Programming in American Life from 1920–1960* (Chicago: Nelson-Hall, 1979), 265–66.

27. Horten, "Unity on the Air?"

28. Ibid., 17, 22.

29. Federal Bureau of Investigation file on WEVD. Obtained by author through the Freedom of Information Act.

30. "A Report on the Goals of AJC's Radio Department," 1 January 1939, American Jewish Committee Archives Online, www.ajcarchives.org/main. php?GroupingId=220. Accessed 15 May 2006.

31. American Jewish Congress, *Dear Adolph: Letter from a Foreign Born American* [realaudio] (1942); available at www.ajcarchives.org/main.php?DocumentId= 11150. Accessed 15 May 2006.

32. Marjorie G. Wyler, "The Eternal Light: Judaism on the Airwaves," *Conservative Judaism* 30, no. 2 (Winter 1986–87): 18–19. Quoted in Jeffrey Shandler and Elihu Katz, "Broadcasting American Judaism," in *Tradition Renewed: A History of the Jewish Theological Seminary*, ed. Jack Wertheimer (New York: JTS Publications, 1997), both quotations on 367; "'The Eternal Light' Program Series Drawn from Jewish Culture, Begins on NBC Oct 8" [press release], 29 August 1944, heterograph, JTS Archives, Record Group 11C, Box 26, Folder 38.

33. Radio script, "The Maccabees," by Morton Wishengrod. Originally broadcast 1944; rebroadcast Sunday, 29 November 1964, Zvee Scooler Papers, Museum of the City of New York.

34. The earliest radio reference to Hitler occurred in 1933, when the theater impresario Maurice Schwartz gave a speech titled "Hitler as a Writer" on the *Forward Hour*. WEVD Broadcast License Renewal Application, 25 February 1933, Federal Communications Commission Broadcast License Series, Federal Radio

Commission Closed Segment of Active Stations 1927 through 7–11–34, WEVD Station File; FCC Archives, Record Group 173, NARA, Sutland, MD.

35. *Jewish Daily Forward*, 16 December 1938. Also *Yidish-daytchflikhtling program*, YIVO Sound Archives, New York.

36. Ibid.

37. Jack Alicoate, ed., *Radio Annual* (New York: Radio Daily, 1941, 1943). Jacob Landau, a young Jewish journalist founded the Jewish Telegraphic Agency (JTA) at the end of World War I, when he recognized the need for increased communication between the Jews of Europe and the Jews of America. Essentially, the JTA functioned as a Jewish wire service and continued to do so. For a personal account of work for the JTA in the Soviet Union, see Boris Smolar, *In the Service of My People* (Baltimore, MD: Baltimore Hebrew College, 1982).

38. Radio script, "Der Grammeister," 23 November 1940, Box 8, File 41, Zvee Scooler Papers, YIVO Archives.

39. Radio script, *Zayn vaybs yidine*, Episode 12, Tuesday, 23 January 1940, Congress for Jewish Culture, New York.

40. *Bay tate mames tish*, Episode 14, New York Public Library for the Performing Arts, New York; also, YIVO Sound Archives, New York.

41. *Dreydl* is the Yiddish term for the top and comes from the Yiddish verb *dreyen*, meaning "to spin."

42. Radio script, "Der grammeister," 21 December 1940, Zvee Scooler Papers, Box 8, File 82, YIVO Archives.

43. Radio script, *Zayn vaybs yidine*, Episode 20, Tuesday, 19 March 1940, Congress for Jewish Culture, New York.

44. *Millions for Defense* debuted on 2 July 1941.

45. *Jewish Daily Forward*, 9 May 1943; 20 June 1943. See also *American Jewish Hour*, 4 March 1945, audiorecording, YIVO Sound Archives..

46. "Treasury Hour," 26 December 1942, Moe Asch Acetates (CD 178, ACT 1324), Smithsonian Folkways Archive, Washington, DC.

47. John Dunning, *On the Air* (New York: Oxford University Press, 1998), 681.

48. *Der gehenom*, United States Treasury Program, 3 November 1943, Moe Asch Acetates (ACT 1324), Smithsonian Folkways Sound Archive. *Der gehenom* debuted on the radio in January and broadcast every Sunday afternoon for the entire year. *Jewish Daily Forward*, 25 January 1943.

49. *Der gehenom*, United States Treasury Program, 3 November 1943.

50. *Jewish Treasury Hour*, n.d., Moe Asch Acetates (ACT 1324), Smithsonian Folkways Sound Archive.

51. WEVD (1943, 1946–47), Records of the Jewish Labor Committee (U.S.), Part I, Holocaust Era Files, Wagner 025; Box 20, Folder 10, Tamiment Library/

Robert F. Wagner Labor Archives, Elmer Holmes Bobst Library, New York University Libraries.

52. *Meet Miriam Kressyn,* 29 November 1947, audiorecording, Museum of Radio and Television, New York.

53. *Der grammeister,* n.d., cat. no. 27.6, YIVO Sound Archives.

54. Esther Leibowitz Collection, YIVO Archives, New York. The collection is full of scripts in her dense handwriting.

55. Radio script, "Jaffa," 12 March 1948, Molly Picon Collection, Box 32, File 574, American Jewish Historical Society, New York.

56. Christopher Sterling and John Kitross, *Stay Tuned: A Concise History of Broadcasting in America* (Belmont, CA: Wadsworth, 1990), 212.

57. Weekly listings in the *Forward* listed a program's sponsor right next to the program name. Unsponsored programs appeared next to a blank space. By this time, there were very few blanks.

58. "Der 'forverts' durkh radyo" (The *Forward* over the Radio), *Jewish Daily Forward,* 25 May 1947.

59. Ibid.

60. His programs included *Di mames tokhter* (The Mother's Daughter), *An eydem oyf kest* (A Son-in-Law on the Dole), and *Sheker un shlimazel* (translated idiomatically as "Cheat and Schlemiel"), Stutchkoff's only foray into comedy.

61. *Der tog,* 13 November 1942, 9.

62. Listings from *Der tog* in 1943.

63. *Der tog,* 24 January 1943.

64. Ibid., 5 November 1944.

65. Simon Frith, *Sound Effects* (New York: Pantheon Books, 1982). For an account of the impact of World War II on foreign-language radio, see Jennifer Fay, "Casualties of War: The Decline of Foreign-Language Broadcasting during World War II," *Journal of Radio Studies* 6, no. 1 (1999): 62–80.

66. New York's WINS had Alan Freed, Chicago's WIXY had Jack Armstrong, and Buffalo's WKBW had George "Hound Dog" Lorenz, to name a few. For a more thorough account of the rise of black radio and its personalities, see William Barlow, *Voice Over: The Making of Black Radio* (Philadelphia: Temple University Press, 1999).

67. Susan Douglas, *Listening In: Radio and the American Imagination* (Minneapolis: University of Minnesota Press, 2004), 236.

68. *New York Times,* 18 June 1967.

69. Jack Alicoate, ed., *Radio Annual* (New York: Radio Daily, 1938).

70. Douglas, *Listening In.*

71. "Constitution of the Yiddish Radio Guild of America," ratified 27 March 1944, Sholom Perlmutter Collection, Letters, File 235, YIVO Archives.

72. Ibid.

73. The YRGA file in Sholom Perlmutter's collection is filled with scraps of paper with jottings and notes about stations, lengths of programs, and prices.

74. Sterling and Kitross, *Stay Tuned*.

75. Common Council for American Unity, *Foreign Language Radio Stations* (New York: Common Council for American Unity, 1958).

76. Bob Becker, *Haynt* (2006), available at www.haynt.org/chap10.htm. Accessed 7 June 2006. The Web site contains an entire English translation of Chayim Finkelstein's history of the Polish Yiddish newspaper *Haynt* (Today), *Haynt: a tsaytung bay yidn 1908–1939* (Haynt: A Jewish Newspaper). The citation about Zylbercweig appears on p. 208.

77. Mickey Katz, *Papa, Play for Me: The Hilarious, Heartwarming Autobiography of Comedian and Bandleader Mickey Katz* (New York: Simon and Schuster, 1977).

78. Ibid., 157.

79. Ruth Glazer, "From the American Scene: The World of Station WEVD," *Commentary* 19, no. 2 (1955): 162–70.

80. Ibid.

81. Ibid.

82. Sholom Rubenstein, 19 January 1993, speech at the New School for Social Research, New York, National Jewish Archive of Broadcasting, Jewish Museum, New York.

6. LISTENING FOR YIDDISH IN POSTWAR AMERICA

Epigraph: Joshua Fishman, *Yiddish: Turning to Life* (Amsterdam: John Benjamins, 1991), 115.

1. A glance through the *Forwards* during these years presents a robust and lively picture of life on the radio. The *Forward* tried any number of formats, including daily and weekly listings, but by any measure, WEVD remained quite active as an outlet for Yiddish programming though the early 1980s.

2. I explore some of these themes more thoroughly in a separate article. See Ari Y. Kelman, "The Acoustic Culture of Yiddish," *Shofar: An Interdisciplinary Journal of Jewish Studies* 25, no. 1 (Fall 2006): 127–51.

3. C. Morris Horowitz and Lawrence Kaplan, *The Estimated Jewish Population of the New York Area, 1900–1975* (New York: Federation of Jewish Philanthropies of New York, 1975).

4. B. Gutmans, "Di shprakh fun a Yidisher radio-stantzye in nyu york" (The Speech of a Yiddish Radio Station in New York), *Idishe shprakh*, October 1958.

5. Ruth Glazer, "From the American Scene: The World of Station Wevd," *Commentary* 19, no. 2 (1955): 162–70.

6. *New York Times*, 9 July 1964.

7. This was originally the slogan of the Bronx-based multilingual radio station, WBNX.

8. *New York Times*, 17 April 1962, 53.

9. American Council for Nationalities Service, *Foreign Language Radio Stations* (New York: American Council for Nationalities Service, 1964).

10. Fishman, *Yiddish: Turning to Life*, 465, table 21, "Mother Tongue of the Native or Foreign of Mixed Parentage for 25 Languages, 1910–1970."

11. The Yiddish-speaking ultra-Orthodox communities in the United States have instead invested in the creation of their own circuits of Yiddish-language media, including newspapers, videos, CDs, and Web sites that are not for large-scale broadcasts as much as they are vehicles for speaking between and among the communities themselves.

12. Sapoznik had been playing Appalachian music, and in 1973, he began a relationship with Tommy Jarrell, an aging fiddle and banjo player and a master of the genre. Jarrell, at one point, discovered that Henry was Jewish and asked him, "Hank, don't your people got none of your own music?" The story is told in greater detail in Henry Sapoznik, with Pete Sokolow, *The Compleat Klezmer* (Cedarhurst, NY: Tara Publications, 1988), 15. See also the Klezmorim, *East Side Wedding* (Arhoolie Records, 3006, 1977).

13. Mark Slobin, "The Klezmorim: East Side Wedding," *Ethnomusicology* 22, no. 2 (May 1978): 392.

14. Michael Strassfeld and Sharon Strassfeld, eds., *The Third Jewish Catalog* (Philadelphia: Jewish Publication Service, 1980), 202.

15. Joshua Fishman, "Three Centuries of Heritage Language Education in the United States," in *Heritage Languages in America: Preserving a National Resource*, ed. S. McGinnis, J. K. Peyton, and D. A. Ranard (McHenry, IL, and Washington, DC: Delta Systems and Center for Applied Linguistics, 2001), 81–97.

16. Herbert Ganz, "The 'Yinglish' Music of Mickey Katz," *American Quarterly* 5, no. 3 (Autumn 1953): 213–18. See also Josh Kun's introduction to *Papa, Play for Me* (Amherst, MA: Wesleyan University Press, 2002), the reissued autobiography of Mickey Katz. For a provocative account of how Katz's acoustic contributions fit into broader notions of music, ethnicity, and race, see Josh Kun, *Audiotopias: Music, Race and America* (Berkeley: University of California Press, 2005).

17. *New York Times*, 12 December 1984, C1.

18. Ibid., 18 May 1990.

19. *New York Times*, 2 August 2001, B7.

20. Jack Kuglemass, *Miracle on Intervale Avenue* (New York: Schocken Books, 1986); Barbara Myerhoff, *Number Our Days* (New York: Simon and Schuster, 1978).

21. Tony Kushner, Michael Chabon, Dara Horn, Jonathan Safran Foer, and Myla Goldberg, just to name a few.

22. The Klezmatics, Yale Strom, Andy Statman, John Zorn, New Orleans Klezmer All Stars, the Klezmorim, the Klezmer Conservatory Band, David Krakauer, Golem, and Solomon and Socalled are only a few of the groups making contemporary klezmer music. Seth Rogovoy, *The Essential Klezmer: A Music Lover's Guide to Jewish Roots and Soul Music, from the Old World to the Jazz Age to the Downtown Avant-Garde* (Chapel Hill, NC: Algonquin Books, 2000). Rogovoy's book is only one of many that have come out over the past decade or so addressing and reconstructing the music and culture of klezmer music.

23. Jeffrey Shandler, *Adventures in Yiddishland: Postvernacular Language and Culture* (Berkeley: University of California Press, 2005).

CONCLUSION

Epigraphs: Robin Cohen, *Global Diasporas* (Seattle: University of Washington Press, 1997), 2; Michael Chanin, *Repeated Takes: A Short History of Recording and Its Effects on Music* (London: Verso, 1995), 39.

Bibliography

NEWSPAPERS

Brooklyn Examiner (English), 1929–56
Chicago Jewish Chronicle (English), 1928–49
Idisher kryer (Chicago; Yiddish), 1887–1947
Idishe velt (Cleveland; Yiddish), 1913–54
idishe velt, Di (Philadelphia; Yiddish), 1922–42
Jewish Daily Forward (New York; Yiddish), 1887–1990
Jewish World (West Palm Beach, FL; English), 1986–89
Kalifornyer idishe shtime (Los Angeles; Yiddish and English), 1925–73
Los Angeles Times
Milvokher vokhenblatt (Milwaukee, WI; Yiddish), 1927–48
New York Times
Philadelphia Inquirer
tog, Der (New York; Yiddish), 1914–48

PERIODICALS

Broadcasting
Congressional Record
Kin-Te-Rad (Warsaw, Poland; Yiddish), 1926
Radio Annual (New York)
Radio Digest
Radio Service Bulletin
Sing Out!
Teater un radio velt (New York; Yiddish), 1935–36

COLLECTIONS

Dressner, Howard. Papers. Used by permission of the Dressner family.
Federal Communications Commission Collection. NARA, College Park, MD.
Federal Communications Commission Collection. NARA, Sutland, MD.
Federal Radio Commission Collection. NARA, College Park, MD.
Gornish, Jean. Collection. National Museum of American Jewish History, Philadelphia.
Gornish, Jean. Collection. Philadelphia Jewish Archives.
Jewish Labor Committee. Collection. Tamiment Library/Robert F. Wagner Labor Archives, Elmer Holmes Bobst Library, New York University Libraries.
Konigsberg, Benjamin and Pearl. Collection. Yeshiva University Archives, New York.
Lazarsfeld, Paul. Papers. Butler Library, Columbia University, New York.
Liebowitz, Esther. Collection. YIVO Archives, YIVO Institute, New York.
National Archive of Jewish Broadcasting. Jewish Museum, New York.
Osherovitch, Mendel. Collection. YIVO Archives, YIVO Institute, New York.
Packer, Victor. Papers. YIVO Archives, YIVO Institute, New York.
Perlmutter, Sholom. Collection. YIVO Archives, YIVO Institute, New York.
Picon, Molly. Collection. American Jewish Historical Society, New York.
Ran, Leyzer. Collection. YIVO Archives, YIVO Institute, New York.
Secunda, Sholom. Collection. YIVO Archives, YIVO Institute, New York.
Schweid, Mark. Collection. YIVO Archives, YIVO Institute, New York.
Scooler, Zvee. Papers. Museum of the City of New York.
Scooler, Zvee. Papers. YIVO Archives, YIVO Institute, New York.
Thomashevsky, Boris. Collection. Dorot Jewish Division, New York Public Library.
Vladeck, Baruch Charney. Papers. Tamiment Library, New York University.

WEDC Collection. Chicago Historical Society.

WEVD Collection. Tamiment Library/Robert F. Wagner Labor Archives, Elmer Holmes Bobst Library, New York University Libraries.

William E. Wiener Oral History Library of the American Jewish Committee. Dorot Jewish Division of the New York Public Library.

RECORDINGS

American Jewish Congress. *Dear Adolph: Letter from a Foreign Born American.* [realaudio]. 1942. Available at www.ajcarchives.org/main. php?DocumentId=11150.

American Jewish Hour. In possession of the author.

Bay tate mames tish ('Round the Family Table) (Yiddish). New York Public Library for the Performing Arts, New York.

Bonds durkh gelekhter (Bonds through Laughter) (Yiddish). Moe Asch Acetates, Smithsonian Folkways Archive, Washington, DC.

Foremost Milk Program (Yiddish). YIVO Sound Archives, YIVO Institute, New York.

Freydele Oysher Interview. YIVO Sound Archives, YIVO Institute, New York.

gehenom, Der (Hell) (Yiddish). Moe Asch Acetates, Smithsonian Folkways Archive, Washington, DC.

Hammer's Beverage Program (Yiddish). YIVO Sound Archives, YIVO Institute, New York.

Interview with Freydele Oysher. YIVO Archives, YIVO Institute, New York.

Ir biterer toes (Her Great Mistake) (Yiddish). Moe Asch Acetates, Smithsonian Folkways Archive, Washington, DC.

Madame Bertha Hart's Amateur Hour. YIVO Sound Archives, YIVO Institute, New York.

Manischewitz Company Commercials. YIVO Sound Archives, YIVO Institute, New York.

Meet Miriam Kressyn. Museum of Television and Radio, New York.

"Radio Reminiscences." Interview with Seymour Rexite, Miriam Kressyn, Sholom Rubenstein, and Henry Sapoznik. YIVO Sound Archives, YIVO Institute, New York.

"Radyo Girl." Music and Lyrics, Jospeh Rumshinsky. Recorded by Lucy Levin. YIVO Sound Archives, YIVO Institute, New York.

Shtimen fun der gas (Voices in the Street) (Yiddish). YIVO Sound Archives, YIVO Institute, New York.

Sterling Salt Program (Yiddish). YIVO Sound Archives, YIVO Institute, New York.

Stuhmer's Pumpernikel Program (Yiddish). YIVO Sound Archives, YIVO Institute, New York.

Yiddish Radio Project. www.yiddishradioproject.org.

Yidish bord sholom v'tsedek (Jewish Board of Peace and Justice) (Yiddish). YIVO Sound Archives, YIVO Institute, New York.

ARTICLES, BOOKS, AND FILMS

Aleichem, Sholem. *In amerika: motl peysi dem hazns un andere mayses.* New York: Varheyt, 1918; reprint Amherst, MA: National Yiddish Book Center, 1999.

———. *Motl peysi dem khazns* (Motl, the Cantor's Son). Translated by Hillel Halkin. New Haven, CT: Yale University Press, 2002.

Alicoate, Jack, ed. *Radio Annual.* New York: Radio Daily, 1938–45.

Allport, Gordon, and Hadley Cantril. *The Psychology of Radio.* New York: Harper, 1935.

American Council for Nationalities Service. *Foreign Language Radio Stations.* New York: American Council for Nationalities Service, 1964.

Anderson, Benedict R. *Imagined Communities: Reflections on the Origin and Spread of Nationalism,* rev. and extended ed. London: Verso, 1991.

Archer, Gleason L. *History of Radio to 1926.* New York: Arno Press, 1951.

Arnheim, Rudolph, and Martha Collins Bayme. "Foreign Language Broadcasts on Local American Stations." In *Radio Research,* edited by Paul Lazarsfeld and Frank Stanton. New York: Duell, Sloan and Pearce, 1941.

Baker, Zachary, ed. *The Lawrence Marwick Collection of Yiddish Plays at the Library of Congress: An Annotated Bibliography.* Washington, DC: Library of Congress, 1998.

Barlow, William. *Voice Over: The Making of Black Radio.* Philadelphia: Temple University Press, 1999.

Barnouw, Erik. *A Tower of Babel: A History of Broadcasting in the United States to 1933.* New York: Oxford University Press, 1966.

———. *The Golden Web: A History of Broadcasting in the United States, 1933–1953.* New York: Oxford University Press, 1968.

———. *The Image Empire: A History of Broadcasting in the United States from 1953.* New York: Oxford University Press, 1970.

Barron, Harry. "Leisure-Time Interests, Preferences, and Activities of Children on the Lower East Side of New York City." Master's thesis, Graduate School for Jewish Social Work, 1935.

Baughman, James. *Republic of Mass Culture: Broadcasting in the U.S. since 1941.* Baltimore, MD: Johns Hopkins University Press, 1997.

Bayor, Ronald M. *Neighbors in Conflict: The Irish, Germans, Jews, and Italians of New York City, 1929–1941.* Urbana: University of Illinois Press, 1988.

Berg, Gertrude. *Molly and Me.* New York: McGraw Hill, 1961.

Berroll, Selma Cantor. *Immigrants at School, New York City, 1898–1914.* New York: Arno Press, 1978.

Biale, David, ed. *The Cultures of the Jews.* New York: Schocken Books, 2002.

Black, Edwin. *War against the Weak: Eugenics and America's Campaign to Create a Master Race.* New York: Four Walls, Eight Windows, 2003.

Butsch, Richard. *The Making of American Audiences: From Stage to Television, 1750–1990.* Cambridge, MA: Harvard University Press, 2000.

Cantor, Muriel B., and Suzanne Pingree. *The Soap Opera.* Sage Commtext Series 12. Beverly Hills, CA: Sage, 1983.

Chanin, Michael. *Repeated Takes: A Short History of Recording and Its Effects on Music.* London: Verso, 1995.

Cohen, Lizabeth. *Making a New Deal: Industrial Workers in Chicago, 1919–1939.* Cambridge: Cambridge University Press, 1990.

Cohen, Robin. *Global Diasporas.* Seattle: University of Washington Press, 1997.

Common Council for American Unity. *Foreign Language Radio Stations.* New York: Common Council for American Unity, 1958.

Cowan, Neil, and Ruth Schwartz Cowan. *Our Parents' Lives: The Americanization of Eastern European Jews.* New York: Basic Books, 1989.

Craig, Douglas B. *Fireside Politics: Radio and Political Culture in the United States, 1920–1940.* Baltimore, MD: Johns Hopkins University Press, 2000.

Crocker, Ruth. *Social Work and Social Order: The Settlement Movement in Two Industrial Cities, 1889–1930.* Urbana: University of Illinois Press, 1992.

Czitrom, Douglas. *Media and the American Mind: From Morse to McLuhan.* Chapel Hill: University of North Carolina Press, 1982.

Denning, Michael. *Mechanic Accents: Dime Novels and Working-Class Culture America.* New York: Verso, 1987.

———. *The Cultural Front: The Laboring of American Culture in the Twentieth Century.* New York: Verso, 1998.

Diner, Hasia. *Hungering for America: Italian, Irish, and Jewish Foodways in the Age of Migration.* Cambridge, MA: Harvard University Press, 2001.

Dollinger, Marc. *Quest for Inclusion: Jews and Liberalism and Modern America.* Princeton, NJ: Princeton University Press, 2000.

Dorgan, Howard. *The Airwaves of Zion: Radio and Religion in Appalachia.* Knoxville: University of Tennessee Press, 1993.

Douglas, Susan. *The Invention of American Broadcasting, 1899–1922.* Baltimore, MD: Johns Hopkins University Press, 1987.

———. *Listening In: Radio and the American Imagination.* Minneapolis: University of Minnesota Press, 2004.

Dunning, John. *Tune in Yesterday: The Ultimate Encyclopedia of Old-Time Radio, 1925–1976.* Englewood Cliffs, NJ: Prentice-Hall, 1976.

———. *On the Air: The Encyclopedia of Old-Time Radio.* New York: Oxford University Press, 1998.

Durstine, Roy S. "The Future of Radio Advertising in the United States." *Annals of the American Academy of Political and Social Science. Radio: The Fifth Estate* 177 (January 1935): 147–53.

Eng, Ien. *Desperately Seeking the Audience.* New York: Routledge, 1991.

Erickson, Hal. *Religious Radio and Television in the United States, 1921–1990: The Programs and Personalities.* Jefferson, NC: McFarland, 1992.

Fay, Jennifer. "Casualties of War: The Decline of Foreign-Language Broadcasting during World War II." *Journal of Radio Studies* 6, no. 1 (1999): 62–80.

Fischer, Claude. *America Calling: A Social History of the Telephone to 1940.* Berkeley: University of California Press, 1992.

Fishman, Joshua. *Yiddish: Turning to Life.* Philadelphia: John Benjamins, 1991.

———. "Three Centuries of Heritage Language Education in the United States. In *Heritage Languages in America: Preserving a National Resource,* edited by S. McGinnis, J. K. Peyton, and D. A. Ranard, 81–97. McHenry, IL, and Washington, DC: Delta Systems and the Center for Applied Linguistics, 2001.

Fishman, Joshua, Esther G. Lowy, William G. Milan, and Michael H. Gertner, eds. *Guide to Non-English-Language Broadcasting.* Vol. 2. Edited by Language Resources in the United States. Rosslyn, VA: National Clearinghouse for Bilingual Education, 1982.

Fiske, John. *Power Plays, Power Works.* New York: Verso, 1993.

Fowler, Gene, and Bill Crawford. *Border Radio: Quacks, Yodelers, Pitchmen, Psychics, and Other Amazing Broadcasters of the American Airwaves.* Austin: University of Texas Press, 2002.

Frith, Simon. *Sound Effects.* New York: Pantheon, 1982.

Gabaccia, Donna. *From the Other Side: Women, Gender, and Immigrant Life in the U.S., 1820–1990.* Bloomington: Indiana University Press, 1994.

Gamm, Gerald. *Urban Exodus: Why the Jews Left Boston and the Catholics Stayed.* Cambridge, MA: Harvard University Press, 2001.

Garofalo, Reebee. *Rockin' Out: Popular Music in the USA.* New York: Allyn and Bacon, 1996.

Geertz, Clifford. *The Interpretation of Cultures.* New York: Basic Books, 1973.

Gibson, Campbell. *Population of the 100 Largest Cities and Other Urban Places in the United States.* Population Division Working Paper 27. Washington, DC: U.S. Bureau of the Census, 1988.

Gilroy, Paul. *The Black Atlantic: Modernity and Double Consciousness.* Cambridge, MA: Harvard University Press, 1993.

Gitlin, Todd. "Media Sociology: The Dominant Paradigm." *Theory and Society* 6, no. 2 (1978): 205–53.

Glasser, Ruth. *Music Is My Flag: Puerto Rican Musicians and Their Communities, 1917–1940*. Berkeley: University of California Press, 1997.

Glazer, Ruth. "From the American Scene: The World of Station WEVD." *Commentary* 19, no. 2 (1955): 162–70.

Godfried, Nathan. *WCFL: Chicago's Voice of Labor, 1926–78*. Champaign: University of Illinois Press, 1997.

———. "Struggling over Politics and Culture: Organized Labor and Radio Station WEVD during the 1930s." *Labor History* 42, no. 4 (2001): 347–69.

Goldsmith, Emanuel. *Modern Yiddish Culture: The Story of the Yiddish Language Movement*. New York: Fordham University Press, 1997.

Goldsmith, Peter D. *Making People's Music: Moe Asch and Folkways Records*. Washington DC: Smithsonian Institution Press, 1998.

Goodman, Mark. *The Radio Act of 1927 as a Product of Progressivism*. Mass Media Monographs 2, no. 2 (August–September 1999).

Graeme, Theodore C. *Ethnic Broadcasting in the United States*. Publications of the American Folklife Center, vol. 4. Washington, DC: Library of Congress, 1980.

Gurock, Jeffrey S. *From Fluidity to Rigidity: The Religious Worlds of Conservative and Orthodox Jews in Twentieth-Century America*. Ann Arbor: Jean & Samuel Frankel Center for Judaic Studies, University of Michigan, 1998.

Gutmans, B. "Di shprakh fun a yidisher radyo-stantzye in nyu york" (The Speech of a Yiddish Radio Station in New York). *Yidishe shprakh* (October 1958).

Hadda, Janet. "Yiddish in Contemporary American Culture." In *Yiddish in the Contemporary World: Papers of the First Mendel Friedman International Conference on Yiddish*, edited by Gennady Estraikh and Mikhail Krutiov, 94–105. Oxford: Legenda Press, 1999.

Hall, Stuart. "Encoding/Decoding." In *Culture, Media, Language: Working Papers in Cultural Studies, 1972–79*, edited by Centre for Contemporary Cultural Studies, 128–38. London: Hutchinson, 1980.

Hangen, Tona. *Redeeming the Dial: Radio, Religion, and Popular Culture in America*. Chapel Hill: University of North Carolina Press, 2002.

Harmon, Jim. *Radio Mystery and Adventure and Its Appearances in Film, Television and Other Media*. Jefferson, NC: McFarland, 1992.

Hebdige, Dick. *Subculture, the Meaning of Style*. New York: Routledge, 1989.

Heinze, Andrew. *Adapting to Abundance*. New York: Columbia University Press, 1991.

Helfman, Rhoda Kaufman. "The Yiddish Theater in New York and the Immigrant Jewish Community: Theater as Secular Ritual." Ph.D. dissertation, University of California, Berkeley, 1986.

Hellerstein, Kathryn. "Finding Her Yiddish Voice: Kadya Molodowsky in America." *Sources* 12 (2002): 48–68.

Heskes, Irene, ed. *Yiddish American Popular Songs, 1895 to 1950: A Catalog Based on the Lawrence Marwick Roster of Copyright Entries.* Washington, DC: Library of Congress, 1992.

Higham, John. *Strangers in the Land: Patterns of American Nativism, 1860–1925.* New Brunswick, NJ: Rutgers University Press, 1955.

Hilmes, Michelle. *Radio Voices: American Broadcasting, 1922–1952.* Minneapolis: University of Minnesota Press, 1997.

Hilmes, Michelle, and Jason Loviglio, eds. *The Radio Reader: Essays in the Cultural History of Radio.* New York: Routledge, 2001.

Hoberman, J. *Bridge of Light: Yiddish Cinema between Two Worlds.* Philadelphia: Temple University Press, 1995.

Hoberman, J., and Jeffrey Shandler, eds. *Entertaining America: Jews, Movies and Broadcasting.* New York and Princeton, NJ: Jewish Museum, under the auspices of the Jewish Theological Seminary of America, and Princeton University Press, 2003.

Horowitz, C. Morris, and Lawrence Kaplan. *The Estimated Jewish Population of the New York Area, 1900–1975.* New York: Federation of Jewish Philanthropies of New York, 1959.

Horten, Gerd. "Unity on the Air? Fifth Columnists and Foreign Language Broadcasting in the United States during World War II." *Ethnic Forum* 13, no. 1 (1993): 13–25.

Jaker, Bill, Frank Sulek, and Peter Kanze. *The Airwaves of New York: Illustrated Histories of 156 AM Stations in the Metropolitan Area, 1921–1996.* Jefferson, NC: McFarland, 1998.

Joselit, Jenna Weissman. *The Wonders of America: Reinventing Jewish Culture, 1880–1950.* New York: Hill and Wang, 1994.

Kasson, John. *Amusing the Million: Coney Island at the Turn of the Century.* New York: Hill and Wang, 1978.

Katz, Mickey. *Papa, Play for Me: The Hilarious, Heartwarming Autobiography of Comedian and Bandleader Mickey Katz.* New York: Simon and Schuster, 1977.

Kelman, Ari Y. "The Acoustic Culture of Yiddish." *Shofar* 25, no. 1 (Fall 2006): 127–51.

Kliger, Hannah. *Jewish Hometown Associations and Family Circles in New York.* Bloomington: Indiana University Press, 1992.

Kobrin, Rebecca. "Conflicting Diasporas, Shifting Centers: Migration and Identity in a Transnational Polish Jewish Community, 1878–1952." Ph.D. dissertation, University of Pennsylvania, 2002.

Krasnow, Erwin G. *The Public Interest Standard: The Elusive Search for the Holy Grail* Briefing Paper Prepared for the Advisory Committee on Public Interest Obligations of Digital Television Broadcasters, 1997.

Kugelmass, Jack. *Miracle on Intervale Avenue.* New York: Schocken Books, 1986.

Kwartin, Zevulun. *Mayn leben* (My Life). Amherst, MA: National Yiddish Book Center, 2000. Originally published Philadelphia: Gezelshafatlikhen komitet, 1952.

Land, Jeff. *Active Radio; Pacifica's Brash Experiment.* Minneapolis: University of Minnesota Press, 1999.

Lazarsfeld, Paul, and Frank Stanton, eds. *Radio Research.* New York: Duell, Sloan and Pearce, 1941.

Leach, William. *Land of Desire.* New York: Vintage Books, 1993.

Leibowitz, Rabbi Jacob. *Radyo redes* (Radio Addresses). Brooklyn, NY: Published by the author, 1940.

Levine, Lawrence W., and Cornelia R. Levine. *The People and the President: America's Conversation with FDR.* Boston: Beacon Press, 2002.

Lifson, David. *The Yiddish Theater in America.* New York: T. Yoseloff and Sons, 1965.

Lind, Michael. "American by Invitation." *New Yorker,* 24 April 1995.

Lissak, Rivka Shpak. *Pluralism and Progressives: Hull House and the New Immigrants, 1890–1919.* Chicago: University of Chicago Press, 1989.

Loviglio, Jason. *Radio's Intimate Public: Network Broadcasting and Mass-Mediated Democracy.* Minneapolis: University of Minnesota Press, 2005.

Macdonald, Fred J. *Don't Touch That Dial! Radio Programming in American Life from 1920–1960.* Chicago: Nelson-Hall, 1979.

Marchand, Roland. *Advertising the American Dream: Making Way for Modernity, 1920–1940.* Berkeley: University of California Press, 1985.

Marcus, Jacob R. *To Count a People: American Jewish Population Data, 1585–1984.* Lanham, MD: University Press of America, 1990.

Margoshes, S. "The Jewish Press in New York City." In *The Jewish Communal Register of New York City: 1917–1918,* 596–617. New York: Kehillah (Jewish Community) of New York City, 1918.

McChesney, Robert. *Telecommunications, Mass Media and Democracy: The Battle for Control of U.S. Broadcasting, 1928–1935.* New York: Oxford University Press, 1993.

Metzker, Issac, ed. *A Bintel Brief.* New York: Ballantine Books, 1971.

Michels, Tony. *A Fire in Their Hearts: Yiddish Socialists in New York.* Cambridge, MA: Harvard University Press, 2006.

Miller, Kerby. *Emigrants and Exiles: Ireland and the Irish Exodus to the United States.* New York: Oxford University Press, 1988.

Miller, Spencer, Jr. "Radio and Religion." *Annals of the American Academy of Political and Social Science* 177 (1935): 129–34.

Moore, Deborah Dash. *To the Golden Cities: Pursuing the American Jewish Dream in Miami and LA.* New York: Free Press, 1984.

———. *At Home in America: New York's Second Generation Jews.* New York: Columbia University Press, 1991.

Morrison, David E. "The Transference of Experience and the Impact of Ideas: Paul Lazarsfeld and Mass Communications Research." *Communication* 10 (1988): 185–210.

Muzikant, A. *Dos naye opera bukh* (The New Opera Book). New York: M. Yankovitsh, 1923.

Myerhoff, Barbara. *Number Our Days.* New York: Simon and Schuster, 1978.

Novik, Morris. "Interview with Morris Novik [Novick]." Edited by Seymour Segal and Marcus Cohen. American Jewish Committee, Oral History Library, 1980.

Nugent, Walter. *Crossings: The Great Transatlantic Migrations, 1870–1914.* Bloomington: Indiana University Press, 1992.

Parlin, Charles Coolidge. *The Merchandising of Radio.* Philadelphia: Curtis Publishing Company, 1925.

Peiss, Kathy. *Cheap Amusements: Working Women and Leisure in Turn-of-the-Century New York.* Philadelphia: Temple University Press, 1986.

Penslar, Derek Jonathan. "Transmitting Jewish Culture: Radio in Israel." *Jewish Social Studies* 10, no. 1 (Fall 2003): 1–29.

Perlmann, Joel. *Ethnic Differences: Schooling and Social Structure among the Irish, Italian, Jews, and Blacks in an American City.* Cambridge: Cambridge University Press, 1988.

Picon, Molly. *Molly! An Autobiography.* New York: Simon and Schuster, 1980.

Prell, Riv Ellen. *Fighting to Become Americans: Assimilation and the Trouble between Jewish Women and Jewish Men.* Boston: Beacon Press, 1999.

Radway, Janice. *Reading the Romance.* New York: Verso, 1987.

Razlogova, Elena. "The Voice of the Listener: Americans and the Radio Industry, 1920–1950." Ph.D. dissertation, George Mason University, 2003.

Rogovoy, Seth. *The Essential Klezmer.* Chapel Hill, NC: Algonquin Books, 2000.

Rontch, Isaak, ed. *Di yidishe landsmanshaftn fun nyu york* (The Jewish Hometown Associations of New York). New York: Yiddish Writers Union of the Works Progress Administration, 1938.

———. *Yidishe familiyes un familye krayzn fun nyu york* (Jewish Families and Family Circles of New York). New York: Yiddish Writers' Union of the Works Progress Administration, 1939.

Rosenblatt, Rabbi Samuel. *Yossele Rosenblatt: The Story of His Life as Told by His Son.* New York: Farrar, Straus and Young, 1954.

Rozenwaike, Ira. *Population History of New York City*. Syracuse, NY: Syracuse University Press, 1972.

Rubenstein, Sholom. Speech delivered at the New School University. National Archive of Jewish Broadcasting, Jewish Museum, New York.

Sandrow, Nahma. *Vagabond Stars: A World History of Yiddish Theater*. Syracuse, NY: University of Syracuse Press, 1977.

Sapoznik, Henry. *Klezmer: From the Old World to Our World*. New York: Schirmer Books, 1999.

———. "Brooklyn Yiddish Radio, 1925–1946." In *The Jews of Brooklyn*, edited by Elana Abramovitch and Sean Galvin, 227–30. Hanover, NH: University Press of New England, 2001.

Sapoznik, Henry, and Pete Sokolow. *The Compleat Klezmer*. New York: Hal Leonard Publishing Co., 1987.

Savage, Barbara. *Broadcasting Freedom: Radio, War, and the Politics of Race*. Chapel Hill, NC: University of North Carolina Press, 1999.

Schack, William, and Sarah Schack. "And Now—Yinglish on Broadway." *Commentary* 12, no. 6 (1951): 586–89.

Secunda, Victoria. *Bei Mir Bist du Schön: The Life of Sholom Secunda*. Weston, CT: Magic Circle Press, 1982.

Seidman, Naomi. *A Marriage Made in Heaven: The Sexual Politics of Hebrew and Yiddish*. Berkeley: University of California Press, 1997.

Seller, Maxine Schwartz. *Ethnic Theater in the United States*. Westport, CT: Greenwood Press, 1983.

Shandler, Jeffrey. *Adventures in Yiddishland: Postvernacular Language and Culture*. Berkeley: University of California Press, 2005.

Shneer, David. *Yiddish and the Creation of Soviet Jewish Culture: 1918–1930*. New York: Cambridge University Press, 2004.

Siegel, David, and Susan Siegel. *Radio and the Jews: The Untold Story of How Radio Influenced America's Image of Jews*. Yorktown Heights, NY: Book Hunter Press, 2007.

Silverman, David. "The Jewish Press: A Quadrilingual Phenomenon." In *The Religious Press in America*, edited by Martin Marty, 123–72. New York: Holt, Reinhart, and Winston, 1962.

Singer, Ben. "The Nickelodeon Boom in Manhattan." In *Entertaining America: Jews, Movies and Broadcasting*, edited by J. Hoberman and Jeffrey Shandler. New York and Princeton, NJ: Jewish Museum, under the auspices of the Jewish Theological Seminary of America, and Princeton University Press, 2003.

Slobin, Mark. "The Klezmorim: East Side Wedding. *Ethnomusicology* 22, no. 2 (May 1978): 392.

———. *Tenement Songs: The Popular Music of the Jewish Immigrants*. Urbana: University of Illinois Press, 1982.

———. *Golden Voices: The Story of the American Cantorate*. Bloomington: University of Illinois Press, 2002.

———, ed. *American Klezmer*. New York: Oxford University Press, 2003.

Slotten, Hugh. *Radio and Television Regulation: Broadcast Technology in the United States, 1920–1960*. Baltimore, MD: Johns Hopkins University Press, 2000.

Smith, Erin A. *Hard-Boiled: Working-Class Readers and Pulp Magazines*. Philadelphia: Temple University Press, 2000.

Smulyan, Susan. *Selling Radio: The Commercialization of American Broadcasting, 1920–1943*. Washington, DC: Smithsonian Institution Press, 1994.

Soltes, Mordecai. *The Yiddish Press, an Americanizing Agency*. New York: Teachers College Press, 1950.

Soyer, Daniel. *Jewish Immigrant Associations and American Identity in New York, 1890–1939*. Cambridge, MA: Harvard University Press, 1997.

Spottswood, Dick, ed. *Ethnic Music on Records: A Discography of Ethnic Recordings Produced in the United States, 1893 to 1942*. 7 vols. Urbana: University of Illinois Press, ca. 1990.

Squier, Susan Merrill, ed. *Communities of the Air: Radio Century, Radio Culture*. Durham, NC: Duke University Press, 2003.

Stamps, Charles. *The Concept of the Mass Audience in American Broadcasting*. New York: Arno Press, 1979.

Sterling, Christopher, and John Kittross. *Stay Tuned: A Concise History of Broadcasting in America*. Belmont, CA: Wadsworth, 1990.

Streeter, Thomas. *Selling the Air: A Critique of the Policy of Commercial Broadcasting in the United States*. Chicago: University of Chicago Press, 1996.

Stutchkoff, Nukhem, ed. *Der oytzer fun der yidishe shprakh* (Thesaurus of the Yiddish Language). New York: YIVO Institute, 1951.

Tabak, Roger. "Orthodox Judaism in Transition." In *Jewish Life in Philadelphia: 1830–1940*, edited by Murray Friedman, 48–64. Philadelphia: Ishi Publications, 1983.

Truax, Barry. *Acoustic Communication*. Norwood, NJ: Ablex, 1984.

U.S. Bureau of the Census. *Fourteenth Census of the United States: 1920: Population*. Washington, DC: Government Printing Office, 1923.

———. *Fifteenth Census of the United States: 1930: Population*. Washington, DC: Government Printing Office, 1933.

———. *Sixteenth Census of the United States: 1940: Population*. Washington, DC: Government Printing Office, 1943.

Vaillant, Derek. "Sounds of Whiteness: Local Radio, Racial Formation, and Public Culture in Chicago, 1921–1935." *American Quarterly* 54, no. 1 (2002): 25–66.

Vecoli, Rudolph. "Contadini in Chicago: A Critique of the Uprooted." *Journal of American History* 1, no. 3 (1964): 404–17.

Vecoli, Rudolph, Cathleen Neils Conzen, David Gerber, Ewa Morawska, and George Pozzetta. "The Invention of Ethnicity: A Perspective from the U.S.A." *Journal of American Ethnic History* 12 (1992): 3–63.

Vladeck, Stephen C. "Interview with Stephen C. Vladeck." Edited by Alice Herb. American Jewish Committee, Oral History Library, 1974.

Walker, Jesse. *Rebels on the Air: An Alternative History of Radio in America.* New York: New York University Press, 2004.

Warnke, Nina. "Immigrant Popular Culture as Contested Sphere: Yiddish Music Halls, the Yiddish Press, and the Processes of Americanization, 1900–1910." *Theatre Journal* 48 (1996): 321–35.

———. "Reforming the New York Yiddish Theater: The Cultural Politics of Immigrant Intellectuals and the Yiddish Press, 1887–1910." Ph.D. dissertation, Columbia University, 2001.

Weinreich, Max. *History of the Yiddish Language.* Chicago: University of Chicago Press, 1980.

Weinstein, Miriam. *Yiddish: A Nation of Words.* South Royalton, VT: Steerforth Press, 2001.

Weisser, Michael. *A Brotherhood of Memory: Jewish Landsmanshaftn in the New World.* New York: Basic Books, 1985.

Wenger, Beth S. *New York Jews and the Great Depression: Uncertain Promise.* New Haven, CT: Yale University Press, 1996.

Wertheim, Arthur Frank. *Radio Comedy.* New York: Oxford University Press, 1979.

Willey, George A. "The Soap Operas and the War." *Journal of Broadcasting* 7, no. 4 (1963): 339–52.

Williams, Raymond. *Marxism and Literature.* New York: Oxford University Press, 1978.

Yablokoff, Herman. *Der Payatz: Around the World with Yiddish Theater.* Translated by Bella Mysell. Silver Spring, MD: Bartelby Press, 1995.

Index

271

Text: 10/14 Palatino
Display: Univers Condensed Light 47; Bauer Bodoni
Compositor: BookMatters, Berkeley
Printer and binder: Sheridan Books, Inc.